Power and Law

Power and Law

American Dilemma in World Affairs

Papers of the Conference on Peace Research in History

Edited by
Charles A. Barker

The Johns Hopkins Press, Baltimore and London

"Another American Dilemma: Multilateral Authority versus Unilateral Power"
Copyright © 1970 by Charles A. Barker

Copyright © 1971 by The Johns Hopkins Press
All rights reserved
Manufactured in the United States of America

The Johns Hopkins Press, Baltimore, Maryland 21218
The Johns Hopkins Press Ltd., London

Library of Congress Catalog Card Number 76-135660
ISBN-0-8018-1254-2

Contents

Preface	vii
Contributors	xi
Part I. Power and Restraint as a National Problem	1
Another American Dilemma: Multilateral Authority versus Unilateral Power, CHARLES A. BARKER	3
Anxiety, Ideology, and Order: Reflections on the Making of American Public Policy, CHARLES E. ROSENBERG	22
Part II. The Assertion of Violent Power: An American Crescendo	35
American Foreign Policy in the Early Cold War: The Dilemmas of Historical Continuity, WALTER LAFEBER	37
Law and Order in American Thought: An Ambiguous Heritage, WILLIAM L. NEUMANN	55
Canada and the American Dilemma: Realism versus Idealism, 1945–1964, CAMERON NISH, assisted by STEPHEN ABBOTT	66
Part III. Belief in the Restraint of Power: Trial, Error, and Hope	83
The United States and the Law of Mankind: Some Inconsistencies in American Observance of the Rule of Law, WILLIAM J. BRUCE	85
Law as a Barrier to Change: A Korean Experience, NAM-YEARL CHAI	111
The Right of Revolution: Implications for International Law and World Order, GERALD A. SUMIDA	130
Peace and War: The History of the United States, 1939–1999, ARTHUR I. WASKOW	168
Part IV. The Discussion Reviewed	185
The Historian and the Dilemma, BERENICE A. CARROLL	187

Preface

THESE ESSAYS go to press two months after United States forces entered Cambodia, the farthest reach ever made by American arms. By the same short period of time they follow the climax of protest against the Indochina war which occurred in May 1970, the climax in which students were killed. This was part of the most massive and passionate stage ever attained by the three-century-old antiwar movement in America.

Thus shocking events in 1970 add emotion to the dilemma with which this book opens—the contradiction that Americans have long endured between their assertions of power by unilateral force and their commitments to peace and order. The country will be lucky if present tensions may have been reduced by the time this book reaches the public.

The authors are either historians or political scientists, except for one lawyer who is both historically and politically minded. They shared the papers among themselves and among fellow members of the Conference on Peace Research in History, in a meeting near Plattsburgh, New York, in early September 1968. The time of that meeting, though moderate by present-day comparisons, was tense enough in America's war-or-peace history. Only weeks earlier Senator Eugene McCarthy had lost his campaign to be the Democratic nominee for president, and Senator Robert F. Kennedy had been assassinated. Against that background our meeting was cool as is supposed to be right for scholars. Those events disturbed us but had no part in the organized discussion.

The purpose of this volume is the same as that of the meeting. The aim is to deepen insight into certain streams of events, to take long views in the history of the peace policy and war policy in our country, rather than to analyze current events. Toward such a goal, though with no limitation to American history, the Conference on Peace Research in History has had its being. It first gathered (about seventy members of the American Historical Association at its 1963 convention) in the Friends Meeting House on Cherry Street in Philadelphia. Since then there have been many meetings, or rather sessions, of the CPRH at conventions of both the AHA and the Organization of American Historians. But it has become more than a satellite organization. The independent meeting recorded in these essays will be followed by a second in 1970, again at Plattsburgh. The present volume is the third publication to be sponsored by the conference. This is the place to say with gratitude that the first, Blanche Wiesen Cook's *Bibliography on Peace Research in History* (1969), eliminates any need for a general bibliography in this volume. The second was the 1969, no. 4, issue of the *Journal of Peace Research*, entitled "How Wars End."

A word is required about the philosophy of the conference or, more exactly, about the suppositions on which it has operated. A question which keeps rising is whether it is possible for scholars to unite in a single effort the judiciousness they need and cherish with the involvement that the peace movement entails. We speak with assurance for ourselves alone, but believe we voice a conviction held by the conferees generally, when we say that these qualities can be joined. The one instance when the adverse opinion caused pain to the CPRH was when an honored public figure and scholar refused membership, saying that on working days he was a historian and at night and on weekends a peace advocate but that the two commitments could not be joined. Our own opinion is that whatever ethical considerations may affect an individual historian, the public passions he shares, are often—and often should be—the source of the questions he chooses to study. A historian may well agree with a lawyer in believing that adversary procedure is a prime yielder of truth. But the nature of the historian's operation is such that the adversaries on the issue he is discussing take up residence in his own head. He has always to be at once advocate and judge; he has to entertain both zeal and judgment, ego and superego.

In a preface one may not summarize or select very much. Yet we feel free to point out that while ours was a historical meeting, we entertained considerable departure from conventional molds. The prominence of political scientists as givers and discussants of papers made the occasion bidisciplinary to an unusual degree. The scholar who had the most to say about the future is a historian. Several contributors, though they examined the past of the United States or Canada as is their daily working habit, nonetheless ventured into fields they had not before entered professionally. We believe that this kind of openness of mind leavens the present writings. For instance, the discussion showed how some of the favorite concepts of American diplomatic history, the Monroe and other "doctrines" and various manifestations of "destiny," need be viewed as quite unilateral; also that international law must contain avenues of recourse for persecuted groups and individuals.

The authors of this book have had generous help from other men's time and money. Many colleagues in the CPRH worked hard for the book and the conference. Cooperating closely with Hilary Conroy, who at the time was chairman of the conference, Hugh Hawkins was the chief negotiator with authors and benefactors. Then William J. Bruce and Eugene P. Link, members of the faculty of the State University College of Arts and Science at Plattsburgh, New York, the institution which became our generous host, assumed heavy planning and administrative duties. The college's Pathways to Peace Program, using James N. Rosenberg funds dedicated to "help kindle among students, faculty and world scholars the desire for conversations with men of differing cultural backgrounds and points of view," provided the financial aid necessary to ensure that the conference could meet at Plattsburgh. Thus we had the use of the college's Miner Center at Chazy, north of the main campus, with meeting rooms, sleeping accommodations, and board all together—these essentials plus the amenity of days in beautiful country. Entertaining and feeding three dozen or so men and women who arrived and departed at various hours over three days and nights was no small item. We are sure that all who came are grateful for that hospitality; certainly the authors are for its contribution to the book.

Altogether, besides the authors, about twenty-five persons took part in the discussions. They included:

Margaret K. Bruce	Eugene P. Link	William Toll
Charles Chatfield	Richard D. Lunt	E. Berkley Tompkins
Blanche W. Cook	Saul Mendlovitz	Daniel Walden
Arthur Dudden	Dixon Miyauchi	Charles C. Walker
Richard O. Hathaway	John L. Myers	Solomon Wank
Hugh Hawkins	George Pasti, Jr.	Ralph E. Weber
Larry L. Leonard	Harry R. Rudin	

Finally, we acknowledge with special gratitude the money and advice given the CPRH by the Institute for International Order of New York City. Earl D. Osborn, president of the institute, thought it right that his organization, which serves legal studies mainly and proudly bears the imprint of Grenville Clark's leadership and ideas, should assist a like-minded effort among historians. The institute's grant assisted the writers with their expenses during the summer of 1968; the gift was made conditional on our proceeding promptly to publication. Saul Mendlovitz of the affiliated World Law Fund advised us at several points. But memorably he challenged us with the proposition that history may be too passive a kind of scholarship to serve world order. The authors hope that their book will be somewhat reassuring —to our benefactors and to others—on that disquieting, but we are sure mistaken, point.

F. HILARY CONROY
Chairman of the Meeting

CHARLES A. BARKER
Editor

Contributors

CHARLES A. BARKER is professor of history at The Johns Hopkins University. The history of public thought in America is his field of concentration; in that field he is the author of a biography, *Henry George* (1955), and a general work, *American Convictions: Cycles of Public Thought, 1600–1850* (1970). Close to the present enterprise, he was the first chairman of the Conference on Peace Research in History and coordinated *Problems of World Disarmament* (1963).

CHARLES E. ROSENBERG is professor of history at the University of Pennsylvania, where he specializes in the history of medicine, science, and society in America. His books relate to the intellectual and social assumptions of Americans as displayed in periods of crisis: *The Cholera Years: The United States in 1832, 1849, and 1866* (1962) and *The Trial of the Assassin Guiteau: Psychiatry and Law in the Gilded Age* (1968).

WALTER LAFEBER is Marie Noll Professor of American History at Cornell University. Trained at the University of Wisconsin, where his field of American diplomatic history has been uncommonly energetic, he is the editor of two books on recent affairs and is the author of two others, both concerned with American expansion: *The New Empire: An Interpretation of American Expansion, 1860–1898* (1963) and *America, Russia, and the Cold War* (1967).

WILLIAM L. NEUMANN is professor of history at Goucher College and is active in the peace movement in Baltimore. A specialist in recent history, he has done much research overseas and has written about U.S. policy toward Europe and Asia: *Isolation and Security* (1957), *America Encounters Japan: From Perry to MacArthur* (1963), and *After Victory: Churchill, Roosevelt, and Stalin in the Making of the Peace* (1967). One of the founders of the Conference on Peace Research, he is the present chairman.

CAMERON NISH, a native Montrealer, is associated with Sir George Williams University and the École des Hautes Études Commerciales of Montreal. He specializes in the history of French Canada in both the colonial and modern periods. Among his publications are: *The French Regime* (1965), *The Social Structure of the New France* (1967), *Quebec, 1759–1766: Conquered? Half Conquered? Liberated?* (1967), *Les Bourgeois Gentilshommes* (1968), and *Quebec in the Duplessis Era: Dictator-*

ship or Democracy (1970). At present he is working on a study of entrepreneurship and enterprise in eighteenth century New France.

WILLIAM J. BRUCE is professor of political science and coordinator of international studies at The State University of New York College of Arts and Science at Plattsburgh. He writes about the commitments of the United States to world order and law from career experience in the United Nations as well as from academic expertise to which he was trained at Stanford. He has held several positions in the U.N. Secretariat.

NAM-YEARL CHAI is associate professor of political science at Columbus College in Georgia. A native of Korea, he was trained in the modern history and international relations of East Asia at the University of Pennsylvania.

GERALD A. SUMIDA, who is a research associate of the Princeton Center of International Studies, is practicing law in Hawaii, his native state. He was trained at the Woodrow Wilson School of Public and International Affairs at Princeton and later, with a concentration in international law, at the Yale School of Law.

ARTHUR I. WASKOW is a resident fellow of the Institute of Policy Studies in Washington, a historian of recent America whose numerous writings chiefly concern race relations and disarmament. He appears often in such general journals as *Ramparts, Saturday Review, Commentary, Christian Century,* and *Liberation,* and is the author of *The Limits of Defense* (1962), *From Race Riot to Sit-In, 1919 and the 1960s* (1966), and *Running Riot* (1970). He was one of the founders of the CPRH and its first secretary-treasurer, and he helped organize the Radical Historians at the 1969 convention of the American Historical Association.

BERENICE A. CARROLL is an assistant professor of political science at the University of Illinois at Urbana and is also a historian. She has published *Design for Total War: Arms and Economics in the Third Reich* (1968) and is now engaged in a work on "How Wars End: A Comparative Study." She was secretary-treasurer of the CPRH from 1966 through 1969; her studies and her work for the Conference especially prepared her to have the last say in this volume.

Power and Law

PART I

Power and Restraint as a National Problem

Another American Dilemma: Multilateral Authority versus Unilateral Power
CHARLES A. BARKER

The proposal is made that the issue of war or peace be considered—much as the issue of race discrimination has been—in the light of standards that inhere in the history of American ideas and institutions of government and law.

Anxiety, Ideology, and Order: Reflections on the Making of American Public Policy
CHARLES E. ROSENBERG

Like other great policy issues, the issue of war or peace is governed by emotions universally felt, and these demand multidisciplinary, but especially psychological, research. Uncommon effort will be required to introduce far-reaching policy changes.

Another American Dilemma: Multilateral Authority versus Unilateral Power*

CHARLES A. BARKER

NEARLY A QUARTER century has passed since Gunnar Myrdal produced the book, "An American Dilemma," which to this day more than any other writing helps us to understand the revolution in race relations of our time. Of course Myrdal's central theme was that America's national ideals are incompatible with racial discrimination, and in the 1940s that theme was anything but new. The moral incompatibility had been plain to Thomas Jefferson; it had been more or less alive in America's public consciousness since the birth of the nation. What Myrdal did that was new and different was to speak with perfect timeliness and with the massive comprehensiveness of the social sciences of the twentieth century. While he was writing, World War II was making demands on blacks equal to those on whites. The nation was fighting with such a solidarity as it had never before achieved. Franklin D. Roosevelt amplified the nation's convictions about freedom—freedom from want and freedom from fear besides freedom to speak and to worship. These were universal rights, the president said. Appropriate to that background, the Swedish scholar showed that America's dilemma over race relations penetrated deeply into the common conscience of the people, pressing always to bring practice and idea together.

Meanwhile, since that dilemma has been faced up to—in the book of 1944, in the desegregation decision, in the race revolution now in process—the United States has made and many times restated a commitment, morally as deep as the commitment to equality made in the post-Civil War amendments, to another ideal. Like racial equality, it was accepted and pledged as an aim of the nation during an ordeal of war. The ideal is peace in the world; the United Nations is at once the institutional enactment and the grand symbol of that

---

* Reprinted by permission from *The Virginia Quarterly Review*, 45, no. 2 (Spring, 1969): 230–52.

goal. The principal means chosen to meet the commitment is a multilateral recognition of the rights of all nations and persons and a systematic sharing of obligation and authority. These particulars and many others are embodied in the U.N. Charter and are matched and extended in many other instruments of the past quarter-century. The instruments which, like the charter, have been adopted as treaties are fully and formally a part of United States law.

But of course the commitment to peace made in our time, like the commitment to equality made a century ago, has not become an all-out, exclusive commitment. Hence the subject of the present paper, a second but equal dilemma. The second horn of the second dilemma is no more and no less than our country's practice of unilateral violence against other peoples, especially the people of Vietnam. Do not the following words, which Myrdal applied in 1944 to race relations in the United States, apply now to the contradictions we suffer over simultaneously fighting a war and believing in peace? "Out of the strain comes a sense of uneasiness and awkwardness. . . . The strain is increased in democratic America by freedom left open. . . . The . . . problem . . . would be simpler to handle scientifically, if the moral conflict raged only between valuations held by different persons and groups of persons. The essence of the moral situation is, however, that the conflicting valuations are also held by the same person. *The moral struggle goes on within people and not only between them.*"

The supposition of this essay is that, as the ordeal of World War II helped to internalize in the thought and feeling of the people the race question, the ordeal of the Vietnam war has considerably internalized the war-or-peace problem. I contend that the main current of our national ideals is on the side of our national pledges to peace and multilateralism. But not every American loyalty points in that direction. Thought and selection among loyalties are now in order. A crisis of national conscience is not an easy thing; our age has heard Reinhold Niebuhr say that nations do not have a morality comparable to individual morality. Yet national decisions on matters of morality are made, as in the matter of race. If Americans can determine to resolve the race dilemma—as they now see they must—why should it be impossible to tackle a second and no less crucial dilemma? At any rate a historical estimation of that obligation is the problem we now undertake.

II

Once in the course of its national history, early in the nineteenth century when the slate was clear, the United States managed to find general terms for conducting its foreign relations that proved on the whole satisfactory at home. When we consider the matter as a problem of reaching concurrence in political assumptions, the period around 1800 appears extremely difficult. The new nation had had no more than a quarter-century of experience at independent diplomacy, only a decade under the Constitution. Before 1776 America's only direct share in foreign relations had been the relations of recurrent war with Spain, France, and the Indians. Thereafter shiftiness in relationship and crisis in event had become the American experience. With England the United States fought twice within forty years. With France old enmity changed to alliance in 1778; and during the 1780s and 1790s the relationship went through several stages of unease. In 1797 naval war flared up, but by 1800 President John Adams had damped it down; from then until 1815, Franco-American relations were pretty well governed by Napoleon, or by what governed him. Altogether, logic would suggest that the lessons in making foreign policy that Americans had had time to learn could not have prepared them to deal in a stable way with Europe early in the nineteenth century. The Old World was monarchical and, though Napoleon and Metternich tried, was little organized as a continent. It was subject to revolution and politically archaic, in the American view.

Yet somehow, despite all the trouble from 1783 to 1815, a stable attitude toward Europe is exactly what the United States achieved. The background of relevant thought here was the American expectation that states which have their being in the same community will behave toward one another in more or less predictable ways. The philosopher-statesmen had felt that way about state and interstate politics at home. As readers of *The Federalist* know, the fathers built on the belief of their age that sovereign states, like stars in their courses, move in orbits which may be calculated in accord with political distances and weights. Newtonian figures of speech occurred in the Federalist argument of Alexander Hamilton; they occurred in the reasoning of Federalists less urgent than he, among leaders whose goal was stability more than centralization. Similarly, the most imaginative achievement of 1787 was the unprecedented concession that, as the United States extended westward, new states should be admitted on a basis of equality with the old. More than a dozen years ago Robert Livingston Schuyler suggested that multiple sovereignty in the republic should be understood as being descended from the multiple autonomy which England in the eighteenth century had allowed the American colonies. That old sharing of power under the crown had been extended and rationalized, according to Professor Schuyler, by Jefferson in the "Summary View" and John Adams in the "Novanglus" papers of 1774 and 1775. Finally, multiple autonomy became multiple sovereignty under the Confederation and sovereignty divided and shared under the Constitution of 1787. What needs stressing here is that plural sovereignty in America traces to Old World backgrounds and permissions given in the eighteenth century and that this lineage makes it cousin to the British Commonwealth of Nations and kin to all other systems wherein power is carefully balanced.

What is less recognized about the mentality in which early American statesmanship operated is that, while our national leaders certainly did conceive of affairs in Europe as being managed by dynasts in archaic ways, they nonetheless imagined those affairs to operate along the same base lines as they themselves followed. That is, when they looked westward they envisaged rising states. Kentucky, Tennessee, and Ohio were admitted as full members of the Union by the opening of the nineteenth century. Other new states were already planned in tiers, waiting for populations large enough to justify equal participation in federal institutions and processes. When Americans looked in the opposite direction, eastward across the Atlantic, they likewise envisaged plural sovereignties and changing situations. To put the matter a little differently, the statesmen of the young republic held a reasonably unified view of politics and institutions in both the Old World and the New. As republicans they had been and remained bold; but being believers in government under law did not put them in an altogether different world of ideas from believers in monarchy. As federalizers they were true innovators in world history. But they envisaged underlying relationships of equilibrium and balance, the fount and origin of federalism, to be phenomena that occurred everywhere in the world.

The essential document that displays this attitude is George Washington's Farewell Address, which is both familiar and unfamiliar to twentieth century Americans. As is well known, the address was given in 1796, soon after Jay's treaty had demonstrated that the administration would go far to improve and stabilize relations with England; the president had been advised by both Alexander Hamilton and James Madison well before he spoke. The familiar text has been illuminated by a philosophically minded commentary by Felix Gilbert. In that treatise, *To the Farewell Address: Ideas of Early American Foreign Policy*, the author explains persuasively that the intention of the first president was not mainly to advise against alliances but to explain to colleagues and fellow citizens that as they embarked on international relations they were entering a situation which, like an ocean voyage, could be calculated with some confidence. To reread the Farewell Address today and to examine the Gilbert commentary is to recapture the supposition of the eighteenth century that the peoples of Christendom, however separate and disparate they were, however antagonistic in their actions, were nonetheless peoples essentially equal in their sovereignty and rights and similar to one another in the interests which govern policy.

Today the cutting edge of the idea of equality is often turned inward to excise social injustices at home. But in the Farewell Address the idea was directed outward, toward Europe. As in the Declaration of Independence, the ideal was invoked to assert the parity of peoples or nations: the United States was made to appear equal to England or France, or to any nation on earth. This accorded with the particular needs of American foreign policy. It helped justify Americans as possessors and occupiers of an incomparable interior domain, the very continental domain into which Spain, France, and England had all reached, but which they had been unable to grasp and hold. It abetted the republic's search for new commercial relationships and treaties; it accorded with the policy of neutrality in the wars that the French Revolution precipitated. The overall supposition—that the old enemy in two wars, England, and old friends, France and Holland, and lesser states would all be treated equally—of course differed radically from what had been open to Americans before 1776. By the same token that supposition set an attitude that lasted throughout the nineteenth century, the cool and detached attitude of regarding all nations as being on a par and of seeking favored relations with none.

One of the telling things about Gilbert's elucidation is his evidence that Americans often used the same kind of Newtonian figures of speech for world affairs as they did for American federal relationships. This accorded with the conception of a balance of power, then a universally accepted idea; it accorded likewise with current beliefs about international law and order, those of which Hugo Grotius was the principal author. There is a natural law for the behavior of nations, the same as among persons; war is a crime except in certain situations; when war is legally conducted, it respects human rights and property rights. So had reasoned the great Dutch jurisprudent, and so the prevailing assumptions ran among early American statesmen. The utopian factor in such ideas of world relations was sizable; and the Americans who drew model treaties, hoping that international relations could be confined to mutually beneficial arrangements for trade, shared the utopianism. On the other hand, even the Federalists, who were especially preoccupied with the collision-of-power side of international relations, accepted the principle of equilibrium as operationally correct. As Gilbert sums up the matter, "even the power struggle among [European] states was considered to have its laws. . . . Each state would expand until its forces were halted by counter-pressure. If the world was not in a permanent state of war, the reason was that the force found itself confronted with another force of equal strength. Whereas idealists and reformers inveighed against the idea of the balance of power, the realistic writers on the doctrine of the interest of the states were its enthusiastic advocates; it appeared to them as the one stabilizing factor in a constantly expanding world."

Probably the person and the writings of Henry Wheaton, the country's first international jurisprudent, represent better than any other the congruity between American hopes for equilibrium in the federal system at home and for equilibrium in international relations. Growing up as a Rhode Islander aware of illegal seizures at sea from which Americans suffered, later given enviable experience as Supreme Court reporter at the time when it handed down the Dartmouth College decision and others basic to the Marshall and Story style of federalism, Wheaton as a young man had maximum saturation in principles concerning both the law of the federal union and the law of nations. Before he brought out his *Elements of International Law* in 1836—one of the great textbooks in America's great epoch of producing textbooks on law—he had resided in Europe, as diplomat and scholar. There, versing himself in contemporary and eighteenth century legal writing, he absorbed the tradition of Grotius. "The principal aim of the Author," he explained in the preface, "has been to glean . . . the general principles which may fairly be considered to have received the assent of most civilized and Christian nations, if not as invariable rules of conduct, at least as rules which they cannot disregard without general obloquy and the hazard of provoking the hostility of other communities who may be injured by their violation."

Nine years and many hundreds of pages later, near the close of the American edition of his *History of the Law of Nations in Europe and America*, shortly before the end of his life, Wheaton incorporated a lengthy discussion of Immanuel Kant's plea of 1795 for a confederation of Europe. Kant had said that confederation should wait for the states of Europe to adopt republican forms of government. From Kant Wheaton switched to Hegel as being new and different, and finally pronounced his own conclusions. From them I select the following four: first, that the "practices of war between civilized nations have been sensibly mitigated, and a comparison of the present modes of warfare with the system of Grotius will show the immense improvement which has taken place in the laws of war"; second, that the "sphere, within which the European law of nations operates, has been widely extended by the unqualified accession of the new American states"; third, that the "law of nations, as a science, has advanced with the improvements in the principles and language of philosophy [and] with our . . . deeper researches into the obscurer periods of history"; and finally, "that the law of nations, as a system of positive rules regulating the mutual intercourse of nations, has improved with the general improvement of civilization, of which it is one of the most valuable products."

It says a great deal for the scholarship of Henry Wheaton, and even more for the durability of the idea of natural law as an integral part of international law, that the *Elements of International Law* was published and republished well into the twentieth century and in America was long accepted as the standard work in the field. On the whole, Wheaton's view of international relations was the view of American lawyers and political scientists down to Woodrow Wilson. In Wheaton's time Europe seemed distant and seldom pressing; Asia was more an opportunity than a problem. Overall the outer world seemed not a bad place to venture as national strength increased, and the law of nations provided rules for all who would play the game.

III

Of course idealism was not invariably associated with international order. Often, indeed characteristically, it adhered to national self-interest in expansion, as was the case with Manifest Destiny in the mid–nineteenth century. However, at no time between the War of 1812 and World War I did there rise any such tension between the exercise of government power in foreign relations and the wish of citizens to restrain power, as is familiar in our times. One explanation of this happier situation is that continental expansion and overseas market expansion seldom conflicted with the vital interests of other nations. Throughout an entire century the United States participated in only two foreign wars, and these were so short that in neither case was there time for domestic tensions to become grave.

Yet the period is far from being a blank in the background of the collision of ideas that concerns us. Although the grimness of American policy toward the Indians, subjugating them and moving them from place to place, was largely taken for granted at the time, peace crusaders did sometimes resist the whole business as being incompatible with the principles either of Christianity of or government by consent and under law. But doubtless the episode from before the Civil War that is the most piquant today is the one which Charles Sellers, biographer of President James K. Polk, has commented on with effect. One who revisits the Mexican War today, taking the road of the historical record, he tells us, arrives there with a sense of *déjà vu*. When Polk, who was a strong-willed leader from a southwestern state and a very personification of Manifest Destiny, invaded Mexico by land and by sea, a credibility gap opened at home. Two former presidents and one future president, among many, believed that the man in the White House overstated Mexico's offenses and overpleaded the reasons for fighting a war. "We have a character among the nations of earth to maintain," objected former President Van Buren. "It has hitherto been our pride and our boast, that, whilst lust of power with fraud and violence in the train has led other and differently constituted nations to aggression and conquest, our movements in these respects have always been regulated by reason." Thus spoke the senior Democrat in the country. More specifically to the point of the credibility gap, a thirty-five-year-old Whig congressman from Illinois, Abraham Lincoln, made antiwar speeches casting doubt on President

Polk's truthfulness and judgment. (This provoked home state charges that Representative Lincoln was a "Benedict Arnold.") But it was John Quincy Adams, who shared antislavery feeling with Van Buren and Lincoln and carried it further, who pressed hardest the ethical objection to the Mexican War. The octogenarian statesman "went so far," according to Sellers, "as to express the hope that General Taylor's officers would resign and his soldiers desert, rather than fight such a war."

It is not that such condemnations of the war with Mexico voiced merely a surge of anger which would pass with the event or even that they indicated simple opposition to a territorial expansion of slavery. More than that, people were now organizing in sizable numbers, to reform out of existence two institutions, chattel slavery and war. Henry David Thoreau's *On the Duty of Civil Disobedience* of 1849 illustrates the double conviction.

Much less well remembered than Thoreau's individual protest, the massive peace movement of the nineteenth century began soon after the War of 1812 and was accelerated by the Mexican War. It was a part of the manifold reform movement of that evangelical age, and the fact that many of its leaders were clergymen does not mean that it was less realistic or less informed than, say, the women's rights movement or the antislavery crusade. Ministers discussed international affairs and lawyers and statesmen talked Christian ethics often in the same company of social reform. The Reverend Noah Worcester of the Massachusetts Peace Society, for example, caught the significance for the cause of disarmament of the Rush-Bagot agreement concerning the United States–Canadian boundary; he was also one who condemned the wars against the Seminoles and the Cherokees. During the 1840s, while Manifest Destiny men talked about the future sweep around the world of American-style institutions, American peace seekers, not altogether different in logic, told audiences at home and in Europe that the American government would be the first government and the most fitting one to forgo war as an instrument of national policy. "It is in this country that the martial spirit has received its greatest check," wrote a contributor to the *Democratic Review*. "It is here that the pacific principles will be first adopted."

Today a very short story that the expert on the American peace movement, Merle Curti, tells suggests the inner tensions of the 1840s over the issue of rule by the assertion of power versus rule by consent. The story concerns an American Indian of the midcontinent, George Copway, who traveled and spoke in Europe in the service of world peace. Copway was a chieftain by origin and a Methodist by conversion; he went to Frankfurt-am-Main in 1850 as a delegate to the peace congress organized there by Elihu Burritt, the peripatetic American antiwar speaker and organizer. Rising before an international meeting, which was held in the great St. Paul's Lutheran Church where the Frankfurt Parliament in 1848 had met, wearing his tribal dress and speaking in broken English, Copway pleaded for self-determination as a method of justice for peoples wherever oppressed. Voicing the same doctrine of equality among peoples that occurs in the Declaration of Independence, Copway "carried the audience away," according to a witness.

It seems fair, then, to discern in the voices of midcentury peace crusaders a renewal in evangelical passion of the main ideas of the Revolutionary epoch—government by the people and multiple sovereignty. Restating the principle of equilibrium among peoples, the reformers asserted in addition that political equilibria should be strengthened and structured—beyond what the princes of Europe would do—by laws and congresses on the American model.

IV

Coming to the times of Thoreau and Burritt, that is to the midcentury, brings us not without irony to the sad epoch when American democracy suffered its worst disruption. Not the loose old monarchical equilibrium of Europe (though it suffered its strains at center) but the carefully institutionalized equilibrium of the now continent-wide federal system of America fell apart in terrible war. And the Reconstruction period that followed was the time when America's self-contradictions over race relations became entirely plain. Surely the thirteenth, fourteenth, and fifteenth amendments, enacted between 1865 and 1870, are the fullest and most formal commitment the United States has ever made to the principle of equality under the law. But simultaneously and in the following half-century the almost universal refusal of white Americans to treat Negroes equally with themselves denied the principle. In that contradiction the dilemma Myrdal would later identify became built into our institutions.

By contrast, the incompatibility with which this essay is concerned lost visibility for a while, beginning with the Civil War. The old peace movement faded. About 1861, members decided that it was better to fight to destroy slavery and save the Union than to refuse to bear arms. And about twenty years later certain isms appeared that help explain new attitudes less favorable to equilibrium and more favorable to violence than before. The Social Darwinism of the 1880s confirmed people's taste for competition, individual and national; it justified the rule of the strong. Nineteenth-century German political idealism—imported in Hegelian, Fichtean, Rankean, and other packages—added immensely to the sense of scholars and publicists that nations are governed by their collective wills. From such components the spirit of imperialism was brewed. Among American vocalizers of this attitude—who would have to include Josiah Strong and Brooks Adams, Theodore Roosevelt and Albert J. Beveridge—we may pick the naval historian, Admiral A. T. Mahan, for a quotation as summary as any. "The martial spirit . . . alone is capable of coping finally with the destructive forces that from outside and from within threatened to submerge all the centuries have gained. . . . Not in universal harmony, nor in fond dreams of unbroken peace," went on that great scholar in *The Interest of America in Sea Power,* "rest now the best hopes of the world, as involved in the fate of European civilization. Rather in the competition of interests, in that reviving sense of nationality . . . in the jealous determination of each people to provide first for its own . . . are to be heard the assurances that decay has not touched yet the majestic fabric erected by so many centuries of courageous battling."

Of course, peace men did not keep silent while the national will men and the imperialists were building their case. Around 1900 statesmen and intellectuals, including William Jennings Bryan and Senator Hoar, Mark Twain, William Dean Howells, and William Graham Sumner, took vigorous antiwar and anti-imperialist stands. The principal argument sprang from the main stem of the tradition: a democratic republic does not take control of another nation without its consent. Then gradually the argument widened and deepened. In 1905 George Santayana, one of two conspicuous peace men who were members of that most brilliant of all departments in American university history, the Harvard Department of Philosophy, had his say. In the second volume of *The Life of Reason,* which he subtitled *Reason in Society,* Santayana argued that war had become archaic and that international rivalries might be sublimated into competitions like athletic contests between cities and schools. In 1907, speaking from eighteen years at Hull House and from impressions of what militarism was doing to Germany, Jane Addams published *Newer Ideals of Peace*, the strongest plea in our language, probably, that war and the fulfillment of democracy are incompatible processes. Three years later, William James, who was Santayana's most eminent colleague, produced his little classic, *The Moral Equivalent of War*. He proposed that under a national system young men should be assigned to nonmilitary but strenuous and risk-taking services to their country. Today it would be appropriate to honor the Harvard philosophers for peace, the one for having supplied a sporting justification for the race with the Soviet Union to place a man on the moon and the other for having supplied good reasons for a Peace Corps and a VISTA program.

Altogether the dialogue between the imperialists and anti-imperialists, those who were tolerant of war and those who were opposed, had reached an advanced stage by 1910. Overseas expansion is natural and good for America, Mahan and Roosevelt and their kind were saying; war also has its virtues, for it toughens the character of a people. Quite wrong, responded the anti-imperialist and the antiwar people. Overseas rule is foreign to our ideas and institutions, they said, and war, for all its heroic qualities, is barbarous and even more subversive of our historic beliefs.

Such articulation, however, did not put war-or-peace into politics. Before 1916 it was no more an issue than slavery was before 1820, when the Missouri Compromise was enacted. Jane Addams gives us a measure. In 1912, in her own city of Chicago, the "beloved lady" of many humanitarian activities had been applauded into being the number two idol at the Progressive Party convention. She worked hard for Theodore Roosevelt; she believed in his domestic program. We know now, however, that she was embarrassed by his imperialist and navalist record and taste. To stand back from that line of possible severance within the party, Miss Addams—who was far from guessing that within five or six years she would be the most prominent pacifist in a country at war—deliberately suppressed the embarrassment. To her, that is, as to the country at large, war-or-peace had not yet become an operational issue in political affairs.

V

Once the Great War engulfed Europe, however, how rapidly matters changed. After a reading of the fifth volume of Professor Arthur Link's *Wilson*, concerning the leadership of the United States during the years it remained neutral, the word "dilemma" seems weak. It was the president's agony more than anyone else's, because Wilson was Wilson: as a scholar he knew a great deal about national history and held firmly to old doctrines of international law; as a politician and statesman he felt daily the pressures first for military preparedness and then for entering the war. From 1914 to 1917, generally speaking, President Wilson held back. For a long time he insisted on treating the belligerents equally. He wanted not only the United States but all neutrals to retain their commercial and political rights without interference from any nation at war. Reluctant always to lead his country at arms, believing that war was the antithesis of what the United States stood for, Wilson decided to fight only when he considered the war to be hopelessly stalemated and felt free to promise that a peace truly consistent with American ideals could be attained. All these attitudes indicate how strongly Woodrow Wilson held to the view that the power of nations—of all nations, including his own—is something to be channeled and controlled.

Neither at the close of the First World War nor at the close of the Second could the United States deal in a constitutional way with the problem of war as after the Civil War it had dealt with the problem of the Negro. There was no world constitution to provide a sanction for outlawing war as there was an American constitution to outlaw slavery and racial discrimination. Yet after both wars great pledges to peace were given. With President Wilson's role in bringing to birth the League of Nations and with the deeds of later administrations in cooperating with the League, in bringing about actual treaties and stages of naval disarmament, in sponsoring the Kellogg-Briand Treaty, and so on, the United States before 1930 took formal and substantial steps into world multilateralism and toward the antiwar circumvention of national sovereignty. There is no need to recapitulate here how actions of the 1920s, and soon the neutrality laws of the 1930s, were paralleled by the most numerous antiwar movement in United States history up to that time. The polarization of ideas, which had occurred between 1885 and 1915, now burgeoned into a polarization of public opinion. Peace pamphlets poured from the presses. Jane Addams received a Nobel Prize. In the intellectual history of war criticism, Professor Quincy Wright's two-volume *Study of War* was the finest achievement. Brought out in 1942, after we had entered the Second World War, it was a product of the author's teaching, indeed his founding, the academic discipline of international relations during the 1930s. In spirit the book was—and now freshly is, for recently it has twice been republished—a critical, peace-minded study of the prehistory, history, sociology, law, and ideology of war.

But of course, among the very people who joined the peace movements of the 1930s the Nazi Terror in Europe and the Japanese expansion in the Pacific soon compelled a different kind of resolution. It was like the yielding of the peace convictions held by abolitionists when the Civil War came in 1861: excepting hard core pacifists, mostly Christian, Americans quickly consolidated in what seemed then as it still seems to all but a handful of deep dissenters, a war of self-defense and the guarding of essential ideals and loyalties. For all the waste and the horror, participation in the Second World War conferred on nearly all Americans an unforgettable sense of doing what had to be done. The words of Roosevelt and Churchill met the occasion. The tension that is our subject between exercising national power at its most violent and holding back from that exercise lost public meaning for that time. Doubtless the yielding of the American peace movement and the abandonment of American neutrality legislation and ideas—two separate but simultaneous war phenomena of the home front—have abetted the opinion among us that peace convictions must always give way to reasons of state. In fact, the peace movement did not rise again until ten or a dozen years after the war had ended—that is, not until the late 1950s, when the Korean War had also been fought and concluded.

But this bypasses the sizable incorporation of peace-reformist goals into national policy that occurred in San Francisco during the summer of 1945. Certainly the pledge Roosevelt had led the country in making that an allied victory would mean the elimination of great war from the world was handsomely honored in the Charter of the United Nations. The obligation the United States undertook when it ratified the U.N. treaty promptly and with no reservations was more exacting regarding the keeping of world peace than membership in Woodrow Wilson's League of Nations would have been. It is hard for Americans today to recognize how American in name, style, and philosophy the United Nations truly is. It follows the design of our own national and state constitutions of the dozen years that began in 1776. Rights are guaranteed. Plural sovereignties are recognized and assigned obligations. The General Assembly acts out the principle of equality in rights and self-government of all organized peoples. The Security Council contemplates a systematized equilibrium among the great powers. Altogether the Americanism of the United Nations, and the commitment of the government to it, would seem to have no limit.

This brings us to the real birth, I believe, of the dilemma we identified tentatively at the beginning of this paper. Again, the first horn of the dilemma is the pledge of the United States to multilateralism on a global scale. The second horn lies in our wars, in our extended militarization, most of all in our introducing a new order of armaments in the world. Only short weeks after the United Nations Charter had been drafted, atomic bombs burst over Hiroshima and Nagasaki. Where events in San Francisco had created a world system of multilateral authority and had placed new restraints of law on the power of nations, the explosions in Japan occurred as unilaterally as it is possible for events to occur. They represented then, as they still do, the grossest use ever made by man of his power to destroy. The event seemed at the time what the years have proved it to be—pregnant with an arms race beyond comparison with any previous hazards.

Putting together the pieces in the coincidence of 1945, one may well doubt that any pair of events has ever been more incongruous than this. The incongruity restates the dilemma we are examining: multilateral authority in the world and multilateral disarmament, main goals of the United Nations, versus unlimited armaments and unlimited power to kill. Though this is a world predicament, is it not peculiarly an American one? Has even the problem of race relations been more especially ours? Could any other thinkable dilemma be more of American making, more a collision of two achievements characteristic of our national culture, than the dilemma born in 1945?

VI

Three times in early centuries public thought in America has advanced to positions that would lead through politics to relocations of sovereign authority. This happened in the seventeenth century, when three colonies—Massachusetts, Connecticut, and Rhode Island—set themselves up as commonwealths and when all the English colonies attained a degree of self-government unmatched since the colonies of ancient Greece. It happened in the eighteenth century, between 1765 and 1789. It happened a third time during the nineteenth century in the nationalizing events of the Civil War epoch, for which the title given by Charles and Mary Beard, "The Second American Revolution," is still suggestive of complex truth. During at least two of those three relocations historical learning and historical mindedness entered the making of events. It did so brilliantly in the cases of Jefferson, Madison, John Adams, James Dickinson, and others during the final third of the eighteenth century. It did so during the latter half of the nineteenth century in cases stretching from George Bancroft and Francis Lieber to John W. Burgess and Woodrow Wilson.

Partly on account of the precedents, but especially because unilateralists keep coming up with a bizarre view of American history which they intend to have serve their cause, we need to consider this intellectual aspect of our problem. To illustrate, Robert S. McNamara, then Secretary of Defense, expressed an opinion with clarity in the *Atlantic Monthly* of March 1967. "If you read Toynbee," said the powerful secretary, "you realize the importance of a democracy learning to cope with a limited war. The greatest contribution Vietnam is making—right or wrong beside the point—is that it is developing an ability in the United States to fight a limited war, to go to war without the necessity of arousing the public ire. In that sense, Vietnam is almost a necessity in our history, because this is the kind of war we'll almost certainly be facing in the next fifty years."

It is hard to see how Mr. McNamara could have pronounced three sentences more jarring to multilateralists and peace advocates than these. In them: (1) he made a limited war man of Arnold Toynbee, an impossible proposition; (2) he said that the "right or wrong" of the war in Vietnam is beside the point of its other "contributions" to the United States; and (3) he praised fighting limited wars "without ire." This last seems to mean fighting without the passion of believing in a just war and without the feeling of heroism and tragedy and hope for a good peace that in the past have given citizen soldiers their glory. Moreover, by calling the Southeast Asia war "almost a necessity in our history" but by being too honest to pretend that it was a war of self-defense, did not McNamara say that unilateral decisions of the kind we are still making in Asia will continue to be the one way and the right way? But probably the most offensive to peace men of any of the former secretary's notions is the proposition that the Vietnam war is vouchsafed to the United States to help the people unlearn their ancient distaste for war.

These snapshot and crystal ball views of history seem not to represent fairly the total views of the speaker about the destiny of his own people. It now appears that McNamara probably entertains other more human expectations. But whether fully representative of the man or not, these words are important. They open a rare glimpse into the tacit, workaday presuppositions of our expansionists of American power. The glimpse shows how unilateral activism can be justified by a new variant on the old doctrine of national mission. The mission this time is to cut communism short at its outmost reaches. (Fortunately there is no call to strike communism at the central headquarters of the movement.) Though apologists have often likened the operations of this mission to a world police action, or (in the days of John Foster Dulles) to a fire-fighting one, those homely phrases fit neither the unilateralism nor the extralegalism of the effort. If we are to speak in terms borrowed from domestic history, "world vigilantism" would seem a more appropriate wording. Of course, the McNamara way of thinking about American peace-keeping can claim a sizable number of precedents—the Indian wars and the Mexican War of the nineteenth century and our more recent interventions in the Caribbean and the Pacific. Although such expansions offer little analogy to our large-scale operations in Vietnam, they do supply what precedents we have for expanding unilaterally by force of arms American control and influence in new areas.

This aspect of the historical record may nourish McNamara's view of our present-day obligations—the obligations that he said are likely to continue another half-century. But it in no way obliterates from the same record America's early and traditional way of conceptualizing relations among nations, the way of a planned—possibly, an institutionalized—equilibrium of power. If we ask whether or not that view has its believers and sustainers today, nearly two centuries after the philosopher-statesmen, doubtless the most affirmative answers are to be found in the convictions of the leaders of such organizations as the United Nations Association and the United World Federalists. They, and the many scholars who have gone with them, including

Quincy Wright and the recently deceased great international lawyer, Grenville Clark, belong in the lineage of peace crusaders and scholars who volunteered during the nineteenth century. In today's unevangelical ways they are our Wheatons and Sumners, asserters that equilibrium among nations is again, maybe is always, a valid conception. Like their predecessors they would have equilibrium become other than an automatic phenomenon; they would have it built deeply into the surrounding law, institutions, and opinions of the world.

Recently, beside this reformist hope of international equilibrium, we have had a hard-nosed version. This appears in and between the lines of George Kennan's *Memoirs, 1925–1950*. Even though that eminent diplomat was a lonely inside critic throughout his State Department career, he accepted most of the department's values. Thus, though he loved Russian culture, he "never" (he says) believed the Soviet Union "to be a fit ally or associate, actual or potential, for this country." He is famous for his plan to "contain" communism. Even so, he reasoned that the United States must act politically, must impose political restraints short of military ones on the Soviet Union. That is to say, he argued for equilibrium, from the supposition that both nations have needs that transcend reliance on unilateral power. However slow Americans have been to realize the fact, what is true of Kennan has become true of recent mainline American policy toward the Soviet Union. As Norman Cousins said in an editorial that favored acknowledging openly our actual reliance on Moscow, we have had to trust Khrushchev and Kosygin as we do our own leaders not to touch the nuclear button.

Thus Americans do speak and think often on the assumptions of equilibrium. We rely on multilateral procedures at center, though we wage war along the perimeters of power. Doctrinally speaking, our belief in an essential equality among peoples is what is at stake. While we are learning to deal with the Russians as equals in violent power we are learning also, as we sit with them in the United Nations or negotiate test ban and antiproliferation treaties, to act as though they were our equals in doing the business of the world. Recently that lesson has been hard to hold to. Yet one remembers the ways in which Protestants and Catholics in European and American history, and Christians and Muslims earlier, came to manage with one another in a rough equality under an umbrella of toleration. We are far from having reached any such stage with China. Least of all have we come to think that the citizens of the small countries where we intervene have a right to life and property as sacred as anyone's, according to international law.

On such counts the predicament we suffer becomes a fully developed dilemma, as Myrdal employed that word. The stresses divide American society into parcels of intense feeling. One is spared having to illustrate such a point in the wake of the 1968 election and recent demonstrations. Perhaps more critical than the divisions among groups are the divisions of people within.

For whites, and maybe some blacks, this kind of anguish must equal the anguish even of racial discrimination. Does a young man accept the draft? Ought a great doctor defy it? Should we imprison a priest who pours blood on draft records? While people endure making such judgments, moreover, the whole institution of war takes on a new perspective. For the second time in American history, we confront a "peculiar institution." As once slavery came to the point where the ancient apologies for its existence lost the power to convince, so now does the institution of war. As Americans many times in the past have had to bear the tensions between unilateral power and multilaterally dispersed authority, so again they do now. But the contradiction was never before so universally urgent. Never before was it so fully out in the open, in so many ways realized, as it has now become.

Anxiety, Ideology, and Order:
Reflections on the Making of American Public Policy
CHARLES E. ROSENBERG

INSOFAR AS LAW AND ORDER are not embodied in specific institutional practices, they are an emotional cue, one mobilizing deeply felt hopes, fears, and anxieties. In our times this distinction hardly needs to be elaborated.

I am neither a student of legal institutions nor a social psychologist and cannot discuss with great confidence either one of these meanings of the concept. These pages attempt simply to suggest aspects of American history that have seemed to shape and energize concepts of order and to trace some of the ways in which this emotional and intellectual heritage may have affected attitudes and thus decision-making in the foreign policy area.

Relationships between nations are in general defined by power; and ordinarily the rule of law is an ultimate recourse in the sphere of international affairs only when differences are relatively small or power relationships unclear. Yet it is only the ideologue—the worshiper of force for its invigorating spiritual effect or the academic would-be realist—who justifies the exercise of force as a necessary, even therapeutic, part of life. The average educated citizen of any Western country would endorse without hesitation an earnest policy of abiding by the procedures of law and the principles of equity in the solution of international quarrels. But, as Brecht's bourgeois entrepreneur of crime, Mr. Peachum, puts it: "But circumstances will simply never allow it." Particular international relationships tend to be defined so that some competing absolute—religion, human freedom, the national existence—makes an abstract respect for the procedural order of international law inapplicable if not irrelevant.

This inconsistency is not American but human. The problem that faces us as Americans concerned with decision-making in the foreign policy area is a consequence of American power, not of some peculiar inability to make our actions conform to our self-image. It is the reality of this power that makes the decisions of Washington so significant; and it is the need to understand every aspect of the decision-makers' perceptions of reality that makes our present discussion of American concepts of order immediately relevant and imparts a particular urgency to the historian's normal desire to understand the historical roots of particular human actions.

II

One of the oldest and most generally accepted generalizations about America—an observation with the imprimatur of Alexis de Tocqueville and Henry James, among others—is that our new nation lacked strong and reassuringly stable social institutions.[1] America is a nation without decaying castles, the argument runs, but also without an established church, without a well-defined intellectual class, without the mediating influences of assured social roles and stable levels of aspiration. From this perspective, America has always lacked both an elite maintaining high culture and a common people reassured by the felt realities of traditional institutions. An unceasing need for achievement replaces such older securities; moreover, economic and geographic mobility have tended only to exacerbate these strivings. Thus one version of personality and the American social structure.[2]

Another emphasis, employing not inconsistent materials, is far more positive in its implications. This position urges that the major virtue of America and Americans is that they are always in the process of becoming. The elaboration of individually rewarding modes of thought and more responsive institutional practices results from an unending process of social readjustment. From Frederick Jackson Turner to its most articulate recent spokesman, Daniel Boorstin, this point of view

---

[1] On America's lack of stable institutions, the study by Stanley Elkins, *Slavery: A Problem in American Constitutional and Intellectual Life* (Chicago: The University of Chicago Press, 1959), has been extraordinarily influential. Elkins ingeniously elaborates in mid–twentieth century idiom a number of fundamental consequences of anti-institutionalism in American social thought and public life.

[2] The amount of real social mobility in America compared with that of Western Europe is not really relevant. The fact is that both American and European observers have *felt* that such mobility did exist. It is this perception of the possibility for changed status that might be expected to maximize social anxiety. And see the significant study by David C. McClelland, *The Achieving Society* (Princeton: Van Nostrand, 1961).

has always been influential among American historians.³ Scholars of this persuasion emphasize not the cultural erosion and individual stress caused by these constantly changing conditions but the adaptiveness and social flexibility to which they gave rise. The growth of American society thus created an optimism and manipulativeness that made the utopian immanent, domesticating a hope of general virtue and even moral perfection in minds otherwise normal. Thus the peculiar moral intensity of many Americans, an intensity that has often amused sophisticated Europeans. (The archetypal Clemenceau and Wilson anecdotes conveniently illustrate this confrontation.) With the possibility of unalloyed good seemingly realizable, morally committed Americans have often found it difficult to accept the institutional compromises with human nature that make up the necessary fabric of day-to-day life.

Let us extend our catalogue of generally accepted, if in tone inconsistent, generalizations about American personality. Historians commonly emphasize the allegedly characteristic American acceptance of pragmatic attitudes and material values. The argument is hardly novel. The same conditions of change, the same need for practical solutions to the demands of changed environmental and social stimuli, the same need to produce results at the hazard of chaos have made Americans the masters of realism, of accepting that which works because it does. Hence the customary explanations of phenomena as seemingly diverse as Yankee ingenuity and bread-and-butter unionism.

Yet this pragmatic spirit offers little help in explaining the rather unpragmatic—even messianic—views that Americans have entertained of themselves collectively. Beginning with the seventeenth century experience, and through the explicit ideological redefinitions of the late eighteenth century, articulate Americans have always tended to see a better human order embodied in their nation's civic arrangements. And the success of these unique "democratic institutions" rested, it was also assumed, upon the piety and education of America's citizens. Clothed as the United States has been in these mission-justifying absolutes—democracy and individualism, piety and election—it has always been difficult for many Americans to evaluate with clarity their international prerogatives. Citizens of other nations also confuse what they perceive to be their immediate social order with one divinely

---

[3] Daniel Boorstin, *The Americans: The Colonial Experience* (New York: Random House, 1958); *idem, The Americans: The National Experience* (New York: Random House, 1965).

sanctioned. But for many generations a good number of Americans have seemed to accept this belief with comparatively few relativistic qualms and a correspondingly zealous righteousness. America's economic abundance has served only to strengthen and justify these beliefs, has seemed merely the inevitable reward of superior public virtue. Ironically, this very economic strength underlies the power that has made the understanding of American foreign policy in mid–twentieth century so relevant a scholarly enterprise.

III

How does one evaluate the possible influence of emotional and intellectual factors on the assumptions of American decision-makers, assuming that they are not simply dismissed as elusive, inconsistent, and ultimately academic? This is no easy question, for the mixture we have described of individual opportunity and the maximization of anxiety, of piety and the pervasiveness of material aspiration is ill-assorted indeed.

One logical connection lies in the strategic place that concepts of law and order occupy in America. It seems justifiable to assume that among a population in which the achievement motive and the stress of change are maximized, the need of many individuals for order and cultural reassurance is proportionally greater. There is indeed, as we have seen demonstrated with such clarity in recent years, a quality of desperation and repressive moral aggression in demands for law and order. And those who use this rubric refer not to the institutional and procedurally defined meaning of the term but employ it as an incantation, a plea for the legitimization of values and status in the face of change and inner disquietude. Thus the instinctively repressive reaction to such seemingly diverse phenomena as racial conflict and narcotics addiction—symbolic problems that mobilize deeply felt fears of the loss of control. Order must be imposed with an emphatic and revealingly disproportionate violence. These ritualistic gestures of aggression may well express and, in the expression, allay such cultural anxieties. In a society in which the vision of order plays so strategic and cohesive a role, one should not be surprised at the often disproportionate emotionality of response to events perceived as threats to it.

Race and narcotics are examples of domestic concerns in which the imposition of order is an instinctive response of many Americans.

Similarly, in the area of foreign affairs such needs may well have contributed to the pervasiveness of belief in the existence of ultimate conspiratorial threats to our value-incorporating social order.[4] In a nation in which the traditional sources of cultural reassurance are few, it is correspondingly difficult to accept the random or irrelevant; a scenario based on explicitly polarized moral conflict makes international affairs more understandable and hence more acceptable to many Americans. Again we see the need to impose a schematically rational moral order upon the complex, the random, the potentially chaotic.

Again, a willingness to impose order upon the world by assuming the existence of conspiratorial schemes is hardly confined to Americans. Nor are all Americans so prone to such soothing oversimplifications; individual personalities choose among the alternative world views presented to them by their culture. Yet it seems likely that in a society such as ours the number of those in need of this ideological reassurance is high.

IV

A natural place to begin any discussion of these disparate aspects of American thought is Massachusetts Bay in the first half of the seventeenth century. For enduring tensions manifested themselves in these first decades of American history; and perhaps the most central of these was a shifting perception of order, of the relationship between the is and the might be. In this comparatively fluid physical and economic environment the question of an appropriate relationship between institutions and ideology had continually to be rephrased.

By mid–twentieth century standards, the Englishmen who settled Massachusetts Bay lived extremely structured and institutionalized lives. The explicit religious and social beliefs of community leaders reflected and justified a respect for order and status. Familial and social roles were, in theory, defined clearly, while the church helped coordinate and sanctioned the pattern of structured behavioral control. The distribution of land, the selection of public officers, seating in church, and the mode of dress reflected traditional assumptions in regard to the inevitability—and desirability—of an ordered, graded society. Even those institutional practices that have often seemed most

---

[4] The existence of these convictions seems unquestionable in the mid–twentieth century, whether one concedes either that such beliefs are cynically manipulated or that they may have certain bases in reality.

democratic—the town meeting, for example, or church government —acted as agents of social control and the legitimation of deferential status relationships more explicitly and effectively than they did as arenas for the expansion of roles. Voting, too, may be seen as a ritual in which high levels of participation were a measure not necessarily of individual autonomy in the twentieth century sense but of conscious and willing assent in a collective affirmation of order and status.[5] The standing order was an organic, structural manifestation of traditional ideas and practices. And few doubted that this order embodied absolute law.

Yet Massachusetts Bay was beset almost from the beginning by internal tension which made these very institutions an opportunity for change and the expression and expansion of individual roles. There were two primary sources of instability. One lay in an ultimately individualizing aspect of Puritanism itself. If spiritual knowledge was an absolute good, then a conviction of such knowledge might provoke and justify behavior in overt conflict with the mores of society. The danger of individual formulation of social norms was clear enough to men like John Winthrop; the banning of Anne Hutchinson, like the expulsion and eventual capital punishment of sufficiently persistent Quakers, demonstrated that this was the position of many of the colony's leaders.[6]

Winthrop's affirmation of order was a call for the stability of institutions and a warning against the inherent lawlessness of individual moral judgment. For him, order resided in education and rank and traditional modes of government. Yet to some, convinced by their own spiritual insights, the existing order was in one way or another imperfect and material. A true order existed in the mind of God and in the intuitions of those fortunate enough to be granted this higher knowledge.

The ever-present possibilities of spatial and economic expansion meant opportunities for such pious activists to remove themselves

---

[5] The following studies more or less explicitly endorse this position: Michael Zuckerman, "The Social Context of Democracy in Massachusetts," *William and Mary Quarterly*, 25 (1968): 523–44; Sumner Chilton Powell, *Puritan Village: The Formation of a New England Town*. (Middletown, Conn.: Wesleyan University Press, 1963); Charles S. Grant, *Democracy in the Connecticut Frontier Town of Kent* (New York: Columbia University Press, 1961).

[6] For an attempt to correlate ideology and social role in the Hutchinson affair, see Emery Battis, *Saints and Sectaries: Anne Hutchinson and the Antinomian Controversy in the Massachusetts Bay Colony* (Chapel Hill: University of North Carolina Press, 1962).

from the Bay Colony's constricting social order. Even more generally, it meant the creation of new patterns of acquisition and economic life. This was the second source of tension in the Massachusetts Bay Colony. It lay in the very open-endedness of the North American environment. The settled order that governed an English manor or market town, an organic pattern that defined the status of persons and their sexual and occupational roles, could not well remain unchanged under the stimulus of adjusting to new physical and economic circumstances. It seems plausible that North American conditions would have maximized those elements of the achievement motive already existing in seventeenth century England.

The Puritan mixture of pietistic zeal and traditionally structured social life was inherently unstable in the New World environment. The stress between an existing condition of being and a realizable better state—whether construed in individual material terms or more general spiritual and social ones—must have been a necessary source of tension for those poorly or marginally integrated into the existing social order.

A somewhat analogous tension between existing institutions and the demands of the ideal manifested itself during the era of the Revolution and in the first half-century of American political life. Colonial political institutions and attitudes had become surprisingly stable and sophisticated by the mid–eighteenth century. The very parallelism of political events in many of the colonies demonstrates the strength of this pattern of political maturation, a pattern in which the elements of localism, participation, and a structured view of the relationship between social status and political power all played a part.

But as pietistic zeal and economic opportunity clashed with the seventeenth century New Englander's instinctive sense of hierarchy, so the events of the Revolution, particularly its need for rhetorical legitimation, served as a cause of political instability. The revolutionary situation was an occasion for the employment of concepts that impugned the legitimacy and eventually helped undercut the balanced tradition of deference and participation that had made the colonies and the Revolution at once so viable and so conservative. I refer to the emphasis upon natural rights and political equalitarianism. Both were open-ended, both seemed blueprints for a better, more legitimate political order. It was inevitable that these morally compelling rhetorical absolutes would, in a rapidly expanding civic order, be used to achieve tactical advantage within the system and thus strain and reshape existing practices. It is, indeed, a traditional historical view that political institutions in the early and middle periods were remolded at least in part by the tactical deployment of these new imperatives.

V

Still another influence in ante-bellum America reinforced this tension between the real and the ideal. This was an extraordinarily pervasive evangelicalism. (Although it might be impossible to prove, it is likely that a portion of the appeal of this uncompromisingly activist, even millennial, piety lay in the insecurities of American life itself. Economic and geographic mobility implied the need to find means of legitimating status newly acquired or tenaciously maintained; evangelical piety—unlike birth or education—was a free good, demanding only the character to embrace it.) In its perfectionist and, in this sense, ultimately secularized form, such faith helped impart a style of moral outrage to the analysis of public affairs.[7] Thus the fervor of attempts to end drink or prostitution or slavery; these were not simply melioristic and pragmatic reform movements, but implacable and uncompromising portions of a crusade to remake an imperfect world, to impose an ultimate moral order upon an erring nation.

It has been argued that Americans, in the absence of explicit class or ideological schisms, have used issues of style or gesture to assert the legitimacy and status of particular groups in a diverse and rapidly changing society.[8] Though perhaps overschematized, there is at least

[7] Still the most detailed and convincing study of the social aspects of this secularized perfectionism is that by Whitney Cross, *The Burned-over District: The Social and Intellectual History of Enthusiastic Religion in Western New York, 1800–1850* (Ithaca, N.Y.: Cornell University Press, 1950). See also Timothy L. Smith, *Revivalism and Social Reform in Mid–Nineteenth-Century America* (New York and Nashville: Abingdon Press, 1957). Other historians have tended to emphasize the element of social control in the evangelical reforms of the ante-bellum period: Clifford S. Griffin, *Their Brothers' Keepers: Moral Stewardship in the United States, 1800–1865* (New Brunswick, N.J.: Rutgers University Press, 1960); Charles I. Foster, *An Errand of Mercy: The Evangelical United Front, 1790–1837* (Chapel Hill: University of North Carolina Press, 1960); John R. Bodo, *The Protestant Clergy and Public Issues, 1812–1848* (Princeton, N.J.: Princeton University Press, 1954).

[8] See particularly the influential works of Richard Hofstadter, in which this insight plays a central role. For a recent and perhaps overly emphatic attempt to illuminate the way in which the politics of social style creates and feeds upon cultural issues, see Joseph R. Gusfield, *Symbolic Crusade: Status Politics and the American Temperance Movement* (Urbana: University of Illinois Press, 1963).

some truth to this; and thus again appears the irony of American public life with its pragmatic and relatively orderly political institutions providing stability and continuity while a significant minority assumes another point of order, one in which moral behavior and piety were ultimately essential, not "mundane" political and economic role-playing. It seems not implausible to assume that one of the causes of the Civil War lay in this discontinuity, this conflict between the is and the must be.

That the tension between ideal and reality, that the stress of individual choice in an open society affect personality was a truism for nineteenth century social critics. Throughout the century, American psychiatrists—who, in the details of their hypothetical etiologies were necessarily social critics—argued that the incessant need for making decisions in the economic sphere, as well as freedom in politics and extremism in religion, made their countrymen peculiarly susceptible to such stress. There was indeed a rather spirited debate between physicians and some clergymen over the possible role of enthusiastic religion in provoking mental instability. The empirical truth or falsity of this belief is neither relevant nor ascertainable; what is undeniable, however, was the concern of a number of thoughtful Americans with the instability and tensions of the society they lived in and their use of this medical idiom to express such qualms. Men seemed to need order and pattern to maintain their psychic balance. To contemporaries the evidence seemed undeniable that the conditions of life in nineteenth century America were creating unnatural, and to some individuals unbearable, psychic pressures.[9]

It is no accident, moreover, that this form of social criticism was cast in the mode of scientific metaphor. For a majority of Americans have placed an unquestioning faith in the products and values of science and technology. The tangible progress of American industrial technology seemed—and seems—only to document the inherent virtue of the national character. The success of American economic life guaranteed the validity of the nation's spiritual mission; and this aspect of success became to many Americans a real part of their na-

[9] See, for example, Norman Dain, *Concepts of Insanity in the United States, 1789–1865* (New Brunswick, N.J.: Rutgers University Press, 1964); Charles Rosenberg, "The Place of George M. Beard in Nineteenth-Century Psychiatry," *Bulletin of the History of Medicine*, 36 (1962): 245–59; Mark D. Altschule, *Roots of Modern Psychiatry: Essays in the History of Psychiatry* (New York and London: Grune & Stratton, 1957), pp. 119–39.

tion's moral endowment. It was inconceivable to most nineteenth century Americans that the steam engine and morality were not somehow interconnected. It was unthinkable that the failure of, let us say, the Burmese to produce such artifacts was somehow not connected with their lack of evangelical Christianity. Progress and technology were natural elements in the American vision of the nation's higher moral order. The contacts of Americans with other cultures in the so-called developing areas simply dramatized, even in the 1960s, the strength and tenacity of this complex of ideas. The very technological backwardness of the underdeveloped nations seems both to explain and to justify the right of American foreign policy to shape and reorder their social fabric.[10]

This need of Americans to impose a higher, if not ideal, order upon an external world has been demonstrated many times by historians and novelists in terms both social and individual. One thinks, for example, of the frontier mining camp, with its vigilante justice, its hard-won political institutions necessarily ruthless because gained at the threat of anarchy. One thinks, for example, of Faulkner's Thomas Sutpen and his grandly pathetic "design," a vision that provides a striking metaphor for many other aspects of American individual and corporate behavior. Opportunity, insecurity, naïveté, and idealistic aggressiveness have too often created a desire to impose a comforting order over lives, institutions—and foreign nations.

VI

But, if all the preceding suggestions are true in the stylized sense in which such generalizations can be called true, what is their relevance to the understanding of American foreign policy? For this is clearly the goal of any academic group hoping to explore the conditions for a peaceful solution to international problems.

[10] We have not discussed another complex of images and values through which Americans have allayed feelings of national inadequacy—and at times legitimized unilateral foreign policy actions. I refer to the configuration of images and emotions that might for convenience be labeled agrarian primitivism; Americans were better because closer to the true order of nature, leading a simpler, more productive, less effete life. Such ideas had historically coexisted peacefully, if illogically, with a worship of progress and technology. There is no real inconsistency, of course, in appealing simultaneously to both areas of emotional relevance. The themes of social thought are necessarily consistent only in function, not in their formal elements.

As a college student, I was very skeptical of such ideological explanations of American behavior in this area. A child of the thirties, I had grown up with the assumption that our foreign policy was simply the instrument of a dominant capitalist class; inconsistencies either were merely apparent or resulted from a lack of unity and coordination within this preeminent group. Yet this is not a completely adequate explanation. It does not, for example, quite explain Vietnam. Perhaps the ultimate origin of our involvement, certainly the world view of many of the prominent decision-makers, reflects the point of view of American capitalism. Yet the nature of our involvement and its internal dynamic simply cannot be explained on the basis of a rational class interest alone.

The politics of messianism is not dead. Even if one assumes that the rhetoric of Cold War theology has been manipulated with complete cynicism, one must still explain why its emotional relevance is great enough to make it a factor in the execution and ultimate public justification of any controversial policy. From one point of view it is not essential to know whether Dean Rusk really believed in an absolutely desirable American order and the imperative of supporting and propagating it. For these emotionally burdened concepts have been used so often in creating psychic moods that legitimate and justify a foreign policy of force and mission that they are clearly a part of the nation's psychic landscape. And it is our activist policy that conflicts so brutally with the procedural adjudication of international disputes.[11]

VII

We have not yet, of course, analyzed with any degree of precision the final question of the practical relevance of the social attitudes we have tried to describe. These are mere words, it may be argued, and their study is an exercise in verbal agility alone. All these discussions of social malaise are both arbitrary and blandly academic. At best they cannot *prove* anything about the nature of decision-making in our society, and at worst they channel critical energies into areas essentially sterile. And there is some truth to this criticism.

---

[11] Here, of course, is a task for the social psychologist. We can and should study with assiduity the distribution of attitudes such as those discussed in these pages by personality type. With the increasing sophistication of content analytical schemes, it is not inconceivable that the distribution of such attitudes may be studied historically in more than impressionistic terms.

Truth in this sense at least: it would seem that as scholars interested in peace research and as Americans there is no responsibility more important than to analyze the institutional bases of American society. The complex of ideas we have been discussing must finally be seen as structural elements in an intricate configuration of political and social institutions. We must first locate the sites of power in the decision-making process and identify the decision-makers and administrators. Perhaps then it will be possible to study something of the individual and group characteristics of these influential men, their education and shared social values. Only then can one realistically attempt to evaluate the precise role of emotional and ideological factors in the determination of individual social perceptions and thus—ultimately—public policy.

BIBLIOGRAPHICAL NOTE

In the footnotes I cited a few immediately relevant studies. The point of view expressed in this essay is synthetic, however, and incorporates the ideas and emphases of more historians than I could consciously avow. The writings of Richard Hofstadter have exemplified for a generation the use of what might be called metasocial psychology as a tool for explaining events within the sphere of public policy. See particularly *The Age of Reform: From Bryan to F. D. R.* (New York: Knopf, 1956). The emphasis on psychological and emotional explanations of American history so pervasive in the 1950s has had, I think, a permanent effect on those, like myself, who began their graduate education in this decade—even though we were too young to be haunted directly by the bitterly rejected enthusiasms of the thirties. For a summary of some of these explanations, see Daniel Bell, ed., *The New American Right* (New York: Criterion, 1955). Theodor W. Adorno *et al.*, *The Authoritarian Personality* (New York: Harper, 1950), with its definition and, by implication, explanation of bigotry in terms of individual psychodynamics, exerted, I think, a major influence among historians in reinforcing these trends. It has had, of course, a good many successors.

PART II

The Assertion of Violent Power: An American Crescendo

American Foreign Policy in the Early Cold War: The Dilemmas of Historical Continuity
WALTER LaFEBER

Continuity in asserting national power derives from long-run consistency in national leadership. And, while in general the executive is as fully a part of the operation of constitutional checks and balances as are Congress and the judiciary, presidents have for a century and a half made American foreign policy ever more aggressive.

Law and Order in American Thought: An Ambiguous Heritage
WILLIAM L. NEUMANN

Not only at the White House, but also among the people broadly, the mystique of a great national community has been built on our exercise of power in the world. Thus Americans have been both peace-loving and war-loving. A reduction of the war-loving factor would alter our familiar pattern of loyalties.

Canada and the American Dilemma: Realism versus Idealism, 1945-1964
CAMERON NISH
Assisted by STEPHEN ABBOTT

Not the United States by itself, but likewise its most familiar and compatible neighbor, Canada, is torn by the war-or-peace, armament-or-disarmament, issue. National militancy is a catching disease, but, among Canadians, only recently has discussion helped to reveal its prevalence there.

American Foreign Policy in the Early Cold War: The Dilemmas of Historical Continuity

WALTER LaFEBER

IN SEPTEMBER 1968, John Roche, a political scientist who had served for two years as a White House aide, informed the American Political Science Association that history was of little use when policy makers were confronted with such an immediate crisis as, for example, the Soviet invasion of Czechoslovakia.[1] This statement reveals much about American foreign policy in the 1960s and, indeed, about that policy throughout the twentieth century.

There is no such thing as a *tabula rasa* in American (or Soviet) foreign policy. Foreign policy, like law, cannot be formulated successfully without an understanding of the past and the recognition by the formulators that the past imposes inexorable limitations upon them. Roche, ironically, finds support for his view of history (although certainly not for his ideas on foreign policy) from some New Left members, particularly those who have denigrated ideology and turned to "pragmatic" confrontation politics because they have not wished to be restrained by the historical values and judgments that ideological commitments require. Bad sociology replaces "irrelevant" history; those who believe they move forward pragmatically without the restraints of history and ideology move instead toward a dead end within an ideological maze they have unknowingly entered but have never comprehended. The official policies on Vietnam and some New Left attemps to change them stand out as examples of this kind of failure of comprehension.

If adequate insight is to be provided into the dilemmas and alternatives of contemporary foreign policy, an understanding of American diplomatic history is prerequisite. In seeking such understanding, one point of departure might be an analysis of unilateralism in American foreign policy. Comprehending unilateralism leads to an understanding of how academic has been much of the writing and discussion of so-

[1] *New York Times*, Sept. 7, 1968, p. 21.

called American isolationism. Such comprehension also challenges the belief that through important parts of its history the United States functioned within a womb of "free security." Finally, even a brief study of unilateralism can question the "collective security" fallacy that has so long served as a shibboleth for foreign policy officials and observers.[2]

II

Before the United States became a great world power in the 1890s, its attention focused primarily on the American continents. In this carefully defined arena for action, the United States moved from the policy premises that isolationism and free security were myths. Given the views Americans hold of their role as the dominant power in this hemisphere, isolationism and free security were myths indeed.

As it assumed power within the hemisphere during the nineteenth century, the United States believed that all nations were equal neither in the sight of God nor in the view of international power tacticians. Americans took unto themselves a right to determine policy and, at every opportunity, the law for the Western Hemisphere. When Secretary of State Richard Olney announced in 1895 that United States "fiat was law" in the Americas, he made explicit what John Quincy Adams believed to be the case at the time of the Monroe Doctrine's birth.[3] To many American eyes, the limits of multiple sovereignty were apparent in the Floridas between 1809 and 1813, Texas in the 1820s through the mid-1840s, Oregon, California, and in other parts of what used to be Mexican territory. The United States distinguished European nations particularly by the amount of their holdings on and around the North American continent. Jacksonian James K. Polk attacked the British, but so did John Quincy Adams in some of the most cutting and ideologically oriented language ever used by a Washington official to describe a foreign power.

General American histories have not emphasized Adams' attack, in

[2] For a fascinating discussion of "isolationism" and "collective security," see interview with Secretary of State Dean Rusk in the *New York Times*, Dec. 1, 1968, p. 1. William Goetzmann, *When the Eagle Screamed: The Romantic Horizon in American Diplomacy, 1800–1860* (New York: Wiley, 1966) is interesting primarily for the questions raised about the "free security" concept.
[3] Olney to American Ambassador Thomas F. Bayard, July 20, 1895, in *Foreign Relations of the United States, 1895* (Washington, 1896), 1:545–62.

part perhaps because he was most concerned about British (or Spanish) acts not in Europe but on the American continent itself. Since everyone knows how happily that story ended, and because the United States never did get into another war with Great Britain after 1812 (or with Spain until 1898), these matters have too often been described as a part of the American success story, the culmination of a truly fabulous manifest destiny, the triumph of the quest for "security." They have not been regarded, as they should be, as the historical introduction to the Cold War. In the post-1941 years, the primary difference would be the environment in which the policies operated. That the United States did not go to war with European powers between 1812 and 1898 is due less to the American legal and moral view of those powers than to the diplomatic priorities set and political restraints practiced by American and particularly European diplomats and peoples during that era.

III

Important American leaders often operated in the pre-1900 environment without undue concern for the sovereignty of others, either inside or outside the American system. The twentieth century variation of domestic "pluralism" is associated with the federal system developed at the Philadelphia Convention. The "Father of the Constitution," as John Quincy Adams called him, was James Madison, and that Virginian certainly thought as intensively and wrote as comprehensively about the political-economic system as any American since. It is therefore significant that when Madison arose at the Convention to discuss the ultimate problem of sovereignty, he proposed that the central government have an absolute veto "in all cases whatsoever" over the state governments.[4] After the Convention, he worried again that the powers of the central government were not sufficiently extensive. He was particularly concerned that problems might arise in the vast and expanding American domain with which the central government would be unable to cope through only federal means. When Madison and Jefferson obtained Louisiana seventeen years later, they dismissed the idea that republican processes could preserve order and peace in the area. Until, as Jefferson indicated, enough democratically in-

---

[4] Max Farrand, ed., *The Records of the Federal Convention of 1787*, 4 vols. (New Haven: Yale University Press, 1937), 2:305–7, 361, 363–64, 451–52.

clined American settlers moved into the trans-Mississippi region, the administration would rule through military means. Multiple sovereignty obviously had its limits, even within the territorial boundaries of the nation that had produced *The Federalist*. Forty-five years later, after the Jacksonian movement had supposedly promoted the principles of democracy and multiple sovereignty, James K. Polk informed Congress in three different parts of his annual message of 1848 that he as president, not they, best represented the American people because he had been placed in power by the entire electorate while they represented only various and diverse factions of the public.[5] Presidential powers were thereby placed on a much higher level of legitimacy and respect than the political and socioeconomic units of that constituency with which the executive had to deal.

When the United States became a great world power in the late 1890s, two tendencies toward aggressiveness had already appeared: first, the United States had allowed neither law nor the concept of multiple sovereignty to hinder its foreign policies in such critical areas as the Floridas, Indian relations, or dealings with the Mexican government; second, such different men as Madison and Polk, and particularly the latter, were not reluctant to increase presidential control of foreign policy. (It is interesting, however, that Madison's course as president in 1810 and 1811, when he refused to go to war without a clear mandate from Congress, has been judged by most historians as weak and indecisive.)

IV

These two themes have continued to characterize American policy after 1900, but they have operated in a considerably different context. The arena for confrontation has no longer been the American continent but the world. The prizes have no longer been holdings, often peripheral, of European empires, but deeper interests including at times the most vital areas of security. For Americans, however, the power of historical continuity and the euphoria of their own real success on the continent were too strong for any meaningful change in strategy.

[5] James D. Richardson, ed., *A Compilation of the Messages and Papers of the Presidents, 1789–1897* (Washington, 1900), 4:629–70.

In 1910 the environment was even more radically changed by the occurrence of the first of the great twentieth century revolutions. The outbreak in Mexico signaled as dramatically as any single event in history how the course of United States foreign policy in the eighteenth and nineteenth centuries caught up with and confronted Americans of the twentieth century with profound dilemmas. Woodrow Wilson's response was truly in the American tradition when he attempted to teach the Mexicans how to elect good men and then sent a 60,000-man American army south of the border to chastise Mexican bandits.

These problems of revolution and the American response were complex enough in and of themselves to initiate American-Soviet rivalry in 1917–1918 and trigger the Cold War after 1941, first in Europe and then in Asia. The problem was further complicated, particularly in the post–World War II period, by American political spokesmen who insisted upon using the word "revolution" in reference to the American process begun in 1776. True, the spread of the American version of revolution had considerable application as it marched across the continent. But once to the Pacific shore, that version lost much of its relevance as a model for events in the remainder of the world. The other eighteenth century revolution, the French upheaval, became more useful as a historical analogy for the radical changes occurring in the world after 1910. The bloodshed, chaos, and monarchy in France after 1789 were not, however, what Americans had in mind when they lauded revolutions; United States citizens tried to think more positively about such things.

Besides presenting the twentieth century style of revolution, the Cold War environment of the United States differed from that of the eighteenth and nineteenth centuries in yet another way. During the first hundred or so years of the new nation, American foreign policy was often an extension of particular domestic interests, whether those were American farmers settling in the Floridas and Texas, Baltimore merchants dealing with Latin American revolutions and Chinese diplomats, or Protestant missionaries proselytizing in the Willamette Valley and the Hawaiian Islands. This feature particularly marked the conquering of the continent, for in many critical episodes American policy-makers followed after settlers and merchants who had first defined particular geographical areas as holding high value for the United States. The various interests tended to be politically represented through Congress; from that body diverse pressures arose upon the chief executive to take particular steps in foreign policy. But that body and those pressures also could act as a check upon the president in foreign policy. Madison's multiple "factions" could, in such an arena, act to limit both the power of the executive and to control factions that did not represent the national interest. Polk discovered this when he unsuccessfully attempted to move beyond the California ports to all of Mexico and then tried to occupy the Mexican province of Yucatan. Given the national interests of the United States at the time, neither the various socioeconomic interests nor their political representatives would allow Polk to move that far. Despite Polk's pronouncements regarding the supremacy of presidential power, the power of the president in foreign policy was restrained.

Since 1898—and in the context of the Cold War, particularly since the Truman Doctrine of 1947—the chief executive's powers have not been held under such restrictions. The process of American expansion, and consequently the political and decision-making processes themselves, have changed. Expansion has continued, but in quite sophisticated forms and in distant areas; both of these changes have eliminated the immediacy that foreign policy held for Americans before 1898. Combined with this break has been the ideological commitment against revolution, and particularly communism, that united the domestic factions with the presidency in a concerted foreign policy crusade.

Material factors have continued to play a fundamental role but in a considerably different manner. The success of the American corporation has promoted cohesiveness, not factionalism. The corporation, with the decline since the mid–nineteenth century of the influence of the American farmer, missionary, and merchant in the foreign policy realm, has tended to consolidate the interests that formerly restrained presidential powers by restraining one another. The success of the corporation has had another effect in the Cold War: it has become so prosperous and powerful internationally that it has been able to make its way in, for example, the pivotal Western European area, without the complete attention and political assistance of American diplomatic officials. George Ball remarked in May 1967 that the United States no longer needed to pursue the Open Door in Africa; that area, he asserted, could confidently be left to Europeans to worry about politically while the United States pacified and developed other parts of the world.⁶ Left unsaid by Ball—who, given his occupation and interests, must certainly have been aware of it—was that American economic power was so firmly entrenched in Western Europe that any success it experienced in developing Africa would automatically benefit American enterprises.

Because of the political and economic changes and the ideological consensus which have developed since the nineteenth century, the American presidency has shed the restraints in foreign policy that formerly kept the chief executive under at least a semblance of control. Lacking support from either scholars or some socioeconomic factions, Congress has until very recently abdicated its responsibility in examining and restraining presidential powers in foreign affairs. As in the era of Washington, Jefferson, Madison, and Polk, the fight between the executive and the legislative branches of government theoretically continued. But because of the changed international environment in which American foreign policy operated after 1898, and particularly after 1941, that struggle became increasingly theoretical, less and less actual. The process by which American foreign policy was determined had become defactionalized, depoliticized, and de-democratized, each following from the other in that order.

In summary, by the beginnings of the Cold War four significant historical themes had developed that shaped the United States dilemma in foreign policy. First, the American regard for law and sovereignty had often been compromised in the nineteenth century as the young republic conquered a continent. At times, as in the case of relations with the Indians and with Mexico, the United States unilaterally determined the law. Second, just as Americans completed this conquest and prepared to extend their own revolution to other parts of the world, they suddenly confronted a type of revolution different from their own, one containing a socioeconomic and ideological dimension that they interpreted as a fundamental challenge to their own professions of law and sovereignty. Third, several strong presidents successfully consolidated control over foreign policy in the hands of the chief executive. Fourth, the restraints that had limited the nineteenth century president tended to disappear with the century's close, and by the Cold War era the chief executive, often unchecked by factions or Congress, dominated foreign policy formulation to the detriment of the democratic process.

⁶ George Ball, "Multinational Corporations and Nation States," *Atlantic Quarterly*, 5 (Summer 1967): 247–53.

V

Perhaps this last characteristic, indeed all four characteristics, can be exemplifed through the American liking for the word "doctrine" in characterizing foreign policies. As Richard Van Alstyne has observed, when "doctrine" was used to describe President Monroe's pronouncement in 1823, his words became more than a mere policy; they assumed a sacrosanct quality often characteristic of the doctrines of a church.[7]

In 1845, James K. Polk revived the Monroe Doctrine and appropriately gave it, in the term of Dexter Perkins, an injection of "aggression" that was missing from the 1823 message. Sixty years later Theodore Roosevelt added a corollary to the doctrine, significantly doing so on an issue (American control of Santo Domingo's customs houses) on which Congress refused to give its assent. Roosevelt nevertheless went ahead to make the doctrine operative by negotiating an executive agreement.

Since 1947, three of the four presidents have had their names popularly associated with particular doctrines. The Truman Doctrine put containment into effect, aiming at either "the break-up or the gradual mellowing of Soviet power," to use the words of Mr. "X" (George Kennan). The Eisenhower Doctrine of 1957 obtained authorization from Congress to give Middle Eastern nations quick economic and military cooperation including, if necessary and if requested by any of those nations, American military forces. The Johnson Doctrine of May 2, 1965 (coming on the aftermath of the presidential decision to intervene in the Dominican Republic) warned that change in the Western Hemisphere "should come through peaceful process" and that the United States would defend "every free country of this hemisphere" from communism and radical revolution. "American nations," President Johnson solemnly announced, "cannot, must not, and will not permit the establishment of another communist government in the Western Hemisphere." On each of these post-1947 occasions, Congress consented more than it advised. When the Senate tried to ask questions and stall the Eisenhower Doctrine, the State Department and the White House overrode the opposition—though mail from

---

[7] R. W. Van Alstyne, *The Rising American Empire* (New York: Oxford University Press, 1960), pp. 7–9.

constituents at one time ran 8–1 against the doctrine—with the vital help of Majority Leader Lyndon B. Johnson.

The jump from Polk to Johnson, while long in terms of time, is short in terms of strategy. The context within which the policies operate is the most important difference. The transition from the 1840s to the 1960s was continuous; historical continuity can no more be broken than it can be denied. In discussing American policy leading into the Cold War, however, one decade—the years between 1941 and 1950—seems to be unusually fruitful for those who wish to understand how American unilateralism and the growth of presidential power were transferred from the continent to the world.

VI

In midsummer of 1941, Henry Luce, the founder and editor-in-chief of Time-Life, Inc., published a series of editorials entitled "The American Century." Soon issued as a popular book, Luce's views reached a large audience ready to accept his argument that because the United States would emerge from the World War with incomparable economic and military strength, it could shape the world to its liking and thereby create the first "American Century." Only Great Britain, Luce believed, could in any way interpose its power, and with the decline of the British Empire he was confident that London officials would be content to play junior partner in the Anglo-American reconstruction of the postwar ruins.

A month after the publication of Luce's book, President Franklin D. Roosevelt attempted to lay the groundwork for the American Century in his meeting with Prime Minister Winston Churchill at the Atlantic Conference. The principles laid down at that conference, if accepted and followed by the world after the war, would indeed have resulted in at least the beginnings of the American Century. But the Atlantic Charter's provisions that all nations should have equal access to all parts of the world and that all territorial changes should depend upon the acceptance of the populations involved encountered immediate obstacles. In September, Churchill sternly informed the House of Commons that the British Empire would not be affected by such clauses. That same month the Soviet Union accepted the charter but with the highly significant reservation that the document would have to be interpreted in the context of "the circumstances, needs, and historic peculiarities of particular countries."[8] In December, Stalin gave this abstraction reality when he demanded from Foreign Secretary Anthony Eden an immediate British-Russian agreement on postwar Soviet frontiers. These were to be set without regard for either equal access or democratic elections held among those peoples in Eastern Europe who would be affected by the shifting of the boundaries. Eden, and later Roosevelt, stalled the Soviet dictator. In October 1944, Churchill and Stalin worked out a crude percentage arrangement for the division of Eastern Europe (except Poland). Roosevelt informed the other two leaders that the United States would have to maintain its freedom of action and could not agree to the deal for any long period.

By the autumn and winter of 1944, American policy-makers clearly saw the two major obstacles to the successful initiation of the American Century. One barrier was the British Empire, the other the Soviet determination to seal off Eastern Europe. In 1941 Roosevelt had talked about the "two policemen," the British and Americans, who would keep peace and order in the world after the war until reconstruction would allow the international organization to shoulder the task. The president and the State Department then attempted to cut the strength of the British Empire through Article VII of the Lend-Lease agreement. In that provision, the British, after a bitter fight, agreed to discuss allowing equal access to their empire after the war. In 1944 and 1945 the State and Treasury Departments moved through this opening. With the agreement on the British loan arrangements in December 1945, the United States was assured that the old imperial preference system, and most other preferences within the empire that the war-torn British economy might desire, could not be reestablished. Through the agreement, as Assistant Secretary of State William Clayton privately pointed out, the United States had also taken a major step in halting the nationalization of the internal British economy by the newly elected Labor Party. The sovereignty of the other member of the Anglo-American police force had not emerged from the war unimpaired.

[8] For a good discussion of the Atlantic Charter see Martin Herz, *Beginnings of the Cold War* (Bloomington: Indiana University Press, 1966) (much of the following on the 1944–1945 period is based on Herz); Lloyd Gardner, *Economic Aspects of New Deal Diplomacy* (Madison: University of Wisconsin Press, 1964); and my own *America, Russia, and the Cold War, 1945–1966* (New York, 1967).

By late 1942 a third policeman—a Russian—had been added to the force. He too was to be subject to the criteria of the American Century. The Moscow Declaration of 1943, the Declaration of Liberated Europe in early 1945, and the American refusal to agree to postwar boundary settlements indicated the tactics favored by Roosevelt to ensure an open world, free from competing power blocs, after the war. Stalin meanwhile used the Red Army to establish unilaterally his own security arrangements. With the conclusion of the Yalta Conference he could have determined that his partners in the Big Three would not provide the Soviet Union with adequate security in terms of either military buffers or resources for postwar reconstruction.

On March 1, 1945, Roosevelt nevertheless announced to Congress that unilateralism and spheres of influence had been abolished at Yalta. "The Crimean Conference was a successful effort by the three leading nations to find a common ground for peace," he said. "It spells the end of the system of unilateral action and exclusive alliances and spheres of influence and balances of power and all the other expedients which have been tried for centuries—and have failed."[9] Those sentences considerably oversimplified the situation. What had occurred was the climax of an American attempt from 1941 through early 1945 to define the type of postwar world that should emerge and then to influence the other two policemen to agree with that definition. The unilateral definition of American interest impinged upon the interests of at least two other sovereign and powerful policemen. The United Kingdom could not muster the strength to hold off the United States. The Soviet Union, however, was strong enough within her own East European sphere. It refused to accept without significant amendment the American draft of the Declaration of Liberated Europe, and, in the case study of the Cold War's origins, also refused to reorganize the Polish government so the anti-Communist London Poles could gain power equal or superior to that of the pro-Communist Lublin group.

During the six-week period between his address to Congress and his death in mid-April, Roosevelt came to realize what Stalin was accomplishing in Eastern Europe. By the second week of April the American president and the Soviet dictator had exchanged biting

---

[9] L. M. Goodrich and M. J. Carroll, eds., *Documents on American Foreign Relations*, vol. 7: *July 1944 to June 1945* (Princeton: Princeton University Press 1947), pp. 18–28.

words on the other's policy in Poland.[10] A similar American-Russian confrontation was shaping up over Rumania.

In Italy the sides were reversed. There the Americans and British considered the area of such critical strategic value to the West that they refused to allow Soviet participation in the vital control councils. That refusal had occurred before the flare-up over Poland and Rumania; but it intensified when, in the midst of the latter crises, Stalin accused the United States of secretly working out with German officers an Italian surrender that would free a number of Nazi divisions to move from the Italian to the Eastern front. Top level negotiations were indeed going on between German and American agents, and without Russian participation. Roosevelt and other American policymakers evidently desired more Russian cooperation in Eastern Europe than in other areas. Stalin chided President Harry S. Truman for this preference later in April. The Soviet ruler could not understand why Truman was so concerned about Poland; after all, the Russians were not being consulted in the reconstruction of Belgium, and, Stalin observed, Poland was as important to Russian security as Belgium was to British security.[11]

The unilateral American assumption in the Atlantic Charter of a commitment to a particular kind of postwar world was now presenting grave problems. These dilemmas would swell into international crises when the United States attempted to wield its military and economic power to gain the cooperation of the Soviet Union. The United States monopoly of the bomb was doubtless a disturbing spectacle to the Russians, but equally frightening and considerably more effective was American economic power. Unlike the atomic bomb, economic power was constantly brandished directly and overtly by the United States. Also unlike the atomic bomb, which the Soviet Union could offset in part with its massive land armies, the American economic power had no counterpart within the Soviet bloc. In 1946 Foreign Minister V. M. Molotov provided an important insight into the Soviet thinking of the previous months when he observed that to have allowed American economic forces equal access to war-devastated Eastern Europe during the previous two years would have meant

---

[10] *Foreign Relations of the United States, 1945* (Washington, 1967), 5:194–204.

[11] Ibid., pp. 263–64.

United States domination of that area.[12] Economic diplomacy, moreover, allowed American policy-makers to consider themselves to be constructive diplomats (as they believed themselves to be in working out the British loan arrangements). By the Potsdam Conference of July 1945, the State Department "briefing papers" for President Truman noted that the primary hope for American influence in Poland and Eastern Europe would be the manipulation of economic power. When that drive was blocked by the Polish government in August and September 1945, the United States switched its emphasis to missions of the United Nations Relief and Rehabilitation Administration—in which, in Poland for example, Washington held a 72 percent interest. When UNRRA also proved ineffective in keeping the door open, Poland finally sank behind the Iron Curtain. The United States, however, had tried nearly everything short of overt military power.

VII

These American interpretations of the American Century, the Atlantic Charter, the Moscow Declaration, the Declaration of Liberated Europe, the British imperial preference system, Soviet moves in Eastern Europe, and the power of the American economic system indicate the approach the United States followed in attempting to reconstruct a world that would be free of power and economic blocs and that would be peculiarly susceptible to a type of economic power possessed in abundance by Americans.

The unilateral American definition of these problems also indicated the United States view of the United Nations. The U.N. was conceived to maintain peace and order in the world after the three policemen had restored peace and reordered the chaos of war. The policemen, however, could not cooperate. The phrases of the United Nations Charter must be understood within the context of that failure. As early as the San Francisco Conference in the spring of 1945, the lack of cooperation in Poland, Rumania, and Italy convinced many American policy-makers that a U.N. organization was becoming irrelevant. The problem was less how to construct a workable collective security through the United Nations than how to create an organiza-

[12] V. M. Molotov, *Problems of Foreign Policy, Speeches and Statements, April 1945–November 1948* (Moscow, 1949), pp. 210–16.

tion that could not interfere with the American definition of what collective security should be. Leo Pasvolsky, picking up Cordell Hull's work of October 1943 that had resulted in the Moscow Declaration, attempted to develop a collective security organization that would include the Soviet Union. This situation, it was hoped, would force the two great powers to cooperate in the international forum. But Hull had miscalculated. He and his assistants had found the means of cooperation but had not been able to agree with the Russians on the objectives for which that cooperation should strive. The debate on objectives had broken down over issues encompassed by the Atlantic Charter and the Polish dispute.

Other Washington officials attempted to create a United Nations incapable of interfering with the American view of a proper collective security. Having just fulminated against the growing Soviet sphere of influence in Eastern Europe, American spokesmen, led by Senator Arthur Vandenberg and Assistant Secretary of State Nelson Rockefeller, included provisions in the charter, particularly Article 51, which the United States could later use to create a regional organization of its own in Latin America. Similar regional groupings would follow in Western Europe, the Southwest Pacific, Southeast Asia, and the Middle East. As Vandenberg explained, these charter provisions and the later Rio Pact removed any real threat that the Russians would be able to use their veto successfully in Western Hemisphere affairs.

In 1946 the United States attempted to take the next step: elimination of the Soviet veto.[13] If the United States had succeeded, it would have been able to dominate the U.N. on critical East-West issues through a majority controllable by American power and safe from Soviet retaliation. Vandenberg set the tone for this move in April 1946: "No more Munichs! If it is to be impossible for us to get along with the Soviets on such a basis, the quicker we find it out the better. America must behave like the Number One World Power which she is. Ours must be the world's moral leadership—or the world won't have any."[14] Two months later Bernard Baruch, preparing to announce to the United Nations the American plan for the control of atomic energy, carefully explained to President Truman and Secretary

---

[13] This episode involving the Baruch Plan was first analyzed by Professor Lloyd Gardner of Rutgers University and is presented in *Architects of Illusion* (Chicago, 1970).

[14] Arthur H. Vandenberg, Jr., ed., *The Private Papers of Senator Vandenberg* (Boston, 1952), p. 267.

of State James F. Byrnes that his plan, if adopted, would be the first step in weakening the Soviet veto because it provided that important agreements on control and punishment of aggressors could be accomplished through mere majority vote. Truman and Byrnes said they fully understood and approved.

In an important sense, Baruch's attempt to isolate and gravely weaken the Soviet Union within the U.N. was symbolic rather than substantial. The United Nations had ceased to be of primary importance in American policy-making once it became evident that Hull and Roosevelt had failed to get Soviet agreement to American objectives. The world organization from that point was peripheral to the concerns of Washington officials, who viewed its charter as more aspiration than policy guideline. A succession of American and Soviet moves made the international body further irrelevant. The United States initiated the Truman Doctrine, which in its first life was a unilateral aid program for Greece and Turkey. Three months after this doctrine was announced, the Marshall Plan began to coalesce the Atlantic Community. This plan is the foremost postwar example of American unilateralism's giving way to cooperation and producing, on the whole, spectacularly successful results. It should, however, be viewed in perspective. Since the Soviet Union was effectively excluded, it became an ironic denouement to the American hopes of just six years before that an inclusive, not exclusive, world could be created that would be wholly pledged to the tenets of an American Century. At best, the Marshall Plan in this context could be described as the American Century on the piece plan. The Soviets responded with a revitalized Cominform and their counterpart of the plan for Eastern Europe, the so-called Molotov Plan. These moves, intensified by the Berlin crisis and the growing discord over Central Europe, led to the development of the North Atlantic Treaty Alliance in 1949. NATO was by no means the result of unilateral American policies, but its primary feature, the rearmament of West Germany, did result from such policies. In 1950 the British and French wanted no part of German rearmament, and the United States accomplished its objective only after four years of determined effort and empty threats to carry out an "agonizing reappraisal" of its Western European commitments. When German troops entered NATO in 1955, that was another ironic variation on the American Century theme.

VIII

The transformation of American policy from economic aid to military commitment was not unnatural. It had been anticipated by the Truman Doctrine and the Mr. "X" article of 1947, although the author of that article, George Kennan, later claimed that he held a considerably different idea of those military levels than did his superiors in Washington.[15] In 1949–1950 the military policy was rationalized in the famous NSC-68 memorandum, which provided the context for American foreign policies of the next eighteen years. NSC-68 assumed American unilateral action; the United States necessarily occupied the "political and material center with other free nations in variable orbits around it." The economy and society would have to be mobilized and rationalized in the effort to stop communism. A defense budget of $50 billion was presumed necessary, a figure that, the authors of the memorandum confidently asserted, the economy could easily bear.[16] At that point, if not before, the United States took the step Walter Lippmann had warned against three years before when he issued a scathing rebuttal to Mr. "X." To fight a cold war of these dimensions, Lippmann had observed, meant a sociopolitical organization for which the Soviet Union was better suited than the United States.[17]

Little evidence has been found to indicate that the authors of the memorandum were at all concerned about the growing powers of the presidency or the central government in general. In both the international and domestic realms, cooperation with policies set by the executive could be assumed if those policies were sufficiently anti-Communist. The manner in which President Truman and Secretary of State Dean Acheson would operate within their executive powers was vividly illustrated in September 1950 when they committed four divisions of American soldiers to the NATO command. Eighteen months before, Acheson had promised an extremely sensitive Senate that no American troops would be sent to Europe without congressional assent. When Republican senators attempted to write an amendment that would have forced the executive to obtain congressional permission

---

[15] Kennan, *Memoirs, 1925–1950* (Boston: Little, Brown, 1967).
[16] A good brief analysis of NSC–68 is in Cabell Phillips, *The Truman Presidency* (New York: Macmillan, 1966), pp. 305–9.
[17] Walter Lippmann, *The Cold War* (New York, 1947).

before any soldiers could be sent, Acheson's assurance was used as a successful counter. A small Senate rebellion occurred after the administration committed the troops in the autumn of 1950. The outbreak was damped down by a promise that such troop commitments would not happen again without consultation with Congress. Truman meanwhile used his constitutional power as commander-in-chief of the armed forces to maintain the troops in Europe, thereby successfully making a political as well as military commitment of extraordinary significance. Unilateralism could cut two ways, internally as well as externally.

This debate over the commitment to NATO occurred during the early months of the Korean War. In a most valuable essay, the late Arnold Wolfers has shown that American policy in this conflict should not be interpreted as an example of collective security.[18] The United States did not participate in a collective decision with its various allies to enter that war, it provided an overwhelming percentage of the matériel and non-Korean troops needed to fight the war, and it laid postwar plans without consulting any of its allies, including the South Korean government. Ostensibly a United Nations command, the armies that fought to protect the government of Syngman Rhee and American bases in Japan were actually fully controlled by American officials. No formal congressional authorization was obtained for conducting the war, and no congressional permission was received before American military units were sent into battle. Whether it was right or wrong to fight the Korean War is not at issue here; what is at issue is the unilateral American decision, made largely by the executive branch of the government, to commit American men and resources to the conflict. Limited wars require extraordinary patience and support at home. Instead of receiving such support, President Truman confronted a McCarthyism that was revived by the conflict, seemingly continuous congressional investigations into the conduct of the war, and a successful Republican challenge in 1952. Wolfers has observed that the Korean example would be misleading if Americans had to participate in a costly security effort that was truly collective.

The 1941–1950 era is a continuation of the historical process begun in the early days of the American republic. When one ardent Jacksonian bragged that Old Hickory made the law while John Quincy

---

[18] Arnold Wolfers, *Discord and Collaboration* (Baltimore: The Johns Hopkins Press, 1962), pp. 167–80.

Adams merely followed it, he outlined both the dilemma and, given Adams' view of Jacksonian expansion and presidential power, one of the alternatives to the dilemma. That Americans have been Jacksonians, not admirers of Adams, is obvious. It is also natural. Peering out over the great continent, so vast and so rich that man, in Scott Fitzgerald's famous words, had finally discovered something "commensurate with his capacity for wonder," Americans could easily believe themselves above law and immune from history. History, however, caught up with the United States in the last half of the nineteenth century. One can hope that a century later Americans are beginning to comprehend the power of that history, its continuity, and its demand that it be understood if its dilemmas are to be radically transformed.

Law and Order in American Thought: An Ambiguous Heritage

WILLIAM L. NEUMANN

A STIMULATING AND GERMANE thesis has been stated by Charles Barker in this volume, raising many questions that suggest areas for fruitful peace research. Two central elements especially deserve further attention by historians.

The first deals with the content of what Barker calls "our national pledges to peace and multilateralism." What have been these pledges across the decades, and how relevant are they to the peaceful functioning of the international system? Are the pledges uniquely American, or are they found in similar form in the pronouncements of other Western powers?

The second centers on the applicability of the Gunnar Myrdal thesis to the alleged gap between American ideals and national behavior. In what form do these contradictions exist, and do they actually produce a conflict in the American conscience? If so, which Americans have been affected, and what are the results of this conflict on the nation's policy decisions? Historians of the peace movement must ask why these tensions have not been more effective in mobilizing political and other forms of action when wars have been imminent. What has happened in the twentieth century, when peace pledges seem to have proliferated while American power has so frequently been militarily engaged?

Prominent Americans have proclaimed this nation's aspirations for and commitment to the cause of peace from the days of the founding fathers onward. Peace is generally seen as achievable within the existing system of sovereign states, with each respecting the theoretically equal rights of others. It is a peace that in the nineteenth century seemed to require only minimal military strength. The sporadic wars with Indian tribes required little more than frontier garrisons, and only rarely were as many as 1 percent of the American males between the ages of twenty-one and thirty-nine in the armed forces. In the period between the end of Reconstruction and the Spanish-American War this figure remained below 0.5 percent.

II

It was relatively easy for nineteenth century Americans to agree with Benjamin Franklin's oft-repeated dictum that "there has never been nor ever will be, any such thing as a *good* war or a bad peace." This was the period C. Vann Woodward has characterized as an era of "free security," when the Atlantic and Pacific remained wide oceans and when the enemies of the United States were Indian tribes and the weakening American empires of Britain, Spain, and France. The belief in the unique peace-loving character of an innocent nation was deeply established. By ignoring the many small campaigns against the unfortunate original inhabitants of North America, the belief was supportable with historic evidence. No modern nation has yet matched the rate of territorial expansion of the nineteenth century United States with so few combat deaths and so few visible wars. But whether these Americans were unique in their love of peace even then is an open question. The Swedes and Swiss can easily dispute any such claim in the same century. An exploration of American uniqueness must not only involve historic comparisons but a definition of "peace-loving" that can be measured in some way with a degree of objectivity.

Fundamentally, peace has been for Americans—as it must be within the present nationalist ideology—a means rather than an end. Modern governments exist on the assumption that they are essential to the preservation of values that are nowhere else so securely enshrined. National survival becomes thus the highest value that justifies almost any means, including those that require the sacrifice of millions of lives. The American specialist in thinking about the unthinkable, Herman Kahn, has seen the point clearly. With illuminating realism he set out to explore the price Americans seemed willing to pay to keep their nation from becoming Red—the result, presumably, of losing a war to the Soviet Union. Asking the question of participants in his military seminars, Kahn found a general reluctance to go as far as blowing up the entire universe if this were necessary to block a Red victory. A few persons were willing to destroy the solar system. As the scale of destruction moved downward from 100 percent of the world's population, the consent of the majority of those polled was soon achieved. Thus Kahn's seminar, probably loyal members of a nation totaling only 6 percent of the world's population, was ready to have many times the population of the United States destroyed in order to prevent the nation from being subject to the will of another.

Such an effort at calculating the value of nations in human lives cannot be dismissed as mere guesswork. Public opinion polls taken after the bombing of Hiroshima and Nagasaki, late in the war when victory was no longer remote, found that a large majority of Americans was satisfied with the incineration of hundreds of thousands of Japanese in the interests of a quicker victory and the greater protection of the American armed forces. Despite the international fingers of shame later pointed at this American action, it is doubtful whether the citizens of any other great power would have reacted with any more restraint. In time of war all enemies are *Untermenschen*, to use a blunt Hitlerian expression.

If peace is ever an end in itself, it ranks low in the list of national interests and seems never worth more than a tiny fraction of the price demanded by war. President Truman repeated in 1947 what many had said before him when he launched the military aid program for Greece and Turkey, taking the American presence into the traditional sphere of Russian interests. Americans value some things more than peace, said Truman—"freedom: freedom of worship, freedom of speech, freedom of enterprise." Other national spokesmen have proclaimed the higher value of security, prosperity, honor, and inviolable commitments to allies, all to be defended by war or peace, depending upon the circumstances. The peace for which Americans aspire is not merely a condition of no war but a particular state of affairs. Frequently this is stated as a "just peace." The concept is a noble one, but exactly when the *status quo* is just is a highly undecided matter. As Nam-Yearl Chai states so clearly in his essay in this volume, to Africans and Asians the Western concept of the "rule of law" in international relations has often meant subjection and exploitation. Similarly the American tendency to equate a just peace with open frontiers for American investors and exporters requires the acceptance by some peoples of the injustices of economic colonialism. Like nationalists everywhere, Americans have too often been parochial in seeing a good peace for the world as one that best serves their nation's interests.

When the war spirit has swept the United States, the people's commitment to peace has time and again been shown to be limited. On occasion, segments of the public have greeted the expectation or outbreak of war with as much enthusiasm as the allegedly more war-minded peoples of Europe. The outbursts on the eve of the war with Spain in 1898 and in support of the little war with Mexico in 1914 come to mind. Some Americans have always opposed their country's wars, but opposition has also existed in Europe. The British opponents of the Boer War and more recently of the Suez War of 1956 furnish well-known examples. Popular French opposition to the first Vietnamese war and to the Algerian War was even more vigorous and helped bring both these conflicts to a halt.

Foreign observers have questioned the peace-loving character of Americans by pointing to the ferocity with which they have fought wars. From Thomas Aquinas onward, the Christian tradition of a just war has held that even when the victim of an attack fights back, he must do so with moderation and without vengeance. Using different premises, Karl von Clausewitz warned that the ends of war were political and that the military means must be chosen accordingly. But neither of these arguments for restraint has been taken seriously by more than a few American military leaders. The General Custer syndrome of the nineteenth century has carried over into the twentieth century, when the instruments of killing have become vastly more efficient. The assumption that the only good Indian was a dead Indian has a parallel in the attitude during World War II that the only good enemy was a dead enemy. The strategic bombing program to destroy the working class residential areas of German cities originated in large part with the Royal Air Force, but it was supported enthusiastically by the American bombing command and applied as ruthlessly to Japan. During the last months of World War II, when German and Japanese air defenses were shattered, the dumping of bombs on cities went on when the military justifications had practically disappeared. Criticism of the "bomber barons" and their ruthlessness was more the product of armed service rivalries than of moral or political concerns. More recently in the Vietnam War, the Defense Department offered the daily enemy "body count" as a scoreboard for victory until the mass media grew bored and repelled by the grisly statistics. Reading some official testimony on the need for more nuclear missiles, one wonders if one American outlook was not expressed by a line in a 1940 antiwar song, "We won't be safe until everybody's dead."

The seeming readiness to pay an inhuman price for war must be contrasted with an unwillingness to pay what seems a very small price for peace in the form of a limitation of minor national interests. The War of 1812, the Mexican War, and the Spanish-American War were all conflicts where a few more months of patience and conciliation would probably have avoided war and maintained what could still be called "an honorable peace." One can only hope that the Eisenhower regime's discreet ignoring of the "liberation" and "roll-back" slogans in facing the Hungarian revolt in 1956 and the Kennedy administration's somewhat circumspect approach to the Cuban missile situation in 1962 marked a new patience in a more dangerous world.

III

American reluctance to accept peace on other than bargain terms may be the historical result of never having paid the high prices for foreign wars that have been exacted from other powers. American combat deaths have been relatively small. The three wars of the nineteenth century that promised territorial expansion—one unsuccessfully —took a toll of less than 5,000 battle deaths. The cost in human lives that Americans have paid in *all* their foreign wars, including the substantial losses in Vietnam through 1969, has been less than the death toll of Russians in one year of the First or Second World Wars. Total American losses are also far less than the price paid by Britain and France, from much smaller populations, in World War I. For countries like Russia the effect of wars on the sex ratio has been so marked as to be a constant reminder of the price paid. At the turn of the century the number of men and women was approximately equal, but in 1926, after World War I and the civil wars, there were 5 million fewer males than females. After World War II the male deficiency had jumped to 26 million, from 7 million in 1939, leaving the nation with only 74 males for every 100 females.

The United States has also been spared the psychological and physical burdens of military invasions. Since the last foreign troops left the United States in 1815, a country like Russia has experienced the weight of invading armies from six nations; Germany, France and Britain have twice violated the Russian frontiers. Historically minded Americans may still cite the burning of the national capital in 1814 by the British, but every major European capital has been bombed or occupied at least once since that date. Only the conflict of 1861–1865 left a physical scar on the United States, and that was limited to a segment of the South. This fortunate lack of experience may have made it easy to attack antiwar movements as advocates of "peace at any price." The logical corollary, acceptance of war at any price, meant little until nuclear war offered a picture of such total devastation as to bring into question the viability of war as a means to national ends.

For some individuals in all countries the business of mass killing of strangers has always been deeply disturbing. There can be no denying, despite the argument presented here about national behavior, that many Americans have felt the dilemma posed by Professor Barker. Perhaps this explains the richness of rationalizations by which some Americans have consciously or unconsciously attempted that transformation stated bluntly in George Orwell's *1984* as "War is Peace." The variety and character of these rationalizations deserve the careful attention of the peace researcher, historian, or social psychologist. Is there a connection between the American who first called a widely used revolver on the frontier "The Peacemaker" and Woodrow Wilson's invention of "a war to end all wars"? "War is defense" is an association of ideas that may be older than the decision in 1939 or 1940 to call factories producing the implements of war "defense plants." The United States was among the first nations after World War II to abolish its War Department and substitute a Defense Department. A semantic twist made a "threat," once decried in international relations, into a "deterrent." The crowning achievement of rationalization seems to go to the world's most powerful bombing force, the Strategic Air Command, whose motto is "peace is our profession." Such rationalizations have made it possible for much of the idealism associated with peace to be channeled into vigorous support for war. If the Vietnam conflict has had any positive effect it may have been to destroy for some members of this younger generation the rich array of pretenses that threatened to lead this country into fighting "perpetual wars for perpetual peace."

IV

Turning from American concern for peace to the pledges to the principles of multilaterialism, there has been, as Barker notes, a tradition of American respect for international law. As early as 1784 a Pennsylvania court held that the law of nations was "in its full extent . . . part of the law of this State." Chief Justice John Marshall was probably the most influential of those to accept the binding force of international law upon the courts of the United States and to hold that acts of Congress ought never to violate international law.

The law itself, as the studies of Perry Miller and others have shown, has played an important part in American thought. The word "law" seems to evoke deep religious and patriotic connotations despite the "scofflaw" behavior of the average American when it comes to the income tax or traffic regulations. A good citizen is defined first of all as a "law-abiding" citizen. The decisions of the Nuremberg tribunal on allegiance to a higher law, along with the demands of the civil rights movement for justice as against the law, have made unproven impact on popular American thought. One might expect, then, that violations of international law by the government of the United States would be quickly condemned by Congress and the press. A law-respecting society should also express its respect for the norms of the society of nations.

But here, too, rationalization seems to have provided Americans an escape from their dilemma. An "American law of nations," a version of the rules for international order that expresses the values and serves the interests of the United States, has been a helpful creation. Justification for this special law is found in the presumably unique conditions of the Western Hemisphere. The leading nation in this area, the assumption goes, is immune to the evils of the Old World state system and can see, without selfishness and with special responsibility, the proper course of international justice. The absurdity of our denouncing spheres of influence in Europe and Asia—of putting on the robes of the judge after taking up the club of the aggressor—is infrequently recognized by American statesmen.

The modern Monroe Doctrine is the fullest expression of this special American law. Some American statesmen have stated that the Monroe Doctrine is not a part of international law; Secretaries of State Philander Knox, Elihu Root, and Charles Evans Hughes did so on occasion. But even those who make this admission usually claim that the doctrine requires international obedience. Philander Knox said in 1911 that the doctrine "does not depend upon technical legal right, but upon policy and power." Elihu Root admitted the same distinction but went on to say that the doctrine "rests upon the right of self-protection and that right is recognized by international law." A modern American juridical scholar affirms that the United States has not admitted that "any restriction which it seems to apply by virtue of that doctrine is at variance with any requirements" of the law of nations. But as an English scholar, S. L. Brierly, insists, "it is impossible to regard as a rule of law a doctrine which the United States claims the sole right to interpret, which she interprets in different senses at different times, and which she applies only as and when she chooses."

Some Americans have suggested that this country was engaged in making new international law in issuing the Monroe Doctrine. Woodrow Wilson, in one of his oratorical flights in 1917, proposed that "the nations should with one accord adopt the doctrine of President Monroe as the doctrine of the world." But when any other great power has asserted special rights in an area by virtue of contiguity or cultural or historic ties, the United States has consistently rejected them. Japan's effort in 1940 to proclaim a Monroe Doctrine for Asia was quickly dismissed by Secretary of State Cordell Hull as a self-seeking effort at expansion of influence contrary to international tenets.

With rare exceptions, the United States has also repudiated efforts to delimit spheres by bilateral or multilateral agreement. The one exception was the short-lived and ambiguous Lansing-Ishii agreement with Japan in 1917. The Churchill-Stalin arrangement of 1944, which assigned degrees of influence by percentages to various Balkan countries, was anathema to Washington although the United States had only the vaguest concept of its own interests in this area.

When Premier Khrushchev in the summer of 1960 challenged the legitimacy of the Monroe Doctrine in the twentieth century, the State Department said that those principles were "as valid today as they were in 1823." The statement went on to imply that the doctrine had acquired further legitimacy through Article 51 of the United Nations Charter, which provided for regional treaties, and the Rio Treaty of 1947, which supported one version of the Monroe Doctrine. Despite the formation of the United Nations and the Organization of American States, however, the United States has continued to act fundamentally on its own, unilaterally and aggressively, as when it intervened in Guatemala in 1954, in Cuba in 1962, and in the Dominican Republic in 1965.

Although President Kennedy did not mention the Monroe Doctrine in his statement of October 22, 1962, proclaiming the blockade of Cuba, he charged that the Soviet missiles by their presence violated the Rio Treaty, the Charter of the United Nations, and a joint resolution of the 87th Congress. This resolution did affirm the Monroe Doctrine, and for most Americans the action of the Kennedy administration was justified by the historic doctrine. As one man on the street said at the time, the doctrine "just says that nobody can come over here but us, or the countries like England that we like." Few Americans then or since knew that the Soviet Union was violating no international law in giving arms to Cuba, nor in establishing bases on Cuban soil, openly or clandestinely, since it was done with the consent of the Cuban government. The 1967 edition of the Tucker-Kelsen *Principles of International Law*, a generally accepted text, affirmed the legality of the Soviet action. It said that no principle of international law forbids a state from attempting to alter the military balance in its favor as long as its actions do not violate the rights of other states. State Department and Pentagon spokesmen affirmed this principle when they felt it unnecessary to try to justify the establishment of American missile bases on the periphery of the Soviet Union in the late 1950s.

V

Faith in American international law is also supported in nationalist thought by what Charles Rosenberg calls the politics of messianism. To believe to some extent in the existence of a chosen people seems essential to a vigorous nationalist outlook. From that faith can come an almost unlimited variety of rationalizations in support of interests and ambitions. Albert Weinberg in his classic study, *Manifest Destiny*, shows how the previous generations developed effective arguments out of history; but those arguments seem so absurd to college students today that many refuse to believe in the sincerity of the leaders who conceived them.

In our supposedly more sophisticated and skeptical age, however, the same kind of assumptions still operate with little questioning. A freshman student of history would find it difficult to argue that events in any other nation can be explained by those vague and mysterious words like "destiny" and "the hand of history." We think of ourselves as a rational people, now carefully studying the decision-making process and the role of mass media and special interest groups in shaping foreign policies. Yet even as well educated a man as President Kennedy found it useful in his 1962 State of the Union Message to say that "our nation is commissioned by history." And in the Dallas address that assassination left undelivered, the president was going to speak of the United States as "the watchman on the walls of world freedom" appointed to this task "by destiny rather than choice." Vietnam seems particularly to encourage a flight from rationality and a retreat to the unfathomable causes. General Maxwell Taylor in 1966 told a restless country that it "cannot escape its destiny . . . there is no running away from it." Vice President Hubert Humphrey made a similar plea in support of the war in 1967, saying that the nation "cannot back away from the role that history has given us." For President Johnson even bombing was the work of destiny. In praising the work of the pilots aboard the aircraft carrier *Enterprise* while stationed off Vietnam, the president told the crew that they were "cleansing the skies of fear so that men may reach upward safely and surely to grasp their destiny." If Americans accept this view of their actions as being the product of higher, suprahuman forces, there can be no moral dilemma.

Some of the inconsistencies pointed to here should be viewed, as Rosenberg says, not as American but as human. And American behavior might be better viewed not in terms of ideals but as the product of loyalties. In this age of nationalism man has become an excessively loyal and devoted creature. The unquestioned allegiance he once gave to tribe or religion has been reallocated in most of the modern world to that recent invention, the nation. This new god is as jealous as Jehovah. There can be no other god of equal authority. International law, universal ideals, and the code of behavior suggested by the Nuremberg tribunal must all be subordinated to the needs of the nation as seen by its official defenders.

VI

The real dilemma Americans face is in proclaiming higher loyalties while shrinking from disloyalty to the nation. But there must be disloyalty, in the conventional sense of the word, if man is to be freed from that parochial outlook which threatens human survival. How else can there be the rule of law if nations are, for their citizens, above the law? How else can that fourth relocation of sovereign authority, which Barker anticipates, actually take place?

Professors Sohn and Mendlovitz have outlined both transitional-step and big-step approaches to world government; both their approaches seem feasible and desirable. But the legal and political steps are impossible without some psychological changes in a substantial segment of the population of the United States and other major powers. Fundamentally, these psychological changes involve loyalties. It is possible to create loyalty to new political units; the nation-making process still observable in large parts of Africa demonstrates this. African nationalists know also that tribal loyalties must be eroded and eventually destroyed if the tragedy of Nigeria is not to be repeated. Loyalty to nation in the older powers must also be eroded if a system of world law is to function.

Historians like Merle Curti and Carlton Hayes have shown us how loyalties to nation are created in the case of the United States and France. Schoolbook history, the use of the flag and national anthems, the repeated pledges of allegiance, the constant reiteration of "we and they" in a wide range of thought: these and many other practices enter the process of saturating young minds with the nationalist outlook. Research is now needed on the process essential for the next step in civilized thought, the creation of disloyalty or, if discretion is necessary, "unloyalty." Case studies of persons who have surmounted their nationalism is one approach. The historian might make a more vigorous effort to denationalize his writing, particularly in the field of school texts, where the fight against chauvinistic interest groups is both very difficult and very important. Some progress to this end was achieved in the United States in the 1930s and again in the first few years of the United Nations before the Cold War mood produced a great setback.

The direction in which men must act if some level of world peace is to be achieved is clear. Barker in writing of this aspect of the problem notes that former Secretary of Defense Robert S. McNamara has commended the reading of Toynbee. It should now be appropriate to enshrine a statement in the first volume of Toynbee's *Study of History*, that patriotism has become "the last infirmity of noble minds." Only as men free themselves from overriding loyalty to that artificial political unit in which we find ourselves by accident of birth will it be possible to develop allegiance to a world of law and to feel a genuine kinship with the billions of humans who swarm on the surface of this small planet.

Canada and the American Dilemma: Realism versus Idealism, 1945-1964

CAMERON NISH
Assisted by STEPHEN ABBOTT

TRUISMS AND PLATITUDES are the public pillars of Canadian foreign policy. Canada is a "middle power"; Canadian foreign policy is "functional"; Canada is a "bridge" linking Great Britain and the United States; or again, Canada represents a "third force" between the great power blocks. In Canada a further premise often encountered in a variety of guises is: "A new moral force has grown in the World, a new instrument of Providence. It is the strength and purpose and wisdom of the Canadian nation."[1] Two decades ago, A. R. M. Lower, a noted Canadian historian, saw us Canadians as "a dour northern people" having "only one international interest, and that is peace. Surely our role then must be that of an international peace maker."[2]

Another significant trend in Canadian foreign policy and its interpretation may be called Canadian "realism"; Canadians are concerned with the "possible." For example, one study addresses itself to the question, "how did a single 'middle power' conduct itself in a world dominated by Big Powers?"[3] Canadian response to events sometimes is also a vigorous assertion of *independence*." At the time of the Suez crisis, Lester B. Pearson declared that "Canada was not a colonial choreboy running around shouting 'ready, aye ready.' "[4] Quite the contrary, Canada dissociated itself from Great Britain. According to another Canadian foreign policy specialist, Canada has a reputation for independence and objectivity. It has also been written of Canada that the "idea of the medical team in [South Vietnam] fits perfectly into the diplomatic ideal which we have built up in the past two decades. This is the ideal of Canada as the keeper of peace between men who are

[1] Malcolm MacDonald, "Canada, a New Moral Force in the World," *International Journal*, 1, no. 2 (Spring 1946):163 (hereafter cited as *IJ*).

[2] A. R. M. Lower, "Canada, the Second Great War, and the Future," *IJ*, 1, no. 2 (Spring 1946):102 and 111.

[3] Robert A. Spencer, *Canada in World Affairs: From UN to NATO, 1946 to 1949* (Toronto: Oxford University Press, 1959), p. 7.

[4] Cited by James Eayrs, "Canadian Policy and Opinion during the Suez Crisis," *IJ*, 12, no. 2 (Spring 1957):104.

mad, the dispassionate humanitarian middle man."[5] In contrast, "metooism" is also one of the unkinder appellations applied to Canadian foreign policy.

A further staple of Canadian foreign policy is derived from our Western Christian heritage. NATO, for example, was sometimes presented as a "crusade."[6] Louis Saint-Laurent, the prime minister in 1949, is credited with views, ideologies, and spiritual values that were "liberal" and "Christian."[7] These "liberal-cum-Christian-cum-crusade" ideologies are also reflected in the works of James Eayrs. He is one of the most perceptive commentators and is the most pleasurable literary stylist in the literature on Canadian foreign policy.[8]

II

Inasmuch as I am writing for an American audience, I think I should say a few words on the bearing of Canada's parliamentary system on foreign relations. Unlike the foreign relations of the United States, ours are not subject to the ill effects of the division of powers between the executive and legislative branches of government. The will of the executive and the legislative branches of government is always one. It is presumed that the will of the legislative branch reflects the will of the people, for such is the constitutional theory of the Canadian system of representative and responsible government. The people elect the members of Parliament; a committee of the majority party of the House of Commons is the executive or the cabinet. This preliminary remark is required because in the Canadian system it is quite impossible for the executive to suggest and implement policies and then have to face a hostile and negative legislative branch of government, as may occur in the United States. To adjust a line from Plato, "The foreign policy of Canada is what it is because the people are what they are."

Professor Kenneth McNaught, a lively critic of Canadian foreign

[5] John W. Holmes, "Canadian External Policies since 1945," *IJ*, 18, no. 2 (Spring 1963):141; John Grey, "Canadian Role in Vietnam Questioned," *Montreal Star*, Aug. 23, 1968, p. 9.
[6] Spencer, p. 281.
[7] W. E. C. Harrison, *Canada in World Affairs: 1949 to 1950* (Toronto: Oxford University Press, 1959), p. 23.
[8] James Eayrs, *Northern Approaches: Canada and the Search for Peace* (Toronto: Macmillan of Canada, 1961); idem, *Fate and Will in Foreign Policy* (Toronto: University of Toronto Press, 1966).

policy, charitably characterizes our country's behavior as "the *undeclared* 'policy' of drifting into the American orbit."[9] He calls Canada's role in the U.N. "political timidity" and adds, "Middle power functionalism remained a synonym for big power and, increasingly, for American decisions." The implicit and explicit factor in McNaught's argument is contained in the title of his essay: "From Colony to Satellite."[10] There is the assumption that Canada always does her masters' will, that is, the will of Great Britain and the United States. Unfortunately, that Canada's policy might be Canada's will has not been seriously considered, he believes.

One of the postulates of the Canadian external relations is that in 1945 we were committed to multilateral action through an international agency. In fact, our multilateral aid during the war was based on an alliance system for military and political purposes. Our primary link with other members of the nascent United Nations was mutual aid, that is to say, war supplies.[11] The Canadian wartime industrial complex made very significant contributions to the war effort and to the economy of the Canadian nation. The Canadian contributions from 1939 to 1945 were not those of a middle power but rather of a great industrial power. Canadian status, at least that based on economic power, placed Canada in a position to contribute significantly to the postwar period of reconstruction on a multilateral, non-alliance and ideologically uncommitted basis. What did Canada do?

In the fiscal year ending March 31, 1945, Canada contributed $803 million to mutual aid. Of this sum $604.4 million was for military supplies and $14.1 million was for the training of airmen. Nonmilitary mutual aid totaled $184.7 million. Roughly 11 percent of this aid went to the Soviet Union. In the following fiscal year, 1945–1946, $766,916,854.43 was allocated for mutual aid. Approximately $180 million of this total was for nonmilitary supplies. A significant feature of this mutual aid, however, was that as soon as the war ended, Canadian contributions to the Soviet Union dropped from $87.4 million in 1944–1945 to $46.3 million in 1945–1946. Military supplies accounted for about 83 percent of the total in the latter year. In 1947, the first real postwar year, Canadian expenditures for defense amounted

---

[9] Kenneth McNaught, "From Colony to Satellite," in *An Independent Foreign Policy for Canada*, ed. Stephen Clarkson (Toronto: McClelland & Stewart, 1968), p. 175 (italics added).
[10] Ibid., pp. 175–76.
[11] MacDonald, p. 160.

to $387.6 million, or about 14.7 percent of the budget. In the same year, Canadian contributions to nonmilitary aid were $48.7 million to the International Bank for Reconstruction and Development and $1.3 million to international or British Commonwealth organizations. Inasmuch as loans were requested and granted mainly in American dollars, ideologically incompatible countries had only limited access to the bank, that is, to American resources. Canada's economic contributions were committed as early as 1947 to an ideological system.[12]

III

Again we ask: What did Canada do? "It was true," James Eayrs has written, "that Canadian Governments since 1945, unreservedly committed to the Western camp, had refused to seek a middle way between the two great rival blocks, either by trying to mediate directly in Soviet-American conflicts or by heading up some kind of political third force."[13] Another pen sketch of Canadian foreign policy in the early postwar years is that "from mid-1946 until about mid-1947, the approach to the United Nations was tentative and hesitant, suggesting a reluctance to venture too far into the unknown."[14] The title of the book from which this quote has been drawn is perhaps a significant reflection on Canadian foreign policy: *Canada in World Affairs From UN to NATO, 1946–1949*. It might be a more accurate characterization to drop the U.N. from the title of the book. From 1946 to 1949, Canada contributed $471.8 million to the U.N. and foreign aid. In the same period, it dispersed $3.1 billion for national defense.[15] The Canadian option is obvious.

The functionalism, realism, and middle-power status of Canada is often credited to our physical and economic proximity to the United States. Canadian-American relations are said to play a significant role in the elaboration of Canadian foreign policy and in our ideological

---

[12] Government of Canada, *Public Accounts*, 1945, p. xxviii, and *Public Accounts*, 1947 (hereafter cited as *PA*). Most of the statistical data for this paper have been drawn from the reports of the public accounts of Canada. Some numbers are rounded off.

[13] James Eayrs, *Canada in World Affairs: October 1955 to June 1957* (Toronto: Oxford University Press, 1959), p. 3.

[14] Spencer, p. 57.

[15] *PA*, 1946, 1947, 1948, 1949. These figures include Canada's contribution of mutual aid, of which $586.9 million were for military supplies and $180 million for nonmilitary supplies.

commitments. "While backing the main American policies," one study puts it, "the Canadian delegation followed a strongly independent line. . ."[16] An illustration of this strongly independent line is evident in the analysis of Canada's voting record in the United Nations made by a colleague of mine. Canada voted more often with the United States than did any other member of the United Nations.[17] An inordinate amount of time, space, and consideration, in my opinion, has been devoted to the influence of the United States on Canada. The presumption is that Canada would have acted differently if it were not for the United States. Thus Canada can always claim minimal responsibility.

It has been noted, and correctly, that Canadian-American defense agreements predate 1945. Canadian objections, our plaintive whimpers of independence, were not directed to the viability of defense policy and military means but rather to the presence of a few American servicemen on Canadian soil.[18] The military nature of the arctic and subarctic bases was not the issue.[19] An all-engulfing smokescreen allowed Canadians to plod their weary, cautious, and realistic way through the defense orientation of Canadian policy. This fog was so thick that Prime Minister W. L. Mackenzie King was able to convince himself and the Canadian populace that the Canadian-American defense agreements of 1947 were well within the framework of the United Nations Charter.[20] Indeed they did fall within the letter of the charter, but what did they do to the spirit?

Canadian anti-Americanism, so much insisted upon by the intellectual coterie critical of Canadian foreign policy, presumes that Canada was motivated by a saintly and peace-directed ideology. More to the point are the pro-American sentiments of the people and government of Canada; the basic and full-hearted acceptance of American military ideology and policies. This commitment is evident in Gallup poll results. In 1959 Canadians were asked whether they approved or disapproved of an air defense merger between Canada and the United States; 59 percent were favorable while 22 percent took a nega-

[16] Spencer, p. 97.
[17] This information was supplied to the author by Professor Edward McCullough, chairman of the Department of History at Sir George Williams University in Montreal.
[18] D. C. Masters, *Canada in World Affairs: 1953 to 1955* (Toronto: Oxford University Press, 1959), p. 64.
[19] Spencer, pp. 309–10.
[20] Ibid., p. 74.

tive stand. In April 1951, 83 percent of the Gallup sample believed that Communists should be denied political office. Two years later, in 1953, only 26 percent of the sample believed that Communists should have freedom of speech; 62 percent were in favor of denying them this right. On the question of NATO, Canadian opinion was almost overwhelming. In 1952, 78 percent were favorable to the organization, and in 1960 the percentage was 72. Negative reactions to NATO in the same years were 6 percent and 4 percent respectively.[21]

The most striking and significant example of Canadian pro-Americanism is NATO. One of the assumptions that led to Canadian support of this multilateral pact was that peace could only be assured by the military cooperation of the freedom-loving nations against the totalitarian states.[22] It has also been asserted: "Our foreign policy rests on the same basic postulates as the American. Either war is inevitable or can be avoided only by a firm line of containment."[23] Another critical element of this position is that it is impossible to cooperate with the Communists. NATO was a means to peace.[24] Our minimal culpability is sometimes expressed in rather more elegant terms: "The quest for security in a regional grouping" was adopted *"faute de mieux."*[25]

Canada, however, has also claimed for itself a significant role in the elaboration of NATO[26] and the inclusion of clause 2, the non-military clause, which is also called the Canadian clause.[27] There is no statistical evidence of clause 2's ever being implemented. In Canada, we opted for a *force de frappe* and not *faute de mieux*.

Lester B. Pearson credits Louis Saint-Laurent with being one of the initiators of NATO.[28] Saint-Laurent's reason was the failure of

[21] *Montreal Star*, Apr. 18, 1951; May 16, 1953; Jan. 28, 1959; Mar. 19, 1960.
[22] James A. Gibson, "Canadian Foreign Policy: A Forward View," *IJ*, 4, no. 2 (Spring 1949):113.
[23] B. S. Keirstead with the assistance of Muriel Armstrong, *Canada in World Affairs: September 1951 to October 1953* (Toronto: Oxford University Press, 1956), p. 100.
[24] Ibid., pp. 100 and 40.
[25] Spencer, p. 1.
[26] Ibid., p. 274.
[27] Lester B. Pearson, "NATO: Retrospect and Prospects," *IJ*, 14, no. 2 (Spring 1959):30.
[28] Ibid., p. 79.

the U.N. as a means to collective security. In the appreciation of one historian:

> When the history of the twentieth century is written from the vantage point of the twenty-first, Canada's signature of the North Atlantic Treaty on April 4, 1949, may come to be regarded as a more significant event than her entry into the United Nations.[29]

Yet NATO was not a new departure in Canadian foreign policy; it was old wine in an old bottle. "The Canadian-American defence understanding of February, 1949, was the first formal commitment undertaken by future members of the alliance."[30] Collective security within the framework of the U.N. was abandoned at least two years before the signing of the NATO pact. In 1948, Canada sent an observer to the military committee of the Brussels Treaty powers.[31] The same year saw an economic manifestation of this renewed militancy: Canada, by Order-in-Council, implemented the provisions of the General Agreement on Tariffs and Trade (GATT).[32] Canadian foreign policy in the period from 1949 on was postulated on the ethic that "the maintenance, deployment and exercise of military force is part of the conduct of foreign policy."[33] Pronouncements by Canadian statesmen would seem to have been derived from a combination of *Alice's Adventures in Wonderland*, George Orwell's *1984*, and *1066 and All That*. One Canadian writer cited the secretary of state for external affairs as follows: "It is necessary to accumulate enough force now to preserve freedom in order that ultimately freedom can be preserved without force. . . . It was a policy of peace."[34] Prime Minister Saint-Laurent, who was familiarly known as "Uncle Louis," declared:

> The best guarantee of peace today is the creation and preservation of the nations of the free world, under the leadership of Great Britain, the United States, and France, of an overwhelming preponderance of force. . . . This force must not be only military; it must be economic; it must be moral.[35]

---

[29] Spencer, p. 243.
[30] Ibid., p. 89.
[31] Escott Reid, "The Birth of the North Atlantic Alliance," *IJ*, 22, no. 3 (Summer 1967):429–31.
[32] Spencer, pp. 213–15.
[33] Keirstead, p. 129.
[34] Gibson, p. 112.
[35] Harrison, p. 2.

Pearson, however, emphasized the *second best alternative:*

> We should continue to fight for collective security: (1) on the Assembly level of the United Nations, once the Security Council becomes impotent. . . . (2) by arranging, as a second best alternative, a regional Atlantic organization, not only for a collective defence but for collective co-operation in political and economic matters.[36]

From 1950 to 1964 Canada contributed $464.7 million to the Colombo Plan in mutual aid. In the same period Canada contributed $1.8 billion to NATO. In Canada, first and second best alternatives have peculiar meanings.[37]

One Canadian member of Parliament, the "funny-money" adherent Solon Low, while supporting Canada's participation in NATO, had a brilliant insight: he claimed that Canada's reiteration of U.N. support was "hypocrisy."[38] His was a minority view.

Canadian NATO and Colombo Plan contributions began at about the same time. Regional foreign aid and regional military contributions in 1950, according to Plumptre's "Perspective on Our Aid to Others," were $25 million to the Colombo Plan and $300 million to NATO. Of these figures he made a comment, one all too typically Canadian, that "Canada gave, not massively, but with intelligence, sensitivity and humility."[39] Canada gave massive economic support to the *second alternative.*[40]

IV

Pro-Americanism in Canada was not limited to NATO. Let it be clearly understood that Canada was not a satellite; Canada was a willing and ideologically committed ally. The concept of satellitism in Canada implies an other-directed and influenced foreign policy. This is evident in our China and Korea policies.

Canada acquiesced in the unilateral United States action in Korea, albeit, it is said, with grave reservations. On April 8, 1949, in the Security Council, "Canada voted for the admission of the Republic of

[36] Lester B. Pearson, "Forty Years On: Reflections on Our Foreign Policy," *IJ*, 22, no. 3 (Summer 1967):361.
[37] See *PA* for the years 1949–1964.
[38] Spencer, p. 274.
[39] A. F. W. Plumptre, "Perspective on Our Aid to Others," *IJ*, 22, no. 3 (Summer 1967):487–88. It should be noted that Plumptre's figures are inaccurate; see appendices.
[40] See *PA* for 1950 and 1951.

Korea to the United Nations."[41] On a United States resolution "Canada voted to brand Communist China an aggressor—but "reluctantly." Government policy in sending Canadian troops to Korea was supported by 50 percent of a Gallup sample while 31 percent did not approve; 19 percent had no opinion. Canada must be the only mugwump in the world whose mugwump is two-faced.[42]

Of Pearson's China policy, W. E. C. Harrison has written: "On the Yangtze, as on the St. Lawrence, Mr. Pearson's cheerful common sense as an internationalist was enabling him to move faster than his American confederates.[43] This, no doubt, is a perfect illustration of Newton's second law, "change of momentum is proportional to the moving force." Canada's China policy, and there was really only one, well illustrates the Canadian dilemma: "Confronted with . . . serious differences between Canada's principal allies, Mr. Pearson was cautious but clear in his utterances." The caution and clarity resulted in Canada's voting "for the United States resolution shelving the entry of Communist China into the United Nations."[44] Actually, this is a rather cynical presentation of Canada's policy. It should be stated as "trade but no truck" with China. The *momentum* of Canadian policy with regard to China may also be garnered from the *Report of the Department of External Affairs*: "Relations between Canada and China remained unchanged during 1957." In 1958: "Relations between Canada and China remained unchanged during the year." In the reports from 1959 on, there is a significant, and one can only hope embarrassed, omission of any mention of China. An interesting and peculiar aspect of Canada's Chinas policy is the government's insensitivity to public opinion. Between 1953 and 1964 the Gallup poll reveals a shift from a majority opposed both to the seating of China in the U.N. and to Canadian recognition of China to a majority favoring both these proposals. Government policy to date has been consistent: nonrecognition was and remains Canada's position.[45]

Vietnam, and Canada's role as a member of the International

[41] Spencer, pp. 108–10.
[42] Norman Alstedter, "Problems of Coalition Diplomacy: "The Korean Experience," *IJ*, 8, no. 4 (Autumn 1953):257; *Montreal Star*, July 27, 1952.
[43] Harrison, p. 166.
[44] Masters, pp. 113 and 117.
[45] Government of Canada, *Report of the Department of External Affairs*, 1957 and 1958, pp. 34 and 33. See *Montreal Star*, Oct. 28, 1953; Feb. 17, 1954; Jan. 28, 1956; Sept. 27, 1958; Apr. 8, 1961; and Apr. 15, 1964. On Oct. 30, 1968, the *Montreal Star* reported Canada's policy as still unchanged. A stop press was required in October, 1970. Canada officially recognized the government of Mainland China.

Commission there, is another topic upon which much ink has been expended. I wish to limit myself to but two comments: Canada was chosen as the pro-American representative. However, Canada's policy is her own; it just happens to coincide with that of the United States. The second and more disturbing comment is the assumption of a Canadian historian: "The Canadians on the International Commission found the Poles most obstructive in carrying out this aspect of the work [freedom of civilian population movement] of the Commission, while the Indians, in an understandable desire to be impartial, were much too favorable to the Poles."[46] Impartiality, in Canadian terms, means the views of the minority.

Canadian commentators never tire of describing Canada's "middle," "moderating," "effective," "conciliating," "constructive," "realistic," "practical," "mediating," "honest broker," "significant," "independent," etc., role in the United Nations. Such descriptions are sometimes true but also very often false. I have chosen an example of this true-false tendency that is not very significant in terms of world peace. It is only significant in terms of moral rectitude: the racial issue in South Africa.

One writer has claimed that on "moral" issues, Canada often voted with the "cynical majority."[47] Another author has claimed that the Canadian position vis-à-vis the racial issue in South Africa was based on " . . . realistic political considerations."[48] Yet another view of the South African racial issue is evident in calling Canada's position "on first reading . . . a little insipid."[49] Be the Canadian position "cynical" or "insipid," the following citation describes it all too well. When the racial issue was raised in the U.N.,

The Canadian view was that the General Assembly had a right to discuss the question, but Canada did not support the establishment of the commission [to investigate the matter] nor its continuation. Canada voted against the South African resolution denying the competence of the United Nations to consider the matter, abstained on the resolution setting up the commission and voted for a resolution of the Scandinavian countries which merely affirmed that all member states were under the obligation to bring their policies in conformity with their charter obligations.[50]

[46] Masters, p. 90.
[47] Keirstead, pp. 78–80.
[48] Spencer, p. 97.
[49] Keirstead, p. 83.
[50] Masters, pp. 197–98. In October 1968, Canada abstained on a U.N. vote to impose economic sanctions on South Africa and Portugal because of their noncompliance with a previous resolution on Rhodesia.

V

Escott Reid recently wrote that "the next ten years could become a golden decade in Canadian foreign policy comparable to the great decade of 1941–1951." A little further in the same article he said of NATO that "Our successful crusade for that alliance is a bright page in our history."[51] It has already been suggested that the "golden decade" that included the war years was golden mainly in the sense of glinting steel and shining armor. Our task at the moment, however, is to investigate statistically part of Canada's "golden decade" and that "bright page in our history." In other words, what did we spend our money on, war or peace?

The Colombo Plan is without a doubt the best example of Canadian nonmilitary mutual aid. It is a credible, charitable, significant, and humanitarian example of Canada's will to help others. From 1950 to 1964 Canada contributed in the form of outright gifts and loans $464.7 million to Eastern countries. In the same period, Canadian allocations to NATO totaled $1.8 billion. No comment on these figures will be made. International cooperation is another category of Canadian foreign aid. Under this general heading, Canada contributed a total of $639 million in the years 1950–1964. These were contributions to the United Nations and its agencies, the World Bank, and other nonmilitary aid systems. Canadian defense expenditures for the same years were $28.3 billion. Total Canadian nonmilitary aid in this period was $1.1 billion. Contributions to NATO, let alone national defense, were greater than nonmilitary aid in this period.[52]

VI

Let us now try and relate the past few pages to the theme of this conference. Is Canadian policy postulated on the "rule of law" or of "absolute sovereignty?" A Canadian answer must be given, that is, a compromised answer. The Canadian option has been for "relative sovereignty." The "rule of law" has not really ever been attempted. This is one part of the Canadian dilemma, for there is little doubt

[51] Escott Reid, "Canadian Foreign Policy, 1967–1977: A Second Golden Decade?" *IJ*, 22, no. 2 (Spring 1967):171 and 172–73.
[52] All of the statistical data have been gathered from the *PA* for 1945–1967. For more detailed statistical information, see the appendices.

that Canadian politicians and statesmen want peace. However, the means that they use are postulated on war.

Another part of the Canadian dilemma is that we have a schizophrenic foreign policy. The split personalities are war and peace. In terms of dollars, our war personality asserts itself; in terms of stated intent and aspirations, our peace personality predominates.

The Canadian dilemma has also been called a Canadian problem. This is yet a further aspect of the dilemma. There is a tendency to excuse, justify, or rationalize Canadian foreign policy with terms such as "yes, but" and "if only." All too seldom do Canadian politicians and statesmen look for the radical base of the Canadian dilemma, that is, Canadian policy unprotected by the "ifs" and "buts."

This aspect of the Canadian dilemma, Canadian responsibility for its own foreign policy, is, I believe, the one essential facet of the dilemma that must be known and accepted. We are what we do; it's that simple. I am well aware of the arguments used against pacifists, internationalists, World Federalists, and peaceniks, and of those who wonder how we can trust the Russians, Communists, Chinese, Cubans, and so on. We can and we cannot to the same extent that we can and cannot be trusted. It is these kinds of people who say that the synonym for aggressor is enemy. Our side wants peace even if we must have perpetual war to achieve it.

How, then, can we attempt to solve the Canadian dilemma? First, we can begin by appreciating the significance of realism and idealism. Realism, as it is used in the jargon of Canadian foreign policy, means simply a continuation of the *status quo*. Idealism would imply change, something other than we have done in the past. Second, we must accept the dilemma as a Canadian one. Third, we must make use of our economic resources in a more constructive way. We could, without being the least anti-American, make our NATO contributions through clause 2 rather than the more military clauses. Finally, we have to want peace. The last, in this instance, is more important than any other factor. It is that change in our ideology which is basic: everything else flows from that.

APPENDIX

Table 1. Budgetary Expenditures for Defense and International Cooperation
(in millions of Canadian dollars)

Fiscal Year Ended March 31	National Defense		International Cooperation[1]	
	Amount	% of budget	Amount	% of budget
1945	2,938.4	56.0	—	—
1946	1,715.7	33.4	—	—
1947	387.6	14.7	—	—
1948	196.0	9.0	—	—
1949	272.4	12.0	—	—
1950	387.2	16.0	—	—
1951	787.3	27.0	—	—
1952	1,446.5	39.0	—	—
1953	1,973.0	45.0	—	—
1954	1,857.8	43.0	36.6	0.9
1955	1,687.9	39.0	33.2	0.8
1956	1,768.6	40.0	33.2	0.8
1957	1,783.6	37.0	46.8	1.0
1958	1,687.4	33.2	48.3	0.9
1959	1,442.4	26.9	61.1	1.1
1960	1,536.8	26.9	83.0	1.5
1961	1,537.9	25.8	85.3	1.4
1962	1,650.0	25.3	76.1	1.2
1963	1,603.7	24.4	63.2	1.0
1964	1,723.1	25.1	72.2	1.0

SOURCE: Government of Canada, Department of Finance, *Public Accounts* for fiscal years 1945 to 1964. In this and the following tables the system of classification follows the source as closely as possible. But since the system has changed during the period, the more detailed classification has been adopted and the data have been compiled according to this system to ensure a consistent analysis. The data were compiled by Stephen Abbott.

[1] Since expenditures for international cooperation are not itemized in the *Public Accounts* before 1954, it is impossible to give accurage figures in this category until then.

Table 2. *Military Expenditures*

(*in millions of Canadian dollars*)

Fiscal Year Ended March 31	National Defense (including NATO)	NATO		Total Expenditures
		Mutual Aid[1]	Military Costs[2]	
1945	2,938.4	—	—	—
1946[3]	1,715.7	—	—	—
1947	387.6	—	—	—
1948	196.0	—	—	—
1949	272.4	—	—	—
1950	387.2	—	—	—
1951	787.3	195.4	—	195.4
1952	1,446.5	126.4	3.5	129.9
1953	1,973.0	235.1	11.3	246.4
1954	1,857.8	289.7	10.5	300.2
1955	1,687.9	253.4	6.6	260.0
1956	1,768.6	164.0	11.0	175.0
1957	1,783.6	119.5	14.0	133.5
1958	1,687.4	108.0	10.5	118.5
1959	1,442.4	58.3	12.4	70.7
1960	1,536.8	23.3	17.4	40.7
1961	1,537.9	36.1	14.2	50.3
1962	1,650.0	23.2	11.1	34.3
1963	1,603.7	17.9	14.5	32.4
1964	1,723.1	19.4	14.9	34.3

SOURCE: Government of Canada, Department of Finance, *Public Accounts*, 1945–1964.

[1] Mutual aid to NATO countries.

[2] Contributions toward military costs of NATO.

[3] In this year there was also a write-off of $425 million on Air Training Plan loans and advances according to the United Kingdom Financial Agreement Act of 1946.

Table 3. Foreign Aid and Membership Assessment

(in millions of Canadian dollars)

Fiscal Year Ended March 31	Assistance to Other Countries	Membership Assessment[1]	Contribution to International Organizations[2]	Grant to Colombo Plan Fund	Loans[3] Bilateral	Loans[3] Multilateral	Mutual Aid	UNRRA	Military Relief	Miscellaneous
1945	—	0.2	—	—	—	—	792.2	11.1	50.2	32.7
1946	—	2.0	—	—	—	0.04	766.9	142.9	34.5	14.2
1947	—	1.3	—	—	—	48.7	—	—	—	—
1948	5.5	1.4	—	—	—	16.2	—	16.9	—	—
1949	5.5	2.0	—	—	—	—	—	0.3	—	—
1950	6.9	2.7	—	—	—	5.7	—	NO FUNDS ALLOCATED AFTER 1949		
1951	11.4	3.0	—	0.006	—	—	—	—	—	—
1952	1.5	2.7	—	25.3	—	0.2	—	—	—	—
1953	1.4	3.5	—	25.4	—	—	—	—	—	—
1954	6.3	2.9	—	25.4	—	—	—	—	—	—
1955	3.5	2.9	—	25.4	—	—	—	—	—	—
1956	0.1	3.1	2.5	26.4	—	—	—	—	—	—
1957	1.5	5.7	4.4	34.4	—	3.5	—	—	—	—
1958	2.0	3.4	4.6	34.4	16.2	—	—	—	—	—
1959	14.5	3.9	5.1	35.0	18.3	—	—	—	—	—
1960	13.8	4.4	11.7	50.0	0.5	—	—	—	—	—
1961	6.4	4.7	22.2	50.0	—	11.3	—	—	—	—
1962	3.4	6.1	14.5	50.0	—	7.9	—	—	—	—
1963	4.4	6.4	8.8	41.5	—	15.3	—	—	—	—
1964	6.3	8.7	11.9	41.5	—	7.9	—	—	—	—

SOURCE: Government of Canada, Department of Finance, *Public Accounts*, 1945–1964.

[1] By international or British Commonwealth organizations.

[2] Before 1956, Canada's contributions to international organizations are included in the category "Assistance to Other Countries."

[3] Bilateral loans to India, Pakistan, and Ceylon to finance the purchase of wheat and flour. Multilateral loans represent subscriptions to the International Bank for Reconstruction and Development, the International Development Association, and the International Finance Corporation.

BIBLIOGRAPHICAL NOTE

The best single source from which general bibliographical data and information can be garnered on Canadian foreign policy is the Canadian Institute of International Affairs, 230 Bloor Street, Toronto, Ontario, Canada. Under the auspices of the CIIA, Oxford University Press, Toronto, has published a series called *Canada in World Affairs*. The *International Journal*, a quarterly, also is published by the CIIA.

Several other Canadian periodicals often contain material of interest to students of Canadian foreign policy: the *Canadian Historical Review*, the *University of Toronto Quarterly*, *Queen's Quarterly*, and the *Dalhousie Review*. A more popular magazine, *Maclean's*, also carries articles on Canadian foreign policy from time to time.

Among the more significant newspapers that might be consulted are the *Montreal Star* and the *Gazette* of Montreal; *Le Devoir* and *La Presse* also are Montreal newspapers. The *Toronto Star* and the *Globe and Mail* of Toronto are noteworthy as well.

PART III

Belief in the Restraint of Power: Trial, Error, and Hope

The United States and the Law of Mankind:
Some Inconsistencies in American Observance
of the Rule of Law

WILLIAM J. BRUCE

With the founding of the United Nations the United States undertook, and since then has extended, a network of multilateral obligations encircling the world. These obligations, while consistent with the principles of American republican federalism, often conflict with unilateral phases of national policy.

Law as a Barrier to Change:
A Korean Experience

NAM-YEARL CHAI

While the rule of law in the world is an ancient ideal, the modern operations of international law frequently have served justice ineffectively; rather, they have added to the strength of strong nations and increased the dependency of weak ones. Korea, in its relations with Japan and the United States around 1900, is a case in point.

The Right of Revolution:
Implications for International Law and World Order

GERALD A. SUMIDA

International law and world order are necessities, but equally so is accommodation to revolution, especially in the recently colonial or dependent and still underdeveloped nations. Once again, as in the eighteenth century, Americans need to honor political justice, the rule of the ideals of law, rather than old laws and traditions.

Peace and War:
The History of the United States, 1939-1999
ARTHUR I. WASKOW

Movements of social liberation as they have mounted since 1954 open the way to some predictions concerning the main course of American history to the year 2000. Black equalitarianism, urban dissent and reform, and increases in political effectiveness among intellectual and laboring classes encourage reasonable hope that the United States will avoid catastrophic war during the remainder of the twentieth century.

The United States and the Law of Mankind: Some Inconsistencies in American Observance of the Rule of Law

WILLIAM J. BRUCE

TODAY ALL KNOW THAT our globe is shrinking, though we are far from a "one world" community. All recognize that a world without law is not suited to the needs of this century. Accordingly, our peace-building efforts are directly or indirectly related to establishing the kinds of economic, social, cultural, and political relationships among nations that will develop international practices that can be respected by all peoples. In the United States we believe quite generally that the function of law is the ordering of relations among the members of a society. A legal system, we think, reflects the moral and ethical principles of the social order it seeks to regulate, setting forth rules under which peoples organize and act. By extension of this concept, international law is recognized as the legal system that has grown out of the continuous practice in the relations between sovereign, national states —that is, as rules governing their external relations.

Yet there has been an inherent ambiguity in the United States' approach to the rule of law among nations. It is evident to most thinking Americans that the conscience of our people is torn between loyalty to the moral principles of justice and order, as recognized and codified in law, and traditional support for our government's actions in furtherance of the "national interest," especially when many such actions seem out of accord with international law or even with common-sense justice.

The ambivalence in the American attitude toward a rule of law for the world has been greatly complicated since 1900 by two fundamental changes in the international situation. First, the rules that once applied to relations among only the predominantly Western, Christian, and Europe-oriented group of states have had to be expanded to include almost triple the number of states existing at the turn of the century. International law now seeks to represent all the world's cultures, religions, and societies; it attempts to transcend their differing stages of economic, social, and political development. Second, a great part of interstate relations today is concerned with matters that bear directly on internal policy and action—predominantly on economic and financial matters—and that are clearly related to the social and legal institutions and practices of the nations. One need think only of the communications satellite and its impact on freedom of information to begin to see the nature of the current changes in international relations. While the world community is beginning to accept the necessity for international regulation of the production and use of nuclear weapons, we have hardly begun to touch the problems of adjusting national legal and moral systems to an international standard for social equality, for freedom of speech and thought, or for the self-de-determination of peoples.

II

The early 1900s were marked by increased attention to the development of instruments for use as arbitral and judicial processes in international relations.[1] The major nations of Europe and Asia ratified the Hague treaties. The United States played a significant role in the drafting, for instance, of the League of Nations and the Permanent Court of International Justice, but it ratified few of the treaties. Following 1945, with its acceptance of the Charter of the United Nations, there appeared to be a turning point toward active American participation in permanent multilateral agreements.

During the 1950s a series of "defensive alliances" was forged. These were justified in foreign policy statements as necessary to provide mutual security and protection in a given geographic region. The North Atlantic Treaty Organization, the Southeast Asia Treaty

---

[1] This period saw, for example, the entry into force of these Hague Treaties: Pacific Settlement of Disputes and the Permanent Court of Arbitration (1900 and 1910), Law and Customs of War on Land (1902), Rights and Duties of Neutrals (1910), Bombardment by Naval Forces (1910), Certain Restrictions on the Right of Capture (1910), and the Red Cross Conventions (1906, 1929, and 1949). The interwar period produced treaties as well: The Permanent Court of International Justice and the Covenant of the League of Nations (1920), Protocol Prohibiting Biological Warfare (1925), Renunciation of War as an Instrument of National Policy (1928), Limitation and Reduction of Naval Armament (1930), and Anti-War Treaty on Non-Aggression and Conciliation (1935). Following the Charter of the United Nations and the Statute of the International Court of Justice (1945) the treaties on the Treatment of Prisoners of War (1949) and the Convention on the Protection of Civilian Persons in Time of War (1949) were ratified.

Organization, and the Warsaw Pact are commonly justified this way. They might, however, be described equally well as political arrangements among like-minded states directed against what they consider to be a threat from a potential enemy. The State Department argues that these mutual security arrangements, established on a regional basis,[2] fall within the principle of the pacific settlement of local disputes provided for in the United Nations Charter.[3]

The 1960s saw a round of efforts toward disarmament agreements. Although complete world disarmament has been recommended to the Disarmament Commission by the United Nations General Assembly, it is widely regarded as a utopian objective, and a universal treaty does not yet seem likely.[4] This goal has been met only piecemeal, in certain areas of the world. The first recent treaty to incorporate a "local disarmament" concept was developed by the Conference on Antarctica held in Washington between October 15 and December 1, 1959, ratified by the United States Senate in February 1960, and put into effect in June 1961. The preamble states the principle of the treaty: "It is in the interest of all mankind that Antarctica shall not become the scene or object of international discord."

The crucial Treaty Banning Nuclear Weapons Tests in the Atmosphere, in Outer Space, and Under Water was opened for signature in 1963 and, with the famous exceptions of France and China, was soon ratified. The disarmament effort continued to seek agreements for establishing nuclear free zones. Although by 1964 the military aspects of the formula to create a nuclear free zone in Central Europe seemed to be acceptable to the technical advisers, the proposal failed to satisfy the Western powers' political demands for a limita-

---

[2] The Australian–New Zealand–United States Pact (ANZUS), the Arab League, the Baghdad Pact (now Central Treaty Organization, CENTO), the British Commonwealth of Nations, the North Atlantic Treaty Organization (NATO), the Organization of African Unity (OAU), the Organization of American States (OAS), the Rio Pact, the Southeast Asian Treaty Organization (SEATO), the Warsaw Treaty Organization (WTO), and the Western European Union (WEU).

[3] Article 52, paragraph 2, of the U.N. Charter expressly permits regional arrangements "relating to international peace and security" provided they are "consistent with the Purposes and Principles of the United Nations." The charter requires, however (article 54), that the Security Council "be kept fully informed of activities undertaken or in contemplation under regional arrangements or by regional agencies."

[4] For an objective résumé of the disarmament negotiations during this period, see *The United Nations and Disarmament (1945–1965)*, U.N. Publications no. 67.I.9 (1967).

tion on conventional arms and for the reunification of Germany. During this same period nuclear free zones for Africa were recommended by the General Assembly (1961), and a treaty barring nuclear weapons from Latin America, drafted in 1965, was signed in 1968 by all states in the area except Cuba.

In a similar vein, the United Nations General Assembly adopted by acclamation on December 19, 1966, a resolution commending the Treaty on Principles Governing the Activities of States in the Exploration and Use of Outer Space, Including the Moon and Other Celestial Bodies. The treaty, which entered into force on October 10, 1968, was described by President Johnson as the "most important arms control development since the limited test ban treaty of 1963." Ambassador Arthur J. Goldberg felt it would "greatly reduce the danger of international conflict and promote the prospects of international cooperation for the common interest." The ambassador's statement stressed the dilemma faced by the world community: "The greatest danger facing us in outer space comes not from the physical environment, however cold and hostile it may be, but from our human nature and from the discords that trouble our relationships here on earth. Therefore, as we stand on the threshold of the space age, our first responsibility as governments is clear: We must make sure that man's earthly conflicts will not be carried into outer space."[5] Some listeners might well have wondered whether governments do not have a more pressing responsibility closer to home—to apply international law to earthly conflicts.

III

In his 1968 Law Day address at the University of Georgia, Secretary of State Dean Rusk described the increasing importance of law to world affairs. The United States, he said, having entered into some 4,000 international agreements with more than 150 countries and organizations since 1945, has continued to press forward in the building of a community of nations "based on collective action in which each participating country has accepted its responsibility to work toward the common goal." He went on to paint an optimistic picture of U.S. support for a "law of mankind":

[5] *U.S. Participation in the U.N.: Report by the President to the Congress for the Year 1966*, U.S. Department of State Publication 8276 (1967), p. 15.

... All too often, we view the world as a group of independent countries, each pursuing its own policies and following its own interests, like so many stars hurtling through space away from one another. However, this explosive view of world politics neglects to take into account the important ways nations have tied themselves together and continue to do so.... [A compilation of the U.S. international agreements] indicates the degree to which this country has tied its economy, its defenses, and its political outlook to the concept of community action. This multitude of agreements, even those treating rather prosaic subjects, represents the roots that bind us tightly to the fertile soil of world order. It is healthy, I believe, that the countries of the world show signs of recognizing that, no matter how much they wish to live alone, they must live together.

The ever-expanding network of international arrangements comprises what Sir Wilfred Jenks has called the "common law of mankind."[6]

This statement of Secretary Rusk's view of international relations appears to be essentially that of an academic "functionalist." He recognizes a direct correlation between the development of international law and the operations of organizations in various spheres of contemporary life. The functionalist view envisages a progressively larger interrelation among international organizations—private, regional, international, and supranational—each pressing forward to provide order and stability in its own field of activity. These organizations are forced to recognize and promote a growing number of legal and institutional patterns in the international community—so the functionalist reasons—and by the ever greater variety of their structure and scope the world develops a new "common law" of international practice.

Our former secretary of state is far from being alone in this conviction. In a letter transmitting his report to Congress on the first year of American participation in the United Nations, President Harry S. Truman said: "The policy of the United States, as I told the General Assembly in New York on October 23, 1946, is to 'support the United Nations with all the resources that we possess—not as a temporary expedient, but as a permanent partnership.' That policy—in season and out—in the face of temporary failure as well as in moments of success—has the support of the overwhelming majority of the Ameri-

---

[6] Dean Rusk, "Consolidating the Rule of Law in International Affairs," U.S. Department of State *Bulletin*, 58, no. 1509 (May 27, 1968):671-72.

can people."[7] Ten years later, President Dwight D. Eisenhower made a statement carrying only a slightly different meaning: "There can be no winner in any future global war. The world, the entire world, must insist that the conference table, rather than force, is to be used for settlement of international disputes."[8] After a similar interval of time, President Lyndon B. Johnson discussed the topic in a report to Congress, introducing, however, a note of dualism in the United States objective: "Our national interest and the high ideals of our tradition combine in American support of the United Nations. . . . Like other U.N. members, we seek to advance our own interests in this international forum. . . . But using the process of persuasion, we seek also to foster that wide community of interest among nations which is man's best hope of establishing peace with honor and progress with justice. . . . We shall continue that search in the years ahead."[9]

Such presidential statements indicate a strong belief in collective action for peace. When it became apparent that the opposing interests of the United States and the Soviet Union would prevent the Security Council from taking effective action in matters of peace and security, the United States firmly proposed the Uniting for Peace Resolution, which was adopted by the General Assembly on November 3, 1950. The philosophy behind this resolution was that collective measures are not only necessary in the absence of Security Council unanimity but can command sufficient worldwide support to make the "recommendations" of the General Assembly a satisfactory alternative to "decisions" backed by the enforcement powers of the Security Council. Applications of the Uniting for Peace policy and procedures confirm the view that this philosophy has found wide favor in the international community.

Despite such United States pledges to international law, we have shown—since Korea, especially—an increasing readiness to act unilaterally, as a superpower, on the assumption that what is best for the United States is best for the rest of the world.[10] There is no better

[7] U.S. Department of State, *The United States and the United Nations*, Report Series no. 7 (1946), p. iii.
[8] *Participation of the U.S. Government in International Conferences, July 1, 1958—Dec. 30, 1959*, U.S. Department of State Publication 7856 (1959), p. 3.
[9] *U.S. Participation in the U.N., 1966*, p. 2.
[10] See Keith S. Petersen, "The Uses of the Uniting for Peace Resolution Since 1950," in *The Strategy of World Order*, ed. R. A. Falk and S. H. Mendlovitz (New York: World Law Fund, 1966), pp. 254–71, and John G. Stoessinger, *The United Nations and the Superpowers* (New York: Random House, 1965), which present case studies of interaction among the major powers in the United Nations that tend to confirm this view.

way to see how contradictory this has seemed to the world than by considering the views other countries have of us and the part they feel we play in, or rather against, the movement toward the rule of law in the world. The world sees us as a people dynamic and sometimes ruthless, rationalizing unilateral action when multilateral support of our position is denied. It sees us as permitting self-interest to lead us into violation of our basic principles and disdain for our repeated, pledged commitments. It sees, for example, the Connally amendment to the compulsory jurisdiction article of the Statute of the International Court of Justice, in which the United States demands universal acceptance of its national interests in opposition to multilateral declarations on the issue. We profess to be a leader advocating an international bill of human rights for all nations but announce that we will not submit the draft treaty to our Senate for ratification. Or again, our critics see us intervene in Latin America and in Southeast Asia, justifying our actions as necessary for the protection of our national interests. Thus it is not surprising that we appear to many as a dominant world power resisting movements of economic and political change under the guise of protecting stability, law, and order in the world. We say that we are not acting as policemen for the world but that we must resist subversion and aggression by intervening in selected places to maintain either the *status quo* or some form of orderly transition to our liking; at the same time we advocate the principle of the inadmissibility of intervention in the domestic affairs of states. We are thus viewed in the inconsistent position of being an outspoken exponent of the principles of multilateral agreements but acting as a nonparticipant by failing to incorporate those principles into our own law and policy.

IV

In ratifying the Charter of the United Nations in 1945, the United States accepted as well the Statute of the International Court of Justice.[11] In the letter of that law, the court's jurisdiction is indicated as follows:

---

[11] Articles 92 and 93 of the charter provide that the International Court of Justice "shall be the principal judicial organ of the United Nations" and that "all members of the United Nations are *ipso facto* parties to the Statute of the International Court of Justice."

The states parties to the present Statute may at any time declare that they recognize as compulsory *ipso facto* and without special agreement, in relation to any other state accepting the same obligation, the jurisdiction of the Court in all legal disputes concerning:
  a. the interpretation of a treaty;
  b. any question of international law;
  c. the existence of any fact, which, if established, would constitute a breach of an international obligation;
  d. the nature or extent of the reparation to be made for the breach of an international obligation.

The declarations referred to above may be made unconditionally or on condition of reciprocity on the part of several or certain states, or for a certain period of time.[12]

At this time, not having been a party to the Statute of the Permanent Court of International Justice established under the League of Nations in 1920, the United States had to declare its position concerning acceptance of the compulsory jurisdiction of the court.

The history of U.S. participation in the judicial settlement of disputes reveals the ambiguity of our policy. We have consistently championed the ideals of pacific settlement, arbitration, and the rule of law. Often we proudly relate our contributions to peaceful settlement, among which was the drafting of the Statute of the Permanent Court of International Justice by Elihu Root and James Brown Scott. Some of our eminent jurists—Charles Evans Hughes, Frank B. Kellogg, John Bassett Moore, and Manley O. Hudson—have been distinguished judges of that court. On the other hand, during the 1920s and 1930s the Senate proposed reservations concerning advisory opinions by the World Court which would have required an amendment to the statute. Although Elihu Root succeeded in finding a formula which incorporated the Senate's views and was acceptable to the other states that were members of the court, and although Presidents Harding, Coolidge, and Hoover all had urged the Senate to accept it, on January 29, 1935, the Senate refused to ratify the protocol.

Again after World War II we vacillated on an essential commitment to the World Court. The declaration of the United States of August 14, 1946, which accepted the compulsory jurisdiction of the International Court of Justice but in doing so attached the Connally amendment, became the prototype of an acceptance weakened by far-

[12] Article 36, paragraphs 2 and 3, Statute of the International Court of Justice.

reaching reservations. The Connally amendment stipulated that the court would not have jurisdiction in "disputes with regard to matters which are essentially within the domestic jurisdiction of the United States of America *as determined by the United States of America*."[13] Many opponents of the amendment feel that the self-judging reservation is highly detrimental to the U.S. national interests. Justice Phillip C. Jessup has described it as "in a sense, fraudulent because it takes back with one hand what it gives with another."[14] He supports the position of the international lawyer James N. Rosenberg, who argued in 1925 that "the jurisdiction of the Court should be made compulsory and that the decisions of the International Court of Justice should never be enforceable by armed force."[15] Nevertheless, testimony at Senate hearings since 1950, urging the retraction of the self-judging domestic jurisdiction reservation, including a report and recommendation prepared by the Special Committee of the Section on International and Comparative Law of the American Bar Association (1959), have all failed. The Senate has not been moved to repeal the Connally amendment and allow the United States to participate more fully in the court.

From 1950 to 1964, all our presidents and all the chairmen of the Senate Foreign Relations Committee have urged the repeal of the Connally amendment, pointing out that the reciprocal privilege (article 36, paragraph 3) allows other states to use the same reservation and thus defeat U.S. attempts to arrive at settlements through the International Court of Justice. Even such "self-interested" pleas have gone unheeded. Instead, in line with the example set by the United States, of the fewer than forty states that have accepted the compulsory jurisdiction of the court, to date only Nicaragua, Paraguay, and Uruguay have done so without reservation.

One of the earliest problems in interpreting the Charter of the United Nations arose out of the conflict between the purpose "to take effective collective measures," which member states undertake as a responsibility (article 1, paragraph 1), and the restraint imposed on

---

[13] U.S. Department of State *Bulletin*, 15, no. 375 (Sept. 8, 1946):352 (italics added).

[14] Phillip C. Jessup, "Court or Combat," Pathways to Peace Lecture delivered Oct. 3, 1966, at The State University of New York College of Arts and Science, Plattsburgh, N.Y.

[15] James N. Rosenberg, "*Brutum Fulmen*—A Precedent for a World Court," *Columbia Law Review*, 25, no. 6 (1925): 17.

their actions "to intervene in matters which are essentially within the domestic jurisdiction of any state" (article 2, paragraph 7).[16]

On many occasions this "domestic jurisdiction" bar has been raised when U.N. members proposed investigation or action to protect human rights and fundamental freedoms (article 1, paragraph 3) or to provide for the self-determination of peoples (article 1, paragraph 2). At the first session of the General Assembly in 1946, for example, the government of India declared that its relations with South Africa had been impaired by the latter's discriminatory measures against its long-established Indian population. South Africa has continued to maintain, however, that its apartheid policies are domestic matters. Similarly, in the early phases of the debate over Southern Rhodesia, the United Kingdom maintained that Rhodesia was a self-governing territory in which the United Nations had no authority to intervene. Under such circumstances the General Assembly faces the necessity of deciding what type of action, if any, the United Nations should take in cases where a violation of the charter's human rights provisions is alleged. The issue of minority group rights and freedoms remains a perennial item before U.N. organs.

Practice since 1945 shows clearly that, despite the apparent contradiction between its responsibility to "promote . . . universal respect for, and observance of, human rights" (article 55) and the domestic jurisdiction clause, the United Nations has been able to consider, investigate, and pass judgment on specific human rights issues. There is now ample evidence of an international acceptance of the "standard of achievement" adopted December 10, 1948, without a dissenting vote by the General Assembly. The Universal Declaration of Human Rights is now the standard to be supported by at least the moral sanction of the international community. Against this background of interpretation it is understandable, however, that many General Assembly resolutions restate the principle that member states are obligated to "refrain in their international relations from the threat or use of force against the territorial integrity or political independence of any state or in any other matter inconsistent with the purposes of the United Nations" (article 2, paragraph 4).

[16] For an authoritative analysis of the meaning of the phrases "to intervene" and "matters essentially within the domestic jurisdiction of any state," along with statements of positions governments have taken when the issue was raised, see United Nations, *Repertory of Practice of United Nations Organs*, vol. 1, articles 1–22 of the charter (1955); and supplement no. 1, vol. 1, in the sections on article 2, paragraph 7.

On the issue of intervention, U.S. policy has been ambiguous. The Monroe Doctrine, although not based directly on congressional authority, has been accepted in the United States as a unilateral obligation to maintain the freedom and territorial integrity of Latin American states against interference from outside the hemisphere. Yet critics find ample support in the history of the past hundred years for a Latin American view that U.S. intervention arises from self-interest and is only cloaked in the idealism of the Monroe Doctrine. The Rio Pact, which became the Inter-American Treaty of Mutual Assistance in 1947, was one of a series of alliances undertaken by the United States to substitute regional collective security arrangements for unilateral U.S. action. These alliances were concerned with both maintaining the territorial integrity and independence of the members and protecting them against an alien and oppressive social system. In this respect the difference between the views of the United States and those of the Latin American states are of interest. The United States emphasizes article 19 of the Rio Pact, which establishes an inter-American agency with a commitment to act collectively against a security menace; the Latin American states emphasize article 17, in which the territory of an American state "may not be the object, even temporarily, of military occupation or of other measures of force taken by another State, directly or indirectly, on any grounds whatsoever." Latin Americans see the United States as having sought from the inter-American system "the legitimacy of multilateralism," an OAS label of approval for its Monroe Doctrine policies.

This conflict is apparent in the United States reaction to recent developments in Cuba. In 1960 the Cuban foreign minister requested that the Security Council immediately consider "the repeated threats, harassments, intrigues, reprisals and aggressive acts by the U.S. against his government." He stated that the United States had "refused to negotiate on a basis of equality, its differences with Cuba." Ambassador Lodge, our representative on the council, denied the charges and stressed the U.S. belief that the OAS was the proper forum in which to discuss any controversies between American states.

By 1962 this conflict had reached an apogee. A review of the missile crisis of that year enables us to consider the legality of U.S. actions. Looking at the American actions only in relation to international law, was the naval quarantine a "pacific blockade," and was the U.S. aerial surveillance an invasion of Cuban air space? Did these unilateral acts constitute violations of the Inter-American Treaty of

Reciprocal Assistance, which calls for OAS consultation and collective measures? Could these acts be reconciled with the U.N. Charter, which obligates all members to "settle their international disputes by peaceful means" and to "refrain in their international relations from the threat or use of force against the territorial integrity or political independence of any state or in any other manner inconsistent with the purposes of the United Nations"? Scholarly authority finds the U.S. actions highly questionable. In the words of Quincy Wright:

> It cannot be doubted that the United States government acted skillfully to obtain the removal of the missiles from Cuba. . . .
> It cannot be easily argued, however, that the United States lived up to its legal obligations to respect the freedom of the seas, to submit threats to the peace to the United Nations before taking unilateral actions, and to refrain from use or threat of force in international relations except in individual or collective self-defense against armed attack, under authority of the United Nations, or with consent of the state against which the force is to be used. The French jurist Charles Rousseau considered the quarantine inconsistent with generally accepted principles of international law set forth by the World Court in the Corfu Channel case, and Lazaro Cardenas, the former President of Mexico, called it an "illegal unilateral blockade." André Fontaine wrote in *Le Monde* that the United States had "tranquilly violated the most elementary rules of international law."
> The Cuban Quarantine, like the Suez and Hungarian episodes of 1956, demonstrates the reluctance of a Great Power to observe its legal obligations when dealing with unpalatable action or attitudes of a small state, especially when that small state is located in a position of strategic importance to the great power.[17]

Even when the United States turns to international or regional organizations to settle a dispute, many critics feel that this is merely a means of serving American national interests. They point to the U.S. policy for the containment of communism, saying that we used the U.N. label in Korea (1950) and Lebanon (1956) and the OAS label in Cuba (1962) and the Dominican Republic (1954 and 1965) as a cover for unilateral action. It is clear, however, that most Americans view these actions from another perspective. As recently as 1967 there seems to have been tacit acceptance of Secretary Rusk's statement on U.S. policy and action in South Vietnam: "There is no shadow of doubt in my mind that our vital interests are deeply involved in

---

[17] Quincy Wright, "The Cuban Quarantine of 1962," in *Power and Order: Six Cases in World Politics*, ed. John G. Stoessinger and Alan F. Westin (New York: Harcourt, Brace & World, 1964), pp. 210–11.

Vietnam and in Southeast Asia. We are involved because the nation's word has been given that we would be involved. On February 1, 1955, by a vote of 82 to 1 the United States Senate passed the Southeast Asia Collective Defense Treaty. That treaty stated that aggression by means of armed attack in the treaty area would endanger our own peace and safety and, in that event, we would act to meet the common danger."[18] It is just this conflict between our stated "obligations" and others' view of our practice that raises questions about the honesty of our intent.

V

The crisis that developed in Czechoslovakia during 1967 and 1968 invites us to review carefully the events of the past few years and the issues they raised in the United Nations. That crisis and similar ones in which the United States has been involved have prompted widespread debate concerning the principles and practices that would facilitate multilateral agreements—rather than condone unilateral intervention—to solve international conflicts. Out of these situations, will the agreements arrived at through U.N. conference machinery become the "reality of international law," as Wolfgang Friedmann phrases the problem, and will the norms these conferences express operate as a binding code of international behavior "notwithstanding many breaches"?[19]

During the 1960s member states used the United Nations forum to discuss and to recommend courses of action in situations where a dominant power intervened in the domestic affairs of another state. At issue was the whole complex of the purposes and principles written into the U.N. Charter—not only the question of nonintervention in the domestic affairs of a state but also the protection of the independence and sovereignty of member states and the prohibition of the threat or use of force as well as the peaceful settlement of disputes. In our own hemisphere, for example, Panama lodged in January 1964 a complaint against the United States arising out of the canal dispute, and the Security Council appealed to both governments to "bring

[18] From a Jan. 4, 1967, letter of the secretary of state to 100 student leaders who had expressed their concern about aspects of the situation in Vietnam.
[19] For a detailed and critical analysis of the trends in the development of international law, see Wolfgang Friedmann, *The Changing Structure of International Law* (New York: Columbia University Press, 1964).

an end to the exchange of fire and bloodshed" and to "impose restraint over the military forces under their command." In April 1965, the United States notified the Security Council that it had landed troops in the Dominican Republic to protect American citizens there and to escort them to safety; two days later the USSR urgently requested the Security Council to consider the question of U.S. armed intervention there.

In Africa the rights of minorities became a key issue in 1964. In January the secretary general named four experts to study and recommend methods for resolving the situation in South Africa. Based on their report, he appealed in March to the government to spare the lives of those facing death for opposition to apartheid. In June the Security Council repeated this plea, condemned apartheid, and invited the government of South Africa to accept the principle that "all people of South Africa should be brought into consultation and should thus be enabled to decide the future of their country at the national level." This appeal went unheeded, and in December the General Assembly condemned South Africa's policies of apartheid and racial discrimination as a crime against humanity and declared its attempt to annex South-West Africa to be an act of aggression.

In November 1965, when Ian Smith declared the independence of Southern Rhodesia, the United Nations was asked to consider another African case. The General Assembly condemned Southern Rhodesia and invited the United Kingdom to implement U.N. resolutions and put an end to the rebellion. In December, upon request of the U.K., the Security Council recommended an economic embargo on Southern Rhodesian trade.[20]

Also in Eastern Europe and Western Asia the United Nations has been asked to undertake peace-keeping responsibilities. In January and February 1964, Greece and Turkey, the United Kingdom, and Cyprus through the Security Council asked the secretary general to appoint a personal representative to observe the maintenance of law and order in Cyprus. In March the council unanimously recommended the creation of a U.N. peace-keeping force in Cyprus and the appointment of a mediator. In April of that year the Security Council acted

[20] For a summary of the debate and resolutions, see United Nations, General Assembly, Twenty-first Session, *Official Records*, Supplement no. 4 (*Annual Report of the Secretary-General on the Work of the Organization, 16 June 1965 to 15 June 1966*), Doc. A/6301, pp. 30–33.

on a complaint by Yemen and deplored the British attack on its territory, asking the secretary general to help settle the outstanding issues through agreement between both parties. The governments of India and Pakistan in 1965 accused each other before the Security Council of acts of aggression in Kashmir; later they notified the council of an agreement reestablishing a cease-fire and returing to the *status quo ante*. The Security Council later discussed reports on the operations of the U.N. Military Observer Group in India and Pakistan, and in December the two governments agreed on a chairman for the arbitration tribunal that was to consider their disputes.

The Far East, too, was brought to the U.N. forum for discussion during this period. In August 1964, upon a United States report of incidents in the Gulf of Tonkin described as "deliberate attacks of the Hanoi regime on U.S. naval vessels in international waters," the Security Council solicited information on the situation from the governments of both North and South Vietnam. Later that month North Vietnam categorically rejected the United States complaint, contended that U.S. aggression came within the jurisdiction of the 1954 Geneva Conference and not that of the Security Council, and warned that it would consider "illegal, null and void" any council decision in the matter.

By the latter half of 1965, the members of the U.N. recognized the need for international agreement setting out in new detail the steps and procedures states should follow in carrying out their obligations under the charter. From August 27 through October 2 of that year, the Special Committee on Principles of International Law Concerning Friendly Relations and Cooperation among States (established by General Assembly resolution on December 16, 1963) studied several principles of international law that required progressive development and codification: "the principle of refraining from the threat or use of force in international relations; the principle of peaceful settlement of disputes; the duty not to intervene in matters within the domestic jurisdiction of a State; and the principle of sovereign equality of States." At the same time, the USSR requested that the agenda for the 1965 session of the General Assembly include an item entitled "The Inadmissibility of Intervention in the Domestic Affairs of States and the Protection of Their Independence and Sovereignty." In the explanatory memorandum that accompanied this request, the USSR stated that international tensions had been increasing as a result of aggressive acts and open intervention in the domestic affairs of states; it called upon the United Nations to secure "adherence to the principle of non-intervention and to support the peoples of Africa, Asia, and Latin America in their efforts to strengthen their political independence and sovereignty." At that same session the United Kingdom requested that the General Assembly consider an item entitled "Peaceful Settlement of Disputes," explaining that the prohibition of the threat or use of force required U.N. machinery for this purpose.

The trend of opinion was clear. On December 21, 1965, the General Assembly adopted without dissent and with one abstention a Declaration on the Inadmissibility of Intervention in the Domestic Affairs of States and the Protection of Their Independence and Sovereignty. During the debate, the original USSR proposal was amended extensively to include provisions against indirect intervention in the form of subversion and economic or political pressure. A statement was added restricting states from interfering with or hindering the legitimate right of peoples to self-determination, independence, and liberation from colonial domination. In his annual report for the year 1965–1966, the secretary general emphasized the main points of the resolution as follows:

(1) no State had the right to intervene, directly or indirectly, for any reason whatever, in the internal or external affairs of any other State. Armed intervention, threats against the personality of the State or against its political, economic and cultural elements, were condemned; (2) no state should organize, assist, foment, finance, incite or tolerate subversive, terrorist or armed activities directed towards the violent overthrow of the regime of another State, or interfere in civil strife in another State; (3) the strict observance of those obligations was essential to ensure that nations lived together in peace with one another, since the practice of any form of intervention not only violated the spirit and letter of the Charter, but also led to the creation of situations which threatened international peace and security; (4) every State had an inalienable right to choose its political, economic, social and cultural systems, without interference in any form by another State; (5) consequently, all States should contribute to the complete elimination of racial discrimination and colonialism in all its forms and manifestations.[21]

It remained to be seen in 1966 what effect this resolution would have on the actual conduct of states involved in international disputes.

[21] United Nations, General Assembly, *Official Records*, Twentieth Session, Supplement no. 1 (*Annual Report of the Secretary-General on the Work of the Organization, 16 June 1964 to 15 June 1965*), Doc. A/6001, p. 48.

Most Africans and many others were disappointed when resort to law did not resolve the apartheid issue. In July 1966, the International Court of Justice delivered its judgment on two South-West Africa cases in point brought by Ethiopia and Liberia. The issue of whether South Africa's old League of Nations mandate for South-West Africa still was in force was not decided, as the court found that the applicants had no standing in the matter. Accordingly, by the president's deciding vote (the tribunal was divided seven to seven) the court rejected the argument that South Africa had failed to carry out its duties and obligations under the mandate to "promote to the utmost the material and moral well-being and social progress of the inhabitants of the territory."[22]

The year 1966 heard the theme of inadmissibility of intervention replayed with slightly different emphasis. In September 1966, Czechoslovakia asked the General Assembly to provide for the "strict observance of the prohibition of the threat or use of force in international relations and of the right of peoples to self-determination." Although differing interpretations were presented, a large majority of the governments accepted the need to reaffirm these principles. Czechoslovakia asked the General Assembly to provide for the "strict observance of the prohibition of the threat or use of force in internation affirmed the principles and requested the secretary general to forward the record for the item to the Special Committee on Principles of International Law "with a view to the early adoption of a declaration containing the enunciation of these principles."

There was extensive debate on a USSR item asking for implementation of the 1965 Declaration on the Inadmissibility of Intervention in the Domestic Affairs of States. An overwhelming majority of states, however, favored making the declaration effective. By a vote of 114-0-2 the assembly passed a resolution calling on member states to carry out faithfully their obligations to "refrain from armed intervention or the promotion or organization of subversion, terrorism, or other indirect forms of intervention for the purpose of changing by violence the existing system in another State or interfering in civil strife in another State."

[22] For a short summary of the issues and arguments considered by the International Court of Justice, see United Nations, General Assembly, *Official Records*, Twenty-second Session, Supplement no. 1 (*Annual Report of the Secretary-General on the Work of the Organization, 16 June 1966 to 15 June 1967*), Doc. A/6701, pp. 173–77.

The almost unanimous support for the principle of nonintervention by the United Nations, including the United States and the Soviet Union, prompts the question whether we are not witnessing a real recognition that states are members of an international community and that unilateral actions of intervention in domestic affairs are not "in the national interest" of any state. The inconsistency between principle and action leads one to consider whether the pressure of world opinion may not, in time, compel some acceptance of the principle in international law.

VI

The account of the drafting and the unanimous acceptance of the Universal Declaration of Human Rights on December 10, 1948, is now a familiar story. The declaration has had an impact on international law through both the incorporation of its principles in the constitutions of new states and its effect on the administrative and constitutional law of the older states. It has, furthermore, provided a standard of conduct and a basis for recommendations by United Nations organs. Examples are U.N., ILO, and UNESCO conventions on the status of refugees and stateless persons; slavery, the slave trade, and similar institutions; problems of equal remuneration, political rights, and nationality of married women; and such diverse problems as discrimination in employment and occupation, forced labor, consent to and minimum age for marriage, discrimination in education, and the elimination of racial discrimination.

The European Convention for the Protection of Human Rights and Fundamental Freedoms, signed in Rome on November 4, 1950, was the first step in making available a European international judicial procedure for the enforcement of the rights set out in the declaration. Since then no one has been free to say that the Universal Declaration of Human Rights is only a nonbinding pronouncement. Whether or not it would become a part of "international custom," and thus a source of future international law, has been a more difficult problem. In 1966 the second step was taken. On December 19, 1966, years of effort toward creating a standard of international responsibility culminated in the General Assembly's approval of two new covenants, the International Covenant on Economic, Social, and Cultural Rights and the International Covenant on Civil and Political Rights. The history of the difficulties raised, the proposals made, and the agreements reached during the years it took to complete the texts of the two covenants has still to be written. But the influence that nongovernmental organizations brought to bear on governments and on U.N. organs is sure to be an instructive part of that history. Two covenants were adopted because it was agreed that the object of one, civil and political rights, could be secured immediately, whereas the object of the other, economic, social, and cultural rights, could be achieved only in stages, according to each state's available resources. The implementation measures in each of the covenants follow the same pattern, but they differ in the extent of the implementation machinery proposed.

In its substantive provisions, the International Covenant on Civil and Political Rights contains the traditional rights set forth in the 1948 Universal Declaration of Human Rights. It calls for protection to the right of life; it prohibits torture or cruel, inhuman, or degrading treatment or punishment; it prohibits slavery, the slave trade, servitude, and compulsory labor; and it prohibits arbitrary arrest or detention. It provides that all persons deprived of their liberty shall be treated with humanity and that no one shall be imprisoned merely on the grounds of inability to fulfill a contractual obligation. The covenant further provides for freedom of movement and places limitations on the explusion of aliens. It provides in considerable detail for equality before courts and tribunals and for guarantees in criminal and civil procedures. It prohibits retroactive criminal legislation, stipulates the right of every individual to recognition everywhere as a person before the law, and prohibits arbitrary or unlawful interference with privacy, family, home, or correspondence, and unlawful attacks on honor and reputation. Although declaring the right to freedom of thought, conscience, religion, and expression, the covenant states that propaganda for war and any advocacy of national, racial, or religious hatred that constitutes incitement to discrimination, hostility, or violence should be prohibited by law. The covenant recognizes the right of peaceful assembly and the right to freedom of association, including the right to form and join trade unions. It stipulates that every citizen shall have the right and the opportunity to take part in the conduct of public affairs, to vote and to be elected at genuine periodic elections by universal and equal suffrage held by secret ballot, and to have equal access to public services in his country. It further states that all persons are equal before the law, are entitled without any discrimination to equal protection of the law, and shall be guaranteed against discrimination by the law.

The rights set forth in the covenants are not absolute. The Covenant on Civil and Political Rights, in particular, defines the admissible limitations or restrictions on the rights set forth in it. Although the formulation of the limitations differs from article to article, it can be said that the covenant provides that the rights shall not be subject to any restrictions except those that are specified by law and are necessary to protect national security, public order, public health or morals, or the rights and freedoms of others. Some of the rights, however, are not subject to any specific restrictions—for example, the right to freedom of thought, conscience, and religion; but the covenant recognizes that there may be limitations on the right to manifest religion or belief and the right to freedom of expression in accordance with "western" due process of law.

In the International Covenant on Economic, Social, and Cultural Rights, each state agrees to undertake the progressive realization of the recognized rights to the maximum extent of its available resources, using all appropriate means including, particularly, legislative measures. States undertake to recognize the individual's right to work and to the enjoyment of just and favorable conditions of work; the right to join trade unions; the right to social security, including social insurance; the protection of the family, mothers, children, and young persons; the right to an adequate standard of living and the enjoyment of the highest attainable standard of physical and mental health; and the right to education and participation in cultural life. A member nation's responsibility for achieving these rights is set forth in considerable detail. For example, to make compulsory primary education available without charge, states undertake to work out a detailed plan of action within two years and to implement it by stages within a reasonable period.

The two covenants provide for international supervision of the implementation of human rights as well as for a reporting procedure. The United Nations Economic and Social Council, assisted by the Commission on Human Rights and other specialized agencies, is the instrument for implementing economic, social, and cultural rights. Under the Covenant for Civil and Political Rights, this function is entrusted to a Human Rights Committee established by the parties and consisting of eighteen elected members serving not as government representatives but in their personal capacity. This committee receives reports, undertakes studies, transmits its comments to states, and reports to the Economic and Social Council. An optional system that is to operate only on a reciprocal basis provides for state-to-state communication in matters concerning the application of the covenant and the conciliation procedures established for the Human Rights Committee.

The Optional Protocol to the Covenant on Civil and Political Rights provides for another method of implementation. A member agreeing to this protocol recognizes the competence of the Human Rights Committee to consider communications from persons who say they are victims of a covenant violation by that nation. When this procedure becomes effective it will make a large addition to the operations of international law.

VII

In the early years of the United Nations, the United States was often a champion of human rights issues. It played a leading role in the development of the 1948 Universal Declaration of Human Rights, for example. At about the same time the United States took the initiative in introducing a resolution asking the United Nations to endorse the principles employed in the Nuremberg trials. In his 1946 Report to the Congress, President Truman stated: "The time is therefore opportune for advancing the proposal that the United Nations as a whole re-affirm the principles of the Nuremberg Charter in the context of a general codification of offenses against the peace and security of mankind. These principles establish the responsibility and liability to punishment of individuals, as well as of nations, for the waging of aggressive warfare and for crimes against humanity."[23] The 1946 resolution, as passed by the General Assembly, was an affirmation of the legal principles recognized by the Nuremberg tribunal. It directed the committee on the codification of international law appointed by the General Assembly "to treat as a matter of primary importance" plans for the formulation of these principles in the context of an international criminal code or a general codification of offenses against the peace and security of mankind.

This strong position of the late 1940s, which is so different from that of today, held for about two years. In 1953 the United States

[23] U.S. Department of State, *The United States and the United Nations*, p. vii.

proposed what has come to be accepted as an "action program" for human rights. The proposal was offered in three parts: (1) studies of rights as they existed in law and in fact; (2) an advisory service program to provide expert assistance to governments, including provision for seminars, fellowships, and scholarships to acquaint governments and nongovernmental organizations with existing law and practice in human rights; and (3) a system of periodic reports describing the developments and progress achieved in selected groups of rights. This program, established in 1956, enabled U.N. organs to obtain extensive information on existing conditions and difficulties. It provided a basis for U.N. recommendations, including those arising from the intensive concern with the self-determination of peoples and the policies and practices of apartheid.

At the same time, however—during the 1953 session of the Commission on Human Rights, when the drafting of the two human rights covenants was nearly complete—Mrs. Oswald B. Lord, the U.S. representative, stated that although her government welcomed the covenants as a more precise and definite statement of the principles enshrined in the Universal Declaration of Human Rights, "the U.S. Government has come to the conclusion that, in the present state of international relations, it would not ratify them."[24] Furthermore, in 1966, when the two covenants were adopted unanimously by the General Assembly, the American ambassador to the United Nations stated:

> The United States voted in favor of each Covenant and of the Optional Protocol to the Covenant on Civil and Political Rights because we believe that the United Nations must move forward in the field of human rights if it is to fulfill the promise of the Charter to promote and encourage "respect for human rights and for fundamental freedoms for all without distinction as to race, sex, language or religion."
>
> Our affirmative votes do not, of course, express our agreement with or approval of every part of the Covenants.[25]

---

[24] U.N. Doc. E/CN4/SR340 (Apr. 8, 1953).

[25] *U.S. Participation in the U.N., 1966*, p. 143. For a statement of the U.S. position on the covenants up to 1956, see James F. Green, *The United Nations and Human Rights* (Washington, D.C.: The Brookings Institution, 1956), pp. 58–67. He presents the view that the narrow defeat of the Bricker amendment in the Senate has made it unlikely that international treaties on human rights could receive Senate consent. It is argued that such treaties would impose as the "law of the land" federal obligations that were greater than those currently accepted by the states.

The deteriorating position of the United States government can be most pointedly described by recording the status of United Nations human rights conventions reported in the "Remarks of President Lyndon B. Johnson on Signing the Executive Order Establishing Observance of the International Year for Human Rights, 1968." This State Department release contains a table showing that, of the nineteen U.N. human rights conventions listed, as of January 30, 1968, only six had been sent to the Senate and none of these had been ratified, five had been signed by the United States but not sent to the Senate, and nine conventions requiring signature had not been signed by the United States. The list is as follows:

1. Conventions SENT TO THE SENATE but not ratified:

   Freedom of Association (ILO*)
   Genocide (U.N.)
   Forced Labor (ILO)
   Political Rights of Women (U.N.)
   Employment Policy (ILO)
   Political Rights of Women (OAS)

2. Conventions signed by the United States or not requiring signature but NOT SENT TO THE SENATE:

   Discrimination in Education (U.N.)
   Discrimination in Employment and Occupation (ILO)
   Equal Remuneration for Women and Men (ILO)
   Elimination of All Forms of Racial Discrimination (U.N.)
   Consent to Marriage (U.N.)

3. Conventions requiring signature but NOT SIGNED by the United States:

   Civil and Political Convenant (U.N.)
   Economic, Social, and Cultural Covenant (U.N.)
   Status of Refugees (pre-1951 refugees) (U.N.)
   International Rights of Correction (U.N.)
   Protocol Relating to the Status of Refugees (updates earlier convention) (U.N.)
   Convention on the Reduction of Statelessness (U.N.)
   Suppression of the Traffic in Persons (U.N.)
   Status of Stateless Persons (United States did not participate in drafting conference) (U.N.)
   Nationality of Married Women (U.N.)

---

* International Labor Organization

Before the United Nations, in the drafting of the human rights covenants, the United States—like Australia, New Zealand, and India—argued that a federal-state article was needed so that the covenants would not "bring within the jurisdiction of the federal authority any of the matters referred to in the Covenant which independently of the Covenant would not be within the jurisdiction of the federal authority." Constitutional opinion in the United States is not yet clear whether this requirement is truly necessary any longer for U.S. ratification of the covenants. At any rate the social objectives expressed by the government and the protests and demands of minority groups, both rural and urban, that have occupied the attention of the American public during the past few years should move many to ask why the United States has the unenviable record of adhering to only two of the U.N. human rights conventions.[26] Our position as an advocate of human rights in the world must certainly be weakened when others know that we do not practice what we preach, that is, that we fail to incorporate in American domestic law the standards unanimously recommended for all nations.

VIII

We can give an affirmative, if qualified, answer to the question raised in this paper, whether or not the machinery of international relations has operated during this century to bring about agreement on norms of national behavior. While there is a growing, uneasy awareness of the great powers' *pax ballistica*, the world is beginning to sense that the resources of nations must be used to build the kind of international behavior that will preclude a resort to the use of military force. Certain negative norms are quite clearly established, nuclear tests in the atmosphere being the number-one case. At the same time, evidence of international cooperation in building economic and social institutions is accumulating. These are "realities" in international relations. Out of such practices regulations are becoming accepted and new law is developing. Given the continued economic and technological predominance of the United States, it would appear that American programs, especially those that promote economic and social develop-

---

[26] During 1968 the United States ratified the United Nations Convention on the Nationality of Married Women and the (1925) League of Nations Convention on Slavery.

ment to meet the challenge of rising expectations at home and abroad, will exert an important influence on both stability and change.

Other accounts, similar to the one presented here, using themes such as the "permanent sovereignty over natural resources" or the "principles of international peace-keeping operations," are needed to make a full assessment of the contribution of the United States toward the rule of law in this century. There is good reason to hope that during the next several years the United States will take positions in support of collective authority, especially on such U.N. agenda items as "Practices Concerning Cooperation in the Peaceful Uses of Outer Space" and the "Peaceful Uses of the Sea Bed and Ocean Floor Beyond the Limits of National Jurisdiction." The present climate of world opinion seems favorable for arriving at an agreement that multilateral authority should regulate national practices in space and under the sea. Again, as we have seen, effective international principles are being established by certain achievements of economic and social cooperation which correspond to article 55 of the Charter of the United Nations.

We are not likely to see soon a world government with legislative and executive authority. Yet in social, economic, and technical fields, international administrative machinery has in fact been developed and accepted. The whole complex of U.N. agencies is now recognized as a subject of international law; U.N. organs are equipped with an independent international civil service, responsible only to the secretary general. Moreover, in addition to carrying out administrative responsibilities, that official and his staff have been given responsibility for and have demonstrated competence in using their office in political negotiations. On various occasions the "U.N. presence" has demonstrated a capacity to reduce tensions and promote peaceful solutions to issues arising between sovereign states. It remains for these practices to be recognized and consolidated; in time they must be used as building blocks upon which broader structures of multilateral authority and international law can be raised.

BIBLIOGRAPHICAL NOTE

For publications which provide digests and references to sources on U.S. policy, see the following series:

United Nations, General Assembly. *Annual Report of the Secretary-General on the Work of the Organization.* This series, issued in July of each year, provides a terse account of U.N. activities, the issues on the agendas of the Security Council, General Assembly, Economic and Social Council and its commissions, and the administrative and legal problems during the year. The *Introduction to the Annual Report*, issued separately as supplement no. 1 in September for the opening of the General Assembly, enables the secretary general to summarize and comment on the major issues as he sees them.

———. Secretariat. *Repertoire of the Practice of the Security Council, 1946–1951.* Supplement, 1952–1955. Supplement, 1956–1958.

———. *Repertory of Practice of United Nations Organs.* Volumes 1–3 and Supplements no. 1 and 2, volumes 1–3. These studies by the U.N. Secretariat under the direction of the Office of Legal Affairs provide a basis for member states to consider proposals for revision of the Charter of the United Nations. The volumes cover the practices of the organs of the United Nations, arranged according to the Articles of the Charter, and the actions of the organs arising from significant agenda items.

U.S. Department of State. *U.S. Participation in the UN: Report by the President to the Congress for the Year*, 1946–. This series provides an annual summary of items under discussion in U.N. organs and a commentary on the positions the United States has taken.

The following works provide analyses by American and other specialists:

Falk, R. A., and Mendlovitz, S. H., eds. *Strategy of World Order*, vol. 2: *International Law.* New York: World Law Fund, 1966.

Friedmann, Wolfgang. *The Changing Structure of International Law.* New York: Columbia University Press, 1964.

Luard, Evan. *Conflict and Peace in the Modern International System.* Boston: Little, Brown, 1968.

Jessup, Philip C. *A Half Century of Efforts to Substitute Law for War.* 1960.

Russell, Ruth B. *The United Nations and United States Security Policy.* Washington, D.C.: The Brookings Institution, 1968.

U.S. Senate, Foreign Relations Subcommittee. *Human Rights Conventions: Hearings.* 90th Cong., 1st sess., February 23, March 8, and September 13, 1967.

The Washington World Conference. *World Peace through Law.* New York, 1967.

Law as a Barrier to Change: A Korean Experience

NAM-YEARL CHAI

SINCE WORLD WAR II, and especially during the last ten years, the literature of international relations has given much attention to the attitudes of the newly independent Asian and African states toward an international rule of law.[1] This indicates concern over the question of how these states feel about accepting legal norms as obligatory—whether they are receptive, indifferent, or hostile to the idea of building a new world order buttressed by world law.

One can hardly overemphasize our urgent need to gain insight into what these newly independent states really think of this question. We must understand this problem before we can build a new world order, and one can even say that world peace through the rule of law will not come unless the scheme receives solid backing from the newly independent African and Asian states.

Securing the wholehearted support of these states is necessary if we envisage our future world order as voluntary—not something to be imposed by force but a cooperative undertaking through consensual agreements. And no one needs to be reminded that these states make up a majority of the nations today.

This essay attempts to examine the uses of law in Korea, a former colonial area, especially the ways the rules of law were used as legal barriers by Japan and Western powers to frustrate the Korean aspiration for national independence. To place the Korean experience in a telling perspective, some reference first to the attitudes of the newly independent Asian and African states is in order.

The movement toward world peace through the rule of law is gaining momentum today. Athens, Washington, and Geneva were the sites of world conferences on World Peace Through Law in 1963, 1965, and 1967 respectively, and important regional conferences were held

[1] For a full citation of works relevant to this point, see Chapter 1 of Nam-Yearl Chai's "Asian Attitudes toward International Law: A Case Study of Korea" (Ph.D. diss., University of Pennsylvania, 1967).

between 1959 and 1965 in New Delhi, San José (Costa Rica), Tokyo, Lagos, Rio de Janeiro, Rome, and Bangkok. What is more pertinent from the standpoint of our interest is the theoretical underpinning of these conferences. Spokesmen for them would have us believe that what we need is an enlightened public opinion capable of bearing down on their governments to make them abide by the law of the world.

Few people will find fault with the cogency of such an argument. It is easy to follow the reasoning that to achieve a law-oriented world order every member nation must be law abiding and that if every state is law abiding a world ordered by normative rules will emerge.

But however logical the argument may appear, one cannot help but feel that its reasoning is an oversimplified assumption. It is oversimplified in the sense that it leaves some profoundly important questions unanswered: What sort of rule of law (or whose) are we talking about? Are we referring, for example, to the rules of law that governed the interstate relations of the occidental nations before World War II? Are we now asked to renew our pledge to uphold the erstwhile rules of law which generally favored the economic, political, and legal positions of the ex-colonialist powers, thus perpetuating their favored positions? Are we asked to nurture the world order based on the rules of law which embodied only the values of the Graeco-Christian culture? Or are we called upon to forge a law-oriented world order which will embrace the divergent value systems of both the occidental and non-occidental worlds?

Clarification of such questions is as important as it is urgent. I submit that what appears to be a simple phrase like "rule of law" carries a multitude of meanings. It will trigger different reactions in different nations depending upon the kind of experiences they have had in the past.

Thus Professor Pyong Choon Hahm of Korea remarked in a perceptive essay that law to the Koreans was something that was imposed upon them by the foreign colonialist and hence was symbolic of "an instrument of oppression." Hahm explained that the Koreans had to wage "an incessant war against the law" to try to keep freedom and independence within reach. In due course they came to regard it almost as "a patriotic duty" to disregard and violate the law that was thrust upon them.[2]

---

[2] Pyong Choon Hahm, "The Rule of What Law? A Korean Conundrum," *Journal of the International Commission of Jurists*, no. 2 (Winter, 1965):283.

To the Koreans, the rule of law or law itself stood as a barrier to change. That is to say, whenever the Koreans attempted to change the *status quo* imposed upon them by the colonialist, they usually ran into legal difficulties. Thus it becomes extremely relevant to raise the question, "In whose image is world peace through the rule of law to be achieved?"

Korea is one of many former colonial territories in Asia and Africa to regain independence in the post–World War II era. Many of them encountered, among numerous difficulties, certain "legal barriers" in their struggles to achieve statehood. The conclusion thus seems persuasive that some of these barriers resulted in traumatic experiences that today color in one way or another these nations' attitudes toward the rule of law.

On the basis of his familiarity with the historical background of some newly independent Asian states, J. J. G. Syatauw, for instance, observed: "During their struggle for independence the Asian nations ran into great authoritative obstacles which all systems of public order will erect to protect the established system. These obstacles were couched in such traditional terms as sovereignty, colonial dependency, domestic jurisdiction and the like."[3] In view of this, it is only natural for some of these states to demonstrate hostility toward such proposals as "world peace through the rule of law" if this means a new world order in the image of the colonialist-tailored legal norms of the bygone days.

In a sense, all the newly independent Asian states are caught on the horns of a dilemma. They, more than anyone else, need a stable world order. They need it so that they can devote their attention to ordering their newly won statehood with the least bother from big powers. But by the same token the last thing they will do is to accept the existing world order, for that would forever put them in an inferior bargaining position in the world political arena. They would remain bound by unequal treaties and unwanted legal shackles. They are also too eager to start a new national life with a clean slate to permit themselves to be hemmed in by old obligations.

Therefore it is one thing to invite these newly independent Asian and African states to join in the paving of a road toward a world order founded on the rules of law. It is an altogether different thing to ask them to embrace a rule of law heavily favoring the former

[3] J. J. G. Syatauw, *Some Newly Established Asian States and the Development of International Law* (The Hague: Martinus Nijhoff, 1961), p. 113.

colonialists' economic, political, and legal position. One may do well to recall Professor Georges M. Abi-Saab's remark: "The newly independent states do not easily forget that the same body of international law that they are now asked to abide by, sanctioned their previous subjugation and exploitation and stood as a bar to their emancipation."[4] Indeed, it is too much to ask these new states to endorse the proposal unequivocally.

Only saintly individuals willingly accept self-imposed immolation —with the comforting thought that by doing so one earns a blissful life hereafter. Saintly nations have yet to come!

Herein, then, lies the dilemma. The newly independent Asian and African states are revolutionary nations. They owe their birthright to revolutionary nationalism. As Professor Richard A. Falk has so well articulated, these revolutionary elites are committed to radical socioeconomic change. Such a commitment results in a repudiation of those norms of international law that restrict the freedom of a state to shape its national destiny.[5] In this regard, it is instructive to note here a conclusion reached at the Bangkok Conference of Asian Jurists of 1965. As reported by John H. Spencer, it was that "in the former colonial territories, the Rule of Law is viewed more as a malevolent instrument of tyrannical rule than as a force of emancipation or of protection of human rights."[6]

To many newly independent Asian and African states the present calls for "world peace through the rule of law" appear at times a shrewdly calculated effort by a few colonialists to try to advance a resurgence of neocolonialism. Or they may see the West's crusading zeal for order-building as at best a double-entry moral bookkeeping. This point is aptly illustrated by Syatauw's observation:

> In the past when wars were recognized instruments of policy, international law has frequently been used as a justification of violence and aggression once the objective was successfully achieved. To ex-

[4] Georges M. Abi-Saab, "The Newly Independent States and the Rules of International Law: An Outline," *Howard Law Journal*, 8 (Spring 1962):100.

[5] Richard A. Falk, "Revolutionary Nations and the Quality of International Legal Order," in *The Revolution in World Politics*, ed. Morton A. Kaplan (New York: Wiley, 1962), pp. 310–31.

[6] John H. Spencer, review of *The Dynamic Aspects of the Rule of Law in the Modern Age: Report on the Proceedings of the South-East Asian and Pacific Conference of Jurists, Bangkok, Thailand, February 15–19, 1965* (Geneva: International Commission of Jurists, 1965), in *American Journal of International Law*, 61, no. 3 (July 1967):839–40.

pect now of the new states, so often in the past subjected to such violence and aggression, that they should abide by "established rules of international law," often seems like telling a maltreated child, finally grown up and become stronger than the parent, that he should behave. The child may want to do so, but will not necessarily wish to accept all rules of conduct set by the once stronger adult.[7]

Such reasoning may or may not be well founded. Yet one thing does appear certain: the old established nations ought not to press too rashly for an uncritical acceptance by the newly independent nations of the traditional rules of law. In a severely decentralized legal order, voluntary compliance with the transnational legal norms still counts more than anything else. Unruly and hasty insistence on new order-building may result in revolutionary disturbances in an international scene. Hemmed in unwanted legal fences, the new states may well choose the latter course. Or worse still, they may give a death blow to norms quite in keeping with their revolutionary aspiration—as India did when it seized Goa from Portugal.

It is urgent, therefore, that we pay more than lip service to our pledge to keep the rule of law attuned with the aspirations of these new nations. Law must reflect more fairly changing world conditions. It must be harmonized with the economic aspirations of these new states. They need to be convinced that within the framework of the world law they, too, can share the good things of life. They must be given substantial economic and political stakes in the new world order to be built. One of the primary functions of law in an orderly society is to balance constantly the interests of individuals and those of society. What we need now on an international plane is a fair degree of balancing of interests of the newly emerged, poor states and those of the old-established, industrially advanced, wealthy states.

I submit that while we should spare no efforts to keep the movement toward world law a growing concern, we should maintain a proper sense of priority. In particular, we need to reorient our efforts to the urgent task of reexamining the legal bedrock on which the new legal edifice will be erected. In so doing, we must never lose sight of the fact that building a wholesome world order takes more than just the rules of law but, like all good laws, the bedrock of equity and *ex aequo et bono*.

The point of the foregoing discussion is that we need, first of all,

---

[7] Syatauw, *Asian States*, p. 221.

to develop an understanding of the colonial experiences of every newly independent Asian and African state. We need to know very intimately the old uses of law there. But it would go beyond the scope of this paper to try to study the situation in every one of these former colonies. Therefore I shall focus on Korea, with which I am most familiar.

II

Even a cursory survey of Korea's preindependence era reveals numerous instances where law stood as a barrier to change. We have selected for close scrutiny the most significant events in Korea's effort to circumvent domination or to regain independence from Japan. In each instance the effort bore no fruit, because of insurmountable legal barriers erected by the world powers.

Late in the nineteenth century, with the abandonment of a long, unbroken history of isolationism, Korea was, for better or worse, ushered into the family of nations. Between 1882 and 1902, Korea entered treaty relations with a number of Western states, including the United States, Great Britain, Germany, Russia, Italy, Austria-Hungary, Belgium, and Denmark. January of 1888 marked an especially memorable month from the standpoint of Korea's diplomatic history. This was the time when Korea established a diplomatic mission in the West for the first time in her history. On January 17, 1888, the American secretary of state, Thomas F. Bayard, presented the Korean minister, Chong Yang Pak, to President Grover Cleveland. Upon presentation of Pak's credentials to the president, the latter responded with a customary reply.[8]

The establishment during the 1880s of Korea's diplomatic outposts in Europe as well as America might lead one to conclude that Korea's position in the family of nations thus became firmly established. On the contrary, twenty-three years after her entry into the western family of nations, Korea's position as a sovereign nation came to an end.

There was no single cause for Korea's loss of independence. Numerous factors, such as geography, external forces, and a series of internal *faux pas*, appear to have been responsible. When Korea estab-

[8] For a full citation of references relevant to this section, see Chapter III of Chai, "Asian Attitudes toward International Law."

lished a legation at Washington in 1888, there were, for instance, at least six foreign powers vying for influence in the country.

Briefly stated, in the middle of the 1890s, the Japanese victory over China led to the eventual curtailment of the centuries-old Chinese influence in Korea. As a result, Korea became subject to closer Japanese control than ever before. In addition, the ever-intensifying Russian-Japanese rivalry in the Korean peninsula set the two powers on an inevitable collision course. The result was the Russian-Japanese war of 1904–1905. To the surprise of the spectator nations and perhaps to the participants as well, Japan emerged the victor.

Promptly Japan set out to lay the groundwork for placing Korea under a protectorate. In fact, as early as February 1904, Japanese troops ransacked the royal palace at Seoul and managed to secure a Japanese-Korean protocol. This protocol provided that (1) Korea would adopt Japanese advice on the improvement of Korea's internal administration; (2) Japan would guarantee "the independence and territorial integrity of Korea"; and (3) Korea would refrain from entering into treaty relations with any foreign power without Japan's consent or in violation of the protocol.

The February protocol was followed by another agreement of far-reaching consequences, signed on August 22, 1904. Under the terms of this agreement, Korea agreed to accept the counsel of advisers appointed by the Japanese government in the fields of finance and foreign affairs. The logical outcome of the Japanese curtailment of Korean sovereignty, both internally and externally, was the Japanese demand, in the early part of 1905, for the recall of Korean legations abroad.

Alarmed by the rapidly increasing Japanese encroachment on Korea's integrity as an independent nation, the Korean government appealed to the powers with whom the former had treaty relations to intercede. The appeals had no result. Emperor Kojong thereupon decided to appeal directly to President Theodore Roosevelt on the strength of the Korea-United States Amity Treaty of 1882.[9]

On two separate occasions in 1905, personal representatives of the

---

[9] The relevant portion of article 1 of this Treaty reads, in part: "If other Powers deal unjustly or oppressively with either Government the other will exert their good offices, on being informed of the case, to bring about an amicable arrangement, thus showing their friendly feelings." See Henry Chung, *Korean Treaties* (New York: H. S. Nichols, 1919), p. 197.

Korean emperor were sent to America bearing messages to the president. One of these missions was assigned to Yi Sung Man (Syngman Rhee), who was reported to have carried a secret message "concealed in the false bottom of his trunk" to the Korean legation at Washington. While Rhee was urging the Korean cause in America, Secretary of War William Howard Taft set out on a tour of the Orient in June 1905. En route he stopped over in Hawaii and was greeted there by the Korean residents who assembled in his honor. Out of the meeting came a resolution that called on the president of the United States "to safeguard Korean independence by invoking the Treaty of 1882."

Prior to the forthcoming peace conferences between Russia and Japan at Portsmouth, New Hampshire, Rhee and the Reverend Pyong Ku Yun sought out the president at his Sagamore Hill residence. Upon receiving the Korean memorial, Roosevelt made the following remarks:

I would be glad to do anything I can in behalf of your country, but unless this memorial comes through official channels I can't do anything with it. . . . if you will have this sent to me by your legation, I will present it . . . to the Peace Conference. . . . Have your minister take it to the Department of State, and if he doesn't find the secretary of state, let him leave it with anyone, asking that it be sent on to me. That is all that is necessary.[10]

Quite obviously, all that was necessary for Roosevelt to send Rhee and Yun away politely without trying to hurt their feelings, was to make a simple yet impossible suggestion: to transmit the memorial through *official channels*. As later events attest, the memorial never reached the State Department. The chargé d'affaires at the Korean legation refused to transmit it to the State Department on the grounds that he had not received official instructions from the home government. One wonders if President Roosevelt was aware of the fact that by the protocol of August 22, 1904, the Korean Department of Foreign Affairs had already been placed under the supervision of the Japanese-appointed political adviser, D. W. Stevens.

The other secret mission was assigned to an American national, Professor Homer B. Hulbert, who was a long-time trusted friend of the emperor. Hulbert left Korea for the United States in October 1905,

---

[10] Quoted in Robert T. Oliver, *Syngman Rhee: The Man Behind the Myth* (New York: Dodd Mead, 1955), pp. 86–87.

carrying with him a letter from the emperor to the president. Upon arriving in Washington, on November 17, Hulbert immediately set about arranging to see Roosevelt.

Before Hulbert reached Washington, however, the Japanese government had rushed Marquis Ito to Korea. His mission was to conclude the Treaty of Protectorate with Korea. One of the most controversial points in the proposed treaty was article 1, which called for the abolition of Korea's Foreign Office and placed her external relations under the direct control of the Foreign Office in Tokyo. To this demand the Korean emperor and his cabinet members refused to yield. Once, after Marquis Ito had requested an audience, the Korean emperor refused to see him, under the pretext of a sore throat.

Sources are plentiful concerning the step-by-step development of the "negotiations" between the Korean emperor and his cabinet members, on the one hand, and Marquis Ito, Minister Hayashi, and Marshal Hasegawa, on the other. The point that tells us the most here is the circumstance under which the treaty was concluded. Again, sources confirm that the treaty was obtained under duress and threats to the person of the emperor himself. Although the Korean emperor and Premier Kyu Sol Han did not sign the treaty then or later, the Japanese government regarded the treaty as effective on the strength of the agreement of five of eight Korean ministers to sign.

In the meantime, immediately after his arrival in Washington, the emperor's messenger, Hulbert, sent word to the White House that he was bearing an important message from the Korean emperor. To this overture Hulbert received a reply that the president would not receive the message. He rushed to the State Department. But there he was told they were too busy to see him on that day and that he might come again the next day. In Hulbert's own words: "I hurried over to the White House [for the second time] and asked to be admitted. A secretary came out and without any preliminary whatever told me in the lobby that they knew the contents of the letter, but that the State Department was the only place to go."[11]

On the following day, Hulbert managed to see Secretary Elihu Root at the State Department; he delivered the emperor's message to the president. However, this was two days after the Japanese minister, Kogoro Takahira, had handed a complete text of the Protectorate

[11] Hulbert's sworn statement in U.S. Congress, Senate, *Congressional Record*, 66th Cong., 1st sess., 1919, 58, pt. 4:3925.

Treaty of November 17 to Secretary Root. What was worse, by this time the U.S. government had "cut off all communication with the Korean government"; a cable instructing the U.S. legation to withdraw from Seoul had already been sent out.

Sometime later, Hulbert received a formal reply dated November 25 from Secretary Root:

> The letter from the Emperor of Korea which you intrusted to me has been placed in the President's hands and read by him.
> In view of the fact that the Emperor desires that the sending of the letter should remain a secret, and of the fact that since intrusting it to you the Emperor has made a new agreement with Japan disposing of the whole question to which the letter relates, it seems quite impractical that any action should be based upon it.[12]

But Root failed to settle the matter. For one thing, Hulbert received a cable from the Korean emperor the following day, a message which was "secreted out" of Korea and dispatched from Chefoo, China so as to avoid the use of Japanese-controlled wires. Hulbert deposited the cablegram in the hands of the assistant secretary of state, who merely acknowledged by saying that he "would put it on file." It read:

> I declare that the so-called treaty of protectorate recently concluded between Korea and Japan was extorted at the point of the sword and under duress, and therefore is null and void. I never consented to it and never will. Transmit to American Government.[13]

Subsequently Yong Ch'an Min, the Korean minister to France, rushed to Washington and made further appeals to Secretary Root, reiterating the emperor's message in the cablegram. Apparently, feeling obliged to reply to the cable, the State Department gave Min a note of explanation. It pointed out that the existence of the earlier agreements of February 23 and August 22, 1904, the validity of which was never contested by Korea, in fact prevented the U.S. government from interceding for Korea under the Amity Treaty of 1882.[14]

Moreover, in an apparent effort to convince Minister Min that the American government could do nothing further in behalf of Korea, Root pointed out that Chargé Kim, "the regularly accredited" official

---

[12] Ibid.
[13] Ibid.
[14] U.S. Department of State, *Papers Relating to the Foreign Relations of the United States (1905)*, 1905, pp. 629–30.

of the Korean legation at Washington, had communicated to him that the Foreign Office in Seoul had instructed him to transfer his files to the Japanese legation.

This, then, was one of the initial legal rebuffs Korea received in her effort to maintain her place in the family of nations.

III

Hardly had two years elapsed after the Korean emperor's first unsuccessful attempt to safeguard his country's tottering sovereignty when a chance came for him to try again. In spite of his unfruitful effort to invoke article 1 of the Korea–United States Amity Treaty, the Korean emperor decided to make an appeal to the world at large. He decided to appeal to the international peace conference to be held at The Hague in 1907. He appears to have predicated his move on the assumption that if he could convince the world that the Protectorate Treaty of 1905 was a result of intimidation and without his consent, then the powers having treaty relations with Korea might be inclined to restore full diplomatic relations.[15]

The emperor began by dispatching a secret envoy to The Hague. Sources indicate that as early as the middle of 1906 he had appointed Professor Hulbert as ambassador extraordinary and plenipotentiary in the hope that he would have time to visit the major capitals and urge the treaty powers to intercede for Korea at the forthcoming Hague Conference. But it is generally believed that Hulbert declined to play an official role, preferring to be an unofficial adviser, and that he recommended that the emperor not communicate with the powers until just before the conference convened, "to preserve the element of surprise."

So the commission was assigned to three Koreans: Sang Sool Yi, former vice premier; Chun Yi, former judge of the Supreme Court; and Wi Jong Yi, secretary of the Korean legation at Saint Petersburg. On June 29, 1907, these Korean envoys reached The Hague with their credentials. This document read, in part:

As the independence of Korea has been known to all the Powers with which she has ever been in friendly relation, we have, for this reason, the right to send delegates to all international conferences. . . .

[15] See note 8.

But by the terms of the treaty of November 18, 1905, which was extorted from us by force, the Japanese by menace and by a violation of all international equity deprived us of the right of direct communication with the friendly Powers.

Not recognizing this act on the part of the Japanese, we desire hereby to appoint... [the] Delegates Extraordinary and Plenipotentiary..., for the purpose of making clear to the representatives of the Powers the violation of our rights by the Japanese and the dangers which presently threaten our country; and also to reestablish between my country and the foreign Powers the direct diplomatic relations to which we are entitled by the fact of our independence.[16]

Although failure was not altogether unexpected, all efforts of the Korean delegates to present their case before the assembly of world powers were stifled, mainly because of what appeared to be legal barriers. The first of these was the question of invitation. In order to overcome this question, the Korean delegates presented themselves to Count Nelidov, the chief Russian delegate and president of the conference, urging him to grant them admission. This request Nelidov politely but firmly refused, saying that diplomatic usage forbade him from receiving any delegates that were not officially invited by the host government (in this case, the Dutch).

The Korean delegates' subsequent efforts to establish themselves through the Dutch government were of no avail. For one thing, as one of the Japanese cables revealed, the Dutch minister for foreign affairs had assured the Japanese officials at The Hague that he would not grant an interview to the Koreans unless they applied through Japanese channels. Moreover, this minister, Van Tets Van Goudrian, was informed by Ito that the Korean deputation did not have the sanction of the Korean emperor. In spite of the Korean declaration to the contrary through the *Courier de la Conference*, the Korean delegates were denied a hearing.

Like the first conference of 1899, this second conference deliberately excluded from consideration "the order of the things established by treaty." Herein lay the insurmountable legal barrier for Korea, regarded as a Japanese protectorate. As was so well put by Clarence Weems: "The powers recognized that, under the 'Protectorate Treaty' of November 1905, Korea's foreign affairs were handled by Japan.

---

[16] For a photostatic copy of the credential with the original English translation in *Independent* (August 1907), see Sung Kun Lee, *Hankuksa* [*History of Korea*], vol. 6 (Seoul: Eulyu, 1960), p. 945.

These governments were therefore not in position to question the validity of that treaty or to act without regard to it."[17]

This, then, was the second disheartening legal experience that Korea encountered in her struggle for the status of a fully independent state in the ranks of world powers. It would indeed be naïve to conclude that the considerations of diplomatic protocol alone accounted for Korea's inability to make an appeal to the Hague conference. Factors of *Realpolitik* must have weighed heavily. Whatever the reason may be, the point is that the powers assembled at The Hague managed to keep the Korean envoys at arm's length by erecting certain legal barriers.

IV

Deeply incensed by the Hague incident, Japan undertook a number of steps that eventually led to a complete annexation of Korea in August 1910. The Treaty of Annexation completely destroyed any notion that Korea had any legal existence as a nation. This could very well have been the case permanently were it not for the decision by the Korean nationalists to establish a government in exile.

The Provisional Korean Government was established in April 1919, soon after the proclamation of the Declaration of Independence on March 1 of the same year.[18] From then on, Korea's plea to the world assumed a slightly different tone. Before annexation, Korea attempted chiefly to convince the world that the Protectorate Treaty of 1905 was invalid, since it was imposed by intimidation and force and violated previously drawn agreements that guaranteed Korea's independence and national integrity. The pleas were always made in the name of the Korean emperor, who represented Korea. After annexation, however, the question was essentially one of winning diplomatic recognition for a newly formed government. The government was officially called "provisional," and it was to remain so until it would receive official recognition from the other friendly powers of the world.

In a sense, the creation of the provisional government signaled a new start, if for no other reason than that the Koreans no longer had

---

[17] Clarence Weems, ed., *Hulbert's History of Korea*, vol. 1 (New York: Hillary House, 1962), pp. 53–54.

[18] See note 8.

to contend with the "protectorate" status, which so often hamstrung their political struggles. Moreover, the Annexation Treaty dissolved the international status of Korea altogether. By creating a new but provisional government, the Koreans put an end to the much-resented legal barriers that harrassed the Koreans under such strange-sounding jargons as "conflicting" credentials and "protectorate" status. But as subsequent events show, the pleas of the new government also encountered technical difficulties.

One of the momentous tasks the provisional government undertook soon after its formation was to plead for Korea at the Versailles Peace Conference. To this end, even before the formation of the provisional government, Kyu Sik Kim was sent to Paris. When the government was formed, Kim was elected foreign minister. Official credentials designating him ambassador plenipotentiary were sent to him in Paris.

The newly formed provisional government ran into serious legal difficulties at the outset. Syngman Rhee, as president of the government, "sought desperately to get a passport from the [U.S.] State Department to permit him to go to Paris, where he hoped to lay the Korean case squarely before President Wilson and the peace conference."[19] The State Department declined, however, because it considered that all Koreans by this time had acquired Japanese nationality, legally speaking, and that what Rhee needed was a Japanese passport.

Rhee was unable to go to Paris. Moreover, Korea's plea, which was submitted to the peace conference through Kyu Sik Kim on May 12, 1919, was never formally considered, presumably because the conference lacked the legal jurisdiction to look into the matter—or perhaps the provisional government lacked legal competence to even try to direct the conferees' attention to the Korean question. Whatever the reason, Korea once again found another legal millstone firmly attached around her neck.

V

Undaunted by the unfruitful attempt at the Paris Conference, Korea made another plea in the 1920s. To make the petition more auspicious and also to marshal all the legal leverage they could, the Ko-

---

[19] Oliver, *Syngman Rhee*, p. 143.

reans in America and Hawaii formed the Korean Commission to the Conference on Limitation of Armament and retained two legal Counselors, Fred A. Dolph and Charles S. Thomas, former senator from Colorado.[20]

Learning of the Koreans' design to submit a petition to the conference, some Japanese officials promptly declared that the Korean problem was essentially a domestic question of the Japanese empire and hence the forthcoming conference had no jurisdiction to concern itself with it. The Japanese protest notwithstanding, the Koreans made the petition. On two occasions, on December 1, 1921, and on January 25, 1922, the Korean commission presented to the conference letters of petition entitled "Korea's Appeal to the Conference on Limitation of Armament." The appeal rested on Korea's treaties with a number of powers (the United States, Great Britain, Belguim, Italy, and Denmark) in which pledges of "good offices" were inserted to ensure intercession in case of differences with a third power. Since most of the nations at the conference had concluded treaties with Korea, the petitioners felt that this "solemn sanction of treaty obligation" established their right to be heard.

The central points of the petition submitted on January 25, 1922, were that all Koreans pledged their allegiance to the provisional government and that the government therefore should have a chance to be heard at the conference. The petition added that the Koreans had never recognized Japanese authority in Korea and that the Treaty of Annexation was made under duress and against the will of the Korean people.

It must be added here that as early as October 1, 1921, the Korean commission sent a separate appeal to the members of the American delegation to the forthcoming conference. This appeal urged that the conferees "proceed upon the fundamental premise that the covenants of treaties and agreements between nations are and must, until formally repudiated by recognized processes, be faithfully observed by their respective signatories."[21]

Again Korea's efforts were in vain. As was reported later in *Korea Review*, neither the American delegates nor the secretary-general of the conference even acknowledged having received the petition. Since

---
[20] See note 8.
[21] For the text of this appeal, see *Korea Review*, 3, no. 8 (October 1921): 6–8.

the Korean Provisional Government had no official status with the American government, the Korean petition "did not merit the courtesy of an official acknowledgment." What was more, the American government was afraid that acknowledging the petition might be construed as recognizing the provisional government.

VI

A word must be said about efforts by the Korean Provisional Government to gain diplomatic recognition from the United States during World War II.[22] As early as June 6, 1941, Ku Kim, chief executive of the provisional government in Chungking, expressed to President Roosevelt his desire to establish reciprocal friendly relations between the two governments. Kim's aim, of course, was to secure diplomatic recognition for the provisional government.

Kim's communiqué was followed by a letter from Syngman Rhee on February 7, 1942, to the secretary of state. In his letter, Rhee, as chairman of the Korean Commission in the United States, also pleaded for recognition for the provisional government. In addition, the Korean Liberty Conference met in Washington in the early spring of 1942 under the sponsorship of the United Korean Committee and the Korean-American Council. At that meeting a publicity campaign on the Korean question was launched in the hope of winning recognition.

Nothing came of these and the subsequent efforts. Now and then the State Department expressed sympathy, but it was not inclined to extend recognition. More often than not the State Department failed even to acknowledge the communiqués addressed to it.[23] Whenever the State Department found it expedient to acknowledge a communiqué from the Koreans, it always stressed the point that such an acknowledgment should not be construed as any form of recognition, formal or informal.

It is true that certain political, not legal, considerations might have

[22] For background on this section, consult under the heading "Korea and the Question of Recognition of a Provisional Korean Government" in U.S. Department of State, *Foreign Relations of the United States: Diplomatic Papers 1942, 1943, and 1944*, pub. nos. 6995, 7601, and 7859.

[23] For instance, Rhee's letter of March 24, 1942, to the secretary of state was never acknowledged; the statement, "No reply to this letter has been found in Department files," is found in U.S. Department of State, *Foreign Relations of the United States (1942)*, 1:865.

been the factor that led the State Department to reject Korea's pleas. Nevertheless the fact remains that Korea was desperately in need of diplomatic recognition and did not get it. As far as the Koreans were concerned, diplomatic recognition, which was generally sanctioned under traditional international law, stood as an insurmountable legal barrier.

Finally, as is widely known, it was not until December 1943 that the Allied powers—the United States, Great Britain, and China—took official cognizance of Korea's claims to independence. With whatever words of assurance came out of the Cairo Declaration of 1943, the Koreans waited until April 1945 to make another final appeal on behalf of the provisional government at the United Nations Conference in San Francisco. The Koreans did what they could to earn a charter membership for Korea. Again, as before, Korea's efforts bore no fruit, presumably because of a legal technicality—perhaps because nations refused to acknowledge that Korea was ever at war with Japan under international law.

VII

The foregoing examination confirms that Korea encountered numerous insurmountable legal barriers in her struggle to attain independence. Some of these barriers obviously stemmed from Korea's inability to meet certain requirements of traditional international law, some obviously resulted from legal snares concocted by Japan to protect her vested interests— at times with a tacit nod by other powers.

In reference to the African and Asian struggles over colonialism, John G. Stoessinger once observed: "As the adult person is conditioned by the conscious and unconscious memories of his childhood and adolescence, the nation-state is also conditioned by its memories —in other words, its history."[24] Ascertaining precisely the extent to which Korea's colonial history has colored her contemporary attitude toward "rules of law" will be a difficult task. Nevertheless, it would be wrong to pretend that her history bears no relevance to the question. And in this connection we need to mention another facet of Korea's experience. Sources show that even before the annexation Ko-

---

[24] John G. Stoessinger, *The Might of Nations*, rev. ed. (New York: Random House, 1965), p. 69.

reans had never really developed any fondness for law. They had preferred government by a virtuous ruler to one of law; they had, by and large, preferred an out-of-court settlement of a dispute to a legal settlement. Law then was looked upon as an instrument of oppression, as it was during the colonial reign.[25] Thus one may conclude that a serious study of Korea's history, both colonial and precolonial, holds the key to our understanding of Korea and the "rules of law."

Neither should we overlook the following two points. First, in spite of the fact that Korea had had bitter and frustrating encounters with certain rules of law, upon achieving her statehood in 1948 Korea was favorably disposed to international law. This is evidenced by article 7 of the Constitution of the Republic of Korea, promulgated on July 17, 1948: "Duly ratified and published treaties and generally recognized rules of international law shall have the same effect as that of the law of Korea."[26] Commenting on this point, Professor Robert R. Wilson observed: "Of the new constitutions adopted since the beginning of 1957, apparently only that of South Korea (1960) contains a clearly 'incorporative' [rather than hortatory] clause."[27]

Second, we stated at the outset that the Koreans regarded law as an instrument of oppression. Paradoxical as it may seem, however, in making their pleas the Korean nationalists almost always argued, as can be seen throughout this essay, on highly legalistic grounds. Time after time their appeals were couched in heavily legal terms such as *pacta sunt servanda* and duress.

What does all this mean? That the Koreans are not necessarily dogmatic in their antilegal stance. It also means that we could count on Korea—and perhaps on other newly emergent African and Asian states—as potential and ready advocates of the rule of law, provided the legal order they are called upon to support reflected their social and political aspirations.

We need periodically to reexamine certain legal norms that may have lost touch with the world reality of our days. We need to assess the moods of all the participants in the world political arena so as to be able to redefine and adjust, as much as possible, any uncertain

---

[25] Pyong-Choon Hahm, *The Korean Political Tradition and Law: Essays in Korean Law and Legal History* (Seoul: Hollyn, 1967), pp. 1–84.

[26] Republic of Korea, Office of Public Information, *The Constitution of the Republic of Korea* (Seoul, 1955), p. 3.

[27] Robert R. Wilson, "International Law in the New National Constitutions," *American Journal of International Law*, 58 (April 1964):433. Note that article 7 contained in the 1960 constitution is identical with the 1948 version.

norms to forestall future difficulties. In this sense, the two United Nations Conferences on the Law of the Sea of 1958 and 1960 served an extremely useful purpose. Irrespective of their achievements of substance, the conferences served well in facilitating dialogues among so many members of the world on such a timely topic. What we need are Geneva types of multilateral conferences on "unequal treaties," "state succession," "expropriation of foreign-owned properties," and "international standard for aliens," to mention a few. One may speculate that had there been serious dialogues between the old-established nations and the developing nations in the post–World War II era on some of these legal norms, the world would have witnessed fewer controversial unilateral actions such as the declarations of territorial waters in the Indonesian and Philippine archipelagos, and numerous other nationalization decrees.

In the case of unjust domestic law, a machinery for peaceful change is provided for. More equitable laws may be legislated in response to the push and pull of public pressure. There is, however, as yet no effective legislative machinery on an international plane. And this should be a compelling reason for subjecting the transnational legal norms to periodic review, reappraisal, and redefinition through multilateral conferences. Only in this way shall we have a world law of participation, partnership, and promise—promise of good things in life for all.

To cleanse the tarnished old world order and to effect a new world order of peaceful evolution demands a serious effort from the former colonialists and the former colonies. To attain such a goal would require magnanimity and sympathetic understanding on the part of the established nations such as the history of mankind has never known. The developing nations must match such an overture with attitudes of magnanimity and forgiveness in a way never quite achieved before.

The developing nations must stand above pettiness and acrimony. A vicious circle of malice for malice will remain unbroken if those former colonies, smarting with self-pity and self-righteousness, continue to maintain a malice-for-malice stance vis-à-vis their former rulers. To realize world peace through the rule of law, this world of ours needs a healing touch; and perhaps casting a sympathetic eye upon the dilemma-laden history of our neighbors is history's most significant step in the right direction. In the words of Charles A. Barker, "to envisage a dilemma historically is to define, even move in on, a problem." If we succeed in defining our dilemma, we would more than likely have it half-solved.

The Right of Revolution:
Implications for International Law and World Order
GERALD A. SUMIDA

"REVOLUTION," A CRY THAT STRIKES the deepest dread but also inspires the highest ideals in the hearts of men, is the dominant social force pervading both national and international societies in the contemporary era. Such milestones of freedom and justice as the American Declaration of Independence, the French Declaration of the Rights of Man and of the Citizen, and the Virginia Declaration of Rights of 1776 have bestowed upon this concept a special meaning, for enshrined in these documents is the right of revolution. Within the past decade this concept has led to the overthrow of oppressive governments, the disintegration of colonial empires, and, in the broadest sense, the deliberate quest of modernization by the leaders of most of the world's societies.

This "right of revolution" emerged from the natural law tradition that itself is one of the pillars of Western civilization. Although this right has never been formally incorporated into any national or international legal system, it has been a continuous and an important thread running through the political and philosophical history of the West. Indeed, if it is considered a fundamental human right—which, in the natural law tradition, it indubitably is—then the right of revolution has become universal.[1]

Revolution may be regarded as a modality of human action for creating a society that will uphold rather than deny the fundamental rights of men. So important is this goal that this drastic course of action has been transformed into a "right," albeit one to be exercised only as the last resort.

There exist in the present era, however, certain conditions that

I am indebted to Professor Cyril E. Black of Princeton University and especially to Professor Myres S. McDougal of the Yale Law School for valuable advice concerning the writing of this essay. Any errors contained herein, however, are strictly my responsibility.

[1] UNESCO, *Human Rights: Comments and Interpretations* (New York: Columbia University Press, 1949), p. 267.

raise serious questions about the desirability, indeed even the utility, of preserving this particular modality as the ultimate protection of human rights. Nuclear arms have made virtually any use of force among the states that have them tantamount to risking the incineration of the planet. But if this sword of Damocles has tempered the coercive policies of the nuclear states, it has not restrained smaller, as yet nonnuclear states from the threat or the use of force, sometimes to the point of total war in particular regions of the world. That these states tend to be those of the underdeveloped parts of the world —beset with low levels of economic development, chronic political instability, and ethnic and tribal factionalism—does not augur well for internal, regional, or international stability.

To govern the modality of revolution, the states (primarily of Western Europe) have devised a set of rules that attempts to limit any revolution to the country in which it erupts, thereby permitting other states to engage in their normal activities with the minimum of inconvenience. These rules, however, because of their basis in certain fundamental concepts as sovereignty, independence, and the equality of states, are restricted solely to the modality of revolution. They do not encompass an assessment of the reasons advanced by the groups to justify their use of revolutionary means to attain their objectives. But these rules and their rationale have been called into question as the concern of the international community has shifted away from states conceived of as impervious entities toward the individuals within the state. Within the past decade the new states particularly of Africa and Asia, and some in Latin America, have been active in the cause of human rights within the United Nations and have pressed the "necessity" of bringing a quick end to colonialism in all forms.[2] The concepts of sovereignty, independence, and the equality of states, which have hardened into basic doctrines of international law, are no longer unquestioned and can no longer insulate internal events of a state from the scrutiny and intervention of the United Nations.

This trend, and the realization as well that most internal wars today have tangible international aspects, casts doubt on the efficacy and desirability of the international law of revolution. Of course, the

[2] See the Declaration on the Granting of Independence to Colonial Countries and Peoples, adopted by the General Assembly on Dec. 14, 1960 (Res. 1514 [XV]).

effort to fashion a new international legal order that not only will provide universal and effective protection of fundamental human rights but also will meet all the other complex needs of the world encounters so many formidable obstacles that it gives rise to much pessimism and accusations of utopianism. Aside from the prodigious difficulties of taming the great powers and preventing the proliferation of nuclear weapons, there is the problem of defining the fundamental human rights to the extent necessary for implementation in a universal protective system, assuming that one is established. Such a system has been created in Western Europe under the European Convention for the Protection of Human Rights and Fundamental Freedoms. Whether this can be extended on a worldwide scale is problematic at best.

It is only within this context that one can comprehend the role of the right of revolution today and its relationship to international law. Moreover, the modality of revolution must be examined in terms of both the larger social processes that are its immediate context and those doctrines of international law that seek to regulate its exercise and repercussions. Since the trend is to extend the concern and interest on the part of the international community into all areas of a state's conduct, even to that which occurs in its internal arena, the doctrines studied will be those that either immunize the internal arena of a state from the external arena in which the rest of the international community interacts, or extend the international concern and control by participants in the external arena into it. Finally, the policies underlying these two sets of doctrines must be related to those policies supporting the right of revolution. Only after this somewhat elaborate process can the relationship of the right of revolution to international law and its role in the world today be made clear.

II

There is no explicitly defined right of revolution in contemporary international law. Indeed, the exercise of such a right is severely punished as a supreme crime in virtually all municipal legal systems. Yet, this right, formulated as the natural law doctrine of the right of resistance to a tyrannical ruler, is an inherent part of the philosophical tradition from which traditional international law evolved and which still provides a large measure of its theoretical underpinnings.³ Immanent in the political philosophy of the Greeks and the Romans, this doctrine formed a vital part of both the Germanic folk law and the natural law traditions that dominated medieval Western Europe.⁴ Thomas Aquinas, Marsiglio of Padua, and William of Occam, among others, advocated this doctrine, which viewed society as based essentially on a contractual relationship between the ruler and the citizens, on the one hand, and God and the ruler on the other. This relationship imposed certain duties on both ruler and citizens, if the ruler failed to perform his duties or attempted to usurp more power, the relationship ceased to exist, and the citizens were justified in removing him by force if necessary.

The Reformation transformed the right to resist a tyrant into the right to resist a heretical ruler. Although both Luther and Calvin denounced such a concept and argued that citizens and subjects must obey the ruler, no matter how oppressive, a number of "revisionist" Scottish Calvinists interpreted a version of Calvin's *Institutes* to support a version of the right of resistance. Nor were they without support. A common fear of the growth of strong monarchies made philosophical allies of these Calvinists and certain influential Spanish Jesuits. Because of their common heritage in the Christian and natural law traditions, these theorists conceived of the right of resistance as inherent in a fundamentally contractual relationship between God and the ruler and between the ruler and the citizens or subjects. Nevertheless, the explicitness and emphasis of the secular and purely political aspects of this relationship varied greatly from one theorist to another. Those who opposed this right of resistance devised the doctrine of the divine right of kings, the flimsy reasoning of which was quickly exposed. With the onset of the English Civil wars in the 1640s, a new wave of support for the right of resistance came forth. Among

---

³ The history of this tradition, especially as it influenced the development of international law, is traced in Lauterpacht, *International Law and Human Rights* (New York: Praeger, 1950), pp. 73–141. For a general discussion of resistance and revolution, see Carl J. Friedrich, *Man and His Government: An Empirical Theory of Politics* (New York: McGraw-Hill, 1963), pp. 634–56.

⁴ George H. Sabine, *A History of Political Theory* (New York: Henry Holt, 1958), pp. 219, 250; R. W. and A. J. Carlyle, *A History of Medieval Political Theory in the West*, vol. 6, *Political Theory from 1300 to 1600* (London: William Blackwood, 1936), p. 131.

its propounders were the renowned jurists Grotius and Vattel,[5] and later John Locke, whose formulation of this right became the principal justification for the American Revolution.[6]

The American Declaration of Independence of July 1776 is the culmination of a long chapter in the even longer struggle of men to define and to defend their fundamental rights against tyranny and oppression. This document categorically proclaims that:

whenever any Form of Government becomes destructive of these ends, it is the Right of the People to alter or to abolish it, and to institute new Government, laying its foundation on such principles and organizing its powers in such form, as to them shall seem most likely to effect their Safety and Happiness.

So generally accepted was this doctrine that one publicist of international law concluded that "the right of a people to revolt against tyranny is now a recognized principle of international law."[7] Furthermore, this "right of social and political revolution," even if it used violence to change a constitution, a form of government, or a ruling elite, was regarded as one of the most important rights of a state flowing from its sovereignty and independence.[8]

More recently the right of revolution received important recognition during the drafting of the Universal Declaration of Human Rights in the post–World War II period. A special UNESCO commission appointed to explore the theoretical bases of human rights recommended the following provision:

The Right to Rebellion or Revolution

In the event that the government of his nation operates contrary to the fundamental principles of justice and the basic human rights in such fashion that no redress is permitted by peaceful means, man has the right to set up a government more nearly in conformity with justice and humanity.[9]

This provision was not included as such in the Universal Declaration of Human Rights, which was adopted by the General Assembly in

[5] Lauterpacht, *An International Bill of the Rights of Man* (New York: Columbia University Press, 1945), pp. 43, 45–47.

[6] William A. Dunning, *A History of Political Theories from Rousseau to Spencer* (New York: Macmillan, 1920), p. 92.

[7] Ellery C. Stowell, *Intervention in International Law* (Washington, D.C.: John Byrne, 1921), p. 354.

[8] Amos S. Hershey, *The Essentials of International Public Law and Organization*, rev. ed. (New York: Macmillan, 1927), p. 235.

[9] UNESCO, *Human Rights*, p. 271.

1948. But the third paragraph of its preamble recognizes the existence of this right. The paragraph states that:

> *Whereas* it is essential, if man is not to be compelled to have recourse, as a last resort, to rebellion against tyranny and oppression, that human rights should be protected by the rule of law.

The right of revolution has received no further express or implied recognition in official instruments since the declaration. But unceasing efforts within the United Nations have resulted in a vast number of resolutions and international conventions on human rights, which are gradually giving important substantive content to the "consensus of the international community." These expectations about how nations ought to act and what community values ought to be have not yet been accepted as having the force of law. Yet an uncompromising and unequivocal assertion of the inviolability of fundamental human rights is found not only in the "nonbinding" Universal Declaration of Human Rights but more significantly in the binding treaties and international conventions that have derived from this basic document. Most outstanding of this progeny are the European Convention for the Protection of Human Rights and Fundamental Freedoms—thus far the only international institution that provides effective machinery to protect and vindicate *individual* human rights, even against a person's own government—and the International Covenants on Civil and Political Rights and on Economic, Social and Cultural Rights. Both of these documents were recently opened for signature by the United Nations General Assembly,[10] and each will go into effect when thirty-five states have ratified it.

III

In its historical development, the right of revolution seems implicitly to have been restricted to the exercise by a people of its ultimate form of redress against a tyrannical ruler. It is not clear whether this right encompasses only the removal of the oppressive ruler and per-

---

[10] Egon Schwelb, *Human Rights and the International Community: The Roots and Growth of the Universal Declaration of Human Rights, 1948–1963* (Chicago: Quadrangle, 1964), makes the argument that the rights declared in the Universal Declaration of Human Rights have now assumed the binding force of law. An excellent study of the machinery established to protect human rights in Europe is Arthur H. Robertson's *Human Rights in Europe* (New York: Oceana, 1963).

haps the alteration of the form of the government, or whether it extends to a total or "grand revolution" that transforms the entire society—for example, the French, Russian, Chinese, and Cuban revolutions—on the justification that only thus can fundamental human rights be protected and furthered. The significant revolutions of the present era have been undertaken by elites seeking to transform whole societies in order to realize their conceptions of an ideal society and a more desirable world order. It is consequently unrealistic to consider mere supplantations of one ruling elite by another, as occurs in the palace *coup d'état*. Rather, we must be concerned with the more fundamental revolutions carried out in the name of basic human rights.

As a term, "revolution" has been applied to a wide range of rather diverse social phenomena.[11] As a concept, it has successfully eluded any satisfactory definition, although its dynamics and processes have been studied in great detail. The entire continuum of historical events from the palace coup to the "true socioeconomic revolution" to the worldwide system-transforming revolution of modernization has been subsumed under the concept of revolution.[12] These numerous definitions and typologies evince not so much a general intellectual confusion as a preference by each student of revolutions for a formulation that fits his immediate purposes. Moreover, since "social events have no clearly manifest essential character,"[13] it perhaps should not be

[11] The revolutionary activity commonly associated with insurrection, rebellion, revolt, coups, or wars of liberation has variously been called "insurrectionary warfare," "civil strife," or "civil war." The labels all tend to imply that this conflict within a particular state takes place within an encapsulated arena, while just the contrary is true today. The term "internal war," which will be used in this essay, is more accurate: it refers to violent conflicts occurring within the territorial arena of a state but does not thereby exclude any of the interstate aspects of such violence, such as the participation by the great powers in a war by proxy. It is these inextricable interrelationships between the political dynamics of the international arena and the events within the national arena, and vice versa, that constitute a fundamental challenge to international law and world order. On the international aspects of internal war, see James N. Rosenau, ed., *International Aspects of Civil Strife* (Princeton, N.J.: Princeton University Press, 1964) and Harry Eckstein, ed., *Internal War: Problems and Approaches* (New York: Free Press of Glencoe, 1964).

[12] Some recent studies include Crane Brinton, *The Anatomy of Revolution*, rev. ed. (New York: Vintage, 1965); Cyril E. Black, *The Dynamics of Modernization: A Study in Comparative History* (New York: Harper, 1966); Manfred Halpern, "The Revolution of Modernization in National and International Society," in *NOMOS VIII: Revolution*, ed. Carl J. Friedrich (New York: Atherton, 1967), pp. 178–214; Lawrence Stone, "Theories of Revolution," *World Politics*, 18 (1966): 159–76.

[13] Eugene Kamenka, "The Concept of Political Revolution," in *NOMOS VIII*, ed. Friedrich, p. 124.

expected that these necessary oversimplifications that serve as definitions should be identical.

The process of modernization as conceived by Black and Halpern[14] is certainly the most comprehensive conception of revolution in human society, but for our purposes the somewhat more restricted definition of Samuel Huntington is sufficient:

> A revolution is a rapid, fundamental and violent domestic change in the dominant values and myths of a society, in its political institutions, social structure, leadership and government activity and policies.[15]

Revolution thus conceived is to be distinguished from insurrection, rebellion, revolts, coups, and wars of independence, which are the kinds of activity with which international law has been traditionally concerned.[16]

To a great extent it is this avoidance of the real significance of modern revolution that has given rise to one of the most compelling challenges to contemporary international law. It is clear that the right of revolution cannot realistically be limited to insurrections, rebellions, revolts and coups. Instead it extends to "wars of liberation"—as they have occurred in modern times—and to revolutions based on very powerful revolutionary ideologies. For it is these ideologies that provide conceptions not only of an ideal world order but also of some version of the fundamental rights of man.

IV

An elaborate set of rules to govern the conduct of the warring elites and of third states in internal wars comprised an important part of traditional international law. Basically, these rules sought to restrict the bounds of the conflict as much as possible, to ensure the continuation of relations among other states with only the minimum of inconvenience, and to achieve a speedy termination of hostilities. The functional significance of these rules becomes clear when they are conceived of as defining the legal boundaries separating the two arenas of organized

---

[14] See note 12 above.
[15] *Political Order in Changing Societies* (New Haven, Conn.: Yale University Press, 1968), p. 264.
[16] Richard A. Falk, *Legal Order in a Violent World* (Princeton, N.J.: Princeton University Press, 1968), pp. 109–55.

human activity in the world.[17] These are the internal arena of the state, commonly—but inaccurately—regarded as commensurate with its geographical boundaries, and the external arena, in which many diverse participants interact. The most notable of these participants are states and international organizations, both universal and regional, but they also include transnational political parties, pressure groups, private associations, business corporations, public corporations, and individuals as well. Ironically, this new reality renders the "international" in "international system" and "international law" etymologically inaccurate. However, it is clear that the substance of an expanded international law must embrace, as it already has begun to, those participants other than states that are exercising very real influence in the world arena today.[18]

In the sixteenth and seventeenth centuries, as the modern state system began to emerge from the dynastic forms that had prevailed in European society for centuries, the doctrines of sovereignty, independence, and the equality of states were developed as part of the international legal system designed to govern it.[19] In addition to regulating interstate relations, an important task of this new system was

[17] The terms "internal" and "external" are employed instead of the more conventional ones of "national" and "international." The latter imply that states are the sole participants in international society, that the territorial and legal borders of the State are commensurate and impervious, and that the interactions within the international system occur at most on two levels: that of states and that of intergovernmental organizations. The former terms are much more flexible, acknowledging as they do that the territorial and legal boundaries of a state often are not identical for a vast number of interactions involving participants other than states. See the works by McDougal cited in note 18.

[18] See Philip C. Jessup, *A Modern Law of Nations: An Introduction* (New York: Macmillan, 1948); Wolfgang Friedmann, *The Changing Structure of International Law* (New York: Columbia University Press, 1964); C. Wilfred Jenks, *The Common Law of Mankind* (London: Stevens, 1958); Arthur Barber, "Emerging New Power: The World Corporation" and George W. Ball, "Making World Corporations into World Citizens," in *War/Peace Report*, October 1968. Myres S. McDougal is one of the few theorists who have developed comprehensive schemes for studying contemporary international law. See McDougal, "International Law, Power and Policy: A Conception," *Recueil des Cours*, 82 (1953): 137–259; with H. D. Lasswell and I. A. Vlasic, *Law and Public Order in Space* (New Haven, Conn.: Yale University Press, 1963), pp. 3–137; with Lasswell and W. M. Reisman, "The World Constitutive Process of Authoritative Decision," *Journal of Legal Education*, 19 (1967):253–300, 403–37.

[19] Excellent studies include Arthur Nussbaum, *A Concise History of the Law of Nations* (New York: Macmillan, 1947); J. L. Brierly, *The Law of Nations: An Introduction to the International Law of Peace*, 6th ed. (New York: Oxford University Press, 1963); and Jessup, *Modern Law*.

to protect the weaker states against the stronger. At first these principles of international law were utilized by rulers to insulate their countries' internal arenas from disruptive external forces in order to permit them to develop the institutions necessary to support the modern state. In the eighteenth century, but more so in the nineteenth, the state became the principal unit of the international system and was regarded by many as the highest form that civilization could attain. The policies of insulating the internal arena were buttressed by doctrines of international law that not only virtually apotheosized the state but also gave it almost unlimited discretion over its internal policies.

It would be inaccurate to conclude that international law was completely ineffectual during this period. Nevertheless it was subordinated in many critical areas to the more exclusive policies of states. Only after two devastating world wars, followed by long periods when disruption and disorder prevailed in many parts of the world, did men recognize the dangers inherent in any system of international order that denies or greatly restricts the common interests of all peoples, which can only be served by the states' adoption of policies furthering them. As these common interests are defined, extended, and pursued both by states and by intergovernmental organizations, particularly the United Nations, the legal doctrines that formerly served to insulate the internal arena from any efforts of control exercised by the international community must recede or be undermined.

Today a tenuous, inconstant balance exists between the emphasis given to the exclusive, special interests of individual states and the inclusive, common interests of the international community. This balance is not static, nor is the international context within which it is maintained. Whether one or the other set of interests is emphasized in a particular period depends very much on the demands and efforts of the states and of the peoples of the world—what values they choose to pursue and through what modalities.

The rules of international law regulating revolution and internal war are subject to this same process of balance and choice. They will be discussed in terms of which doctrines can serve the objectives of either the established governmental elite or the revolutionary elite in an internal war. In some situations one or the other elite may want to immunize the internal arena from influence or control by participants in the external arena. In other situations external control may be desired. These doctrines of international law are not immutable principles. On the contrary, they embody policies that can be used in varying situations to pursue the goals of a particular elite. Often they are complementary in nature. For example, the principles of nonintervention and domestic jurisdiction, which tend to insulate the internal arena, are complemented by the principle of the minimization and containment of internal violence, which seeks to extend community control into the internal arena when events there threaten the peace of the international community. Once again, the nature of these principles emphasizes the necessity for the peoples of the world to choose the kind of world order they want and the means they will use to attain it.

V

The set of doctrines of international law that seeks to immunize the internal from the external arena can be used by both the governmental and the revolutionary elites. The former seeks to prevent any kind of external assistance to the revolutionary elite, either directly or indirectly by restrictions on their own freedom of action. The latter seeks to prevent any external support of the governmental elite's efforts to suppress the rebels and any restrictions on its own revolutionary activities and on its government should it win the internal war.[20] The pertinent doctrines are those of sovereignty, independence, equality, domestic jurisdiction, and nonintervention.

Few ideas have influenced the thought and history of human society as much as has the concept of *sovereignty*, which itself is susceptible of numerous interpretations.[21] In the present era, except when it signifies the ruling authority in a state (such as a monarch), the

[20] These doctrines, it might be added, are not concerned with the merits of the internal war nor with what comes after a modernizing revolutionary elite has seized effective power and has embarked upon a program of modernization.

[21] A comprehensive study of sovereignty is E. N. van Kleffens, "Sovereignty in International Law," *Recueil des Cours*, 82 (1953):5–131. See also Brierly, *Law of Nations, passim*. Both scholars point out that this concept was developed by political theorists rather than by international lawyers, who regarded the state and sovereignty merely as abstract notions instead of working concepts with a very real application in the relations between states. This criticism is directed mainly at Hobbes and Hegel; van Kleffens exempts Bodin because he not only applied his theory to actual relations between states but also accepted Vitoria's conception of a universal community of states bound by law, a conception that has always been the assumption of the vast majority of international lawyers. See van Kleffens, "Sovereignty," pp. 53–54.

term "sovereignty" refers to the traditional notions of either external or internal sovereignty. The notion of external sovereignty is a claim directed to the participants, especially other states, in the external arena that the state is subject to no superior political authority except that of international law—which presumably includes the prescriptions formulated and applied by the United Nations—and consequently that it is not to be interfered with in the conduct of its external relations. The notion of internal sovereignty is a claim directed to both the internal and external arenas that the ruling elite possesses the supreme authority in the internal arena and that its power there is not to be interfered with by actors in the external arena.

The concept of sovereignty allocates the jurisdiction of spheres of competence to regulate events and relations between the territorial states' ruling elites and the other actors in the external arena. These spheres of competence have shifted with the growing interdependence of all human societies, and the borders of states are clearly very porous walls. Legally, nevertheless, the world is still conceived of as consisting of distinct sovereign states, possessing equal rights and equal independence, whose jurisdiction over their own territory is "necessarily exclusive and absolute," susceptible of no limitation other than that imposed by consent—and by international law.[22] Sovereignty not only is reaffirmed in decisions of international decision-makers but is also recognized as the cornerstone of the new international order established by the United Nations Organization, which "is based on the principle of the sovereign equality of all its Members."[23] Similar statements are found in the constitutive charters of the Organization of American States and of the Organization of African Unity.

The utility of the doctrine of sovereignty to the governmental and revolutionary elites in an internal war is readily apparent. The governmental elite may assert this claim to immunize the internal arena from the external arena, thus precluding any legal assistance to the rebels from other actors in the external arena. In addition, this claim

---

[22] The concept of sovereignty is discussed and treated as fundamental to international law in The Schooner Exchange v. McFadden, 7 Cranch. 116 (U.S. Sup. Ct. 1812); Case of the S.S. "Lotus," [1927] P.C.I.J., ser. A, no. 10; "The Island of Palmas Arbitration," *American Journal of International Law*, 22 (1928):867 (hereafter cited as *AJIL*); and Case of the Austro-German Customs Unions [1931] P.C.I.J., ser. A/B, no. 41; The Corfu Channel Case (Merits), [1949] I.C.J. Rep. 4.

[23] United Nations Charter, Article 2, paragraph 1.

permits the ruling elite to prosecute the internal war as an "internal matter" and inflict heavy criminal penalities upon the rebels. Any assistance to the revolutionaries by other actors constitutes an unjustified interference in the internal affairs of the sovereign state and a grave breach of international law.

The revolutionary elite is likely to use this doctrine to preclude any assistance by other actors to the governmental elite in its struggle against the rebels. This is particularly crucial to the revolutionary elite, since its relative power probably is not great. The revolutionary elite may also use this doctrine to resist any intervention by a third party—be it another state, group of states, regional organization, or the United Nations—if it feels that such an intervention would work toward its defeat.

The principle of the *independence* of states, like that of sovereignty, rests upon the territoriality of the state. As a result it has been characterized as functionally a relative aspect of sovereignty, "the aspect of not being dependent on the authority of another state."[24] The notion of independence as a quality of the state arose during the sixteenth and seventeenth centuries in Western Europe; with the principle of the equality of states, it was part of a legal system designed to protect the weaker states against the stronger.[25] Moreover, it has been recognized and affirmed by authoritative decision-makers[26] and is reaffirmed in the United Nations Charter. Article 2, paragraph 4, of the Charter specifically requires members to refrain from the threat or use of force against the "territorial integrity or political independence of any State." Similar formulations are found in the charters of the OAS and the OAU.

The use of this doctrine by the governmental and revolutionary elites in an internal war is, not surprisingly, very similar to those claims utilizing the principle of sovereignty. The governmental elite may assert that the principle of independence imposes upon third parties the obligation to refrain from engaging in any act that will interfere with its freedom to control its internal arena and external relations. Such interference in any form, except as authorized by the United Nations, constitutes a breach of international law.

[24] Van Kleffens, "Sovereignty," p. 89.
[25] Jessup, *Modern Law*, pp. 36–37.
[26] See the Case of the S.S. "Lotus," note 22 above, and Underhill v. Hernandez, 168 U.S. 250 (Sup. Ct. 1897). The most comprehensive discussion occurs in the Case of the Austro-German Customs Unions; see note 22 above.

The revolutionary elite may assert this doctrine to preclude any assistance to the governmental elite. If the rebels constitute a particular ethnic group within the state, or if they are seeking to overthrow a government tainted with the vestiges of colonialism, they may also use this principle to assert their right to national independence and demand that external actors in no way hinder the exercise of self-determination.

The principle of the *equality of states* was created in the sixteenth and seventeenth centuries by publicists who were seeking to construct a legal system to govern the state system in Western Europe and to ensure the protection of the weak states against the strong.[27] This principle has also been recognized and elucidated by several authoritative decision-makers. They have described the world as being composed of "distinct sovereignties, possessing equal rights and equal independence"[28] and have declared as a fundamental principle of international law "the perfect equality and entire independence of all distinct states" regardless of actual inequalities in size or power.[29] As it has been traditionally formulated, the doctrine conceives of each state both as possessing full independence in its internal arena and as enjoying equality with other states in the external arena wherever there are no conflicting claims, such as in navigation on the high seas. Moreover, this principle has often been couched in terms of a "right to equality," which is really a somewhat misleading statement of the claim that all states must refrain from any action that would interfere with a state's independence or with its equality in situations specifically reserved for inclusive use and enjoyment.[30]

The doctrine of the equality of states may very well be redundant, for the consequences it seeks to achieve are readily explained and

---

[27] Jessup, *Modern Law*, p. 37. Comprehensive treatment of the doctrine of equality may be found in Edwin D. Dickinson's classic work, *The Equality of States in International Law* (Cambridge, Mass.: Harvard University Press, 1920), and in his "Equality of States," in *Encyclopedia of the Social Sciences*, ed. Edwin R. A. Seligman and Alvin Johnson (New York: Macmillan, 1931), 5:580–82. See also Bengt Broms, *The Doctrine of Equality of States as Applied in International Organizations* (Vammala: Vammalan Kirjapaino Oy, 1959), and Herbert Weinschel, "The Doctrine of the Equality of States and Its Recent Modification," *AJIL*, 45 (1951):412–42.

[28] The Schooner Exchange v. McFadden; see note 22 above.

[29] The *Le Louis*, 2 Dods. 210, 165 Eng. Rep. 1464 (1817); see also The Antelope, 10 Wheat. 66 (U.S. Sup. Ct. 1825).

[30] See Hans Kelsen, "The Draft Declaration on Rights and Duties of States: Critical Remarks," *AJIL*, 44 (1950):259–76.

justified by the doctrines of sovereignty and state independence.[31] Even disregarding the actual inequalities of states, this doctrine is being eroded by the growth of international organization, particularly the United Nations, which has granted legal recognition to the factual inequality of states by conferring a special status on the five permanent members of the Security Council. The usefulness of this doctrine may lie, however, in its emphasis on the equality of states before the law; in other words, in the equal protection of the law. Not only may this be a safeguard in international organizations, but it also may serve as a protection against any encroachment by larger powers in other situations.

In conjunction with the doctrines of sovereignty and the independence of states, claims based on the equality of states can be asserted by both the governmental and the revolutionary elites in an internal war to immunize the internal from the external arena. Although the motivations for asserting the claim would not be identical and the external actors to whom the claim is addressed would be different, the pertinent claim here would be the same for both elites: all states are under a duty to refrain from any action that would interfere with the state's full internal independence. In other words, since all states are sovereign and independent, the principle of equality imposes a duty upon each state to treat every other state equally, respecting its sovereignty and independence. A claim that either elite or an external decision-maker might find it beneficial to make is that "[u]nless states are equally protected in the enjoyment of their rights and equally compelled to fulfill their obligations, whatever their condition or status, there can be no reliance upon law in international relations."[32]

In the decentralized international system a doctrine that has played a vital role in allocating competences between national and international decision-makers is that of the *domestic jurisdiction* of the state.[33] It was developed initially in treaties providing for the compulsory arbitration of disputes between states, but at present it is used primarily in an effort to limit the competence of international organizations with respect to the internal arenas of states. It was embodied in Article 15, paragraph 8, of the Covenant of the League of Nations

---

[31] Brierly, *Law of Nations*, p. 132.

[32] Dickinson, "Equality of States," p. 582.

[33] A thorough study is Lawrence Preuss's "Article 2, Paragraph 7 of the Charter of the United Nations and Matters of Domestic Jurisdiction," *Recueil des Cours*, 74 (1949):553–653.

and is similarly set forth in Article 2, paragraph 7, of the United Nations Charter. There it reads: "Nothing contained in the present Charter shall authorize the United Nations to intervene in matters which are essentially within the domestic jurisdiction of any state." The scope of this provision is qualified, however, so that "this principle shall not prejudice the application of enforcement measures under Chapter VII" of the Charter. In the most authoritative statement of the extent to which this principle successfully immunizes the internal arena from the external, it was held that:

The question whether a certain matter is or is not solely within the jurisdiction of a State is an essentially relative question; it depends upon the development of international relations. Thus, in the present state of international law, questions of nationality are, in the opinion of the Court, in principle within this reserved domain.[34]

From the founding of the League of Nations, but more so with developments within the United Nations, the controversy surrounding the concept of domestic jurisdiction is one of achieving a proper balance between the U.N.'s interest in internal developments that might affect international peace and security and the interests of individual states in enjoying full internal sovereignty and independence. Because of the work of the U.N. Security Council and General Assembly, which basically reflects the growing interdependence of all societies, the bounds of this concept have steadily contracted. The argument that any matter affecting the maintenance of international peace is of "international concern" and thus within the competence of the United Nations has now prevailed over the opposing contention that matters protected by Article 2, paragraph 7, must be determined by specific criteria established by international law and not by subjective political ends.[35] However, if there is no irreducible sphere that is somehow inherently

---

[34] Case of the Tunis-Morocco Nationality Decrees, [1923] P.C.I.J., ser. B, no. 4.

[35] See Georges M. Abi-Saab, "The Newly Independent States and the Scope of Domestic Jurisdiction," *Proceedings of the American Society of International Law* (1960), pp. 84–90 (hereafter cited as *Proceedings*); John M. Howell, "Domestic Questions in International Law," *Proceedings* (1954), pp. 90–99; Tae Jin Kahng, *Law, Politics, and the Security Council: An Inquiry in the Handling of Legal Questions Involved in International Disputes and Situations* (The Hague: Martinus Nijhoff, 1964), esp. pp. 25–110. The Security Council has exercised jurisdiction under the "international concern" rationale in the case of the Franco government in Spain (1946), the Indians in South Africa (1946), the Netherlands-Indonesian case (1947, 1949), and most recently the case of Rhodesia (1965).

internal, then the fact that almost all international problems, especially those of an economic or social nature, originate within the internal arena of states leads to the conclusion that all such matters "are susceptible of international legal regulation and may become the subjects of new rules of customary law or treaty obligations."[36]

The utility of this doctrine to both the governmental and revolutionary elites is obvious. Their separate claims to third parties, especially international organizations such as the United Nations, is that the internal war is not a war at all but is simply a matter of domestic jurisdiction that third parties are required—by the concepts of sovereignty, independence, equality, and nonintervention—to recognize and respect. If the internal war is judged to be of "international concern," however, then the United Nations will most likely assume competence over the matter.

The traditional doctrine of *nonintervention* imposes upon each state the duty to refrain from intervening in the internal arena or external relations of another state in violation of its sovereign and independent nature.[37] The critical problem, considering the interdependencies linking all societies, is of course to distinguish permissible from impermissible forms of intervention in the relations between states. The most authoritative statement declares that impermissible intervention is "dictatorial interference by a State in the affairs of another State for the purpose of maintaining or altering the actual condition of things."[38] Such interference must be of a dictatorial character, violating the external independence or the internal sovereignty of a state, and not in accordance with some right under international law.

This principle became a prominent claim against other states especially after the French Revolution, which stressed the rights of internal sovereignty and external self-determination, and in the nine-

---

[36] Preuss, "Article 2, Paragraph 7," p. 568; see also Jenks, *Common Law*, pp. 286–87.

[37] See Henry G. Hodges, *The Doctrine of Intervention* (Princeton, N.J.: Banner, 1915); Ellery C. Stowell, *Intervention*, esp. pp. 317–449, and *International Law: A Restatement of Principles in Conformity with Actual Practice* (New York: Henry Holt, 1931), pp. 69–181; and Karl Loewenstein, *Political Reconstruction* (New York: Macmillan, 1946), esp. pp. 14–48. Several of the essays in Richard A. Falk, ed., *The Vietnam War and International Law* (Princeton, N.J.: Princeton University Press, 1968), treat the problems of intervention and nonintervention in the contemporary context.

[38] Hersh Lauterpacht, ed., *Oppenheim's International Law*, 7th ed. (London: Longmans, Green, 1955), 1:305.

teenth century it facilitated the emergence of states from the disintegrating dynastic forms in Europe. Its actual effectiveness, however, does not appear to have been overwhelming.[39] Moreover, the Spanish Civil War (1936–1939) involved attempts by many states to enforce the traditional prescriptions of nonintervention and neutrality; this effort, as history has recorded, was a failure.[40]

The Covenant of the League of Nations embodied this principle in Article 10, by which "the Members of the League undertake to respect and preserve as against external aggression the territorial integrity and existing political independence of all Members of the League." Coupled with the principle of domestic jurisdiction as set forth in Article 15, paragraph 8, the Covenant doctrinally insulated the state from intervention by other states or by the League itself. This dual proscription of intervention was written into the United Nations Charter in Article 2, paragraph 4, which prescribed that "all Members shall refrain in their international relations from the threat or use of force against the territorial integrity or political independence of any state," and paragraph 7 of the same article.[41] Both provisions are further buttressed by the explicit statement in Article 2, paragraph 1, that the organization is based upon the principle of the sovereign equality of all its members.[42] Similar provisions are found in the charters of the OAS and the OAU.

In practice, the principle of nonintervention has not entirely precluded state intervention in international relations. But with the development of the United Nations the practice of intervention has been made collective and is subject to certain standards, albeit vague and subjective ones. The United Nations has intervened in different modalities in the following "internal" matters: Franco Spain (1946), Greece (1946), Indonesia (1947, 1949), Palestine (1947), Czechoslovakia (1948), Guatemala (1954), Lebanon (1958), and the Congo (1962). In some of these instances great power competition was lurk-

---

[39] Some of the more prominent interventions include the cases of Greece (1827 and later), Portugal (1826, 1834), Hungary (1848), China (1900 and later), the La Plata region in Argentina (1847), Mexico (1861–1867, 1911–1921), Italy (1859), and the Ottoman areas and the Balkans (1840, 1854, 1857, 1886, 1897, 1917, and later).

[40] See Norman J. Padelford, "International Law and the Spanish Civil War," *AJIL*, 31 (1937):226–43, and *International Law and Diplomacy in the Spanish Civil Strife* (New York: Macmillan, 1939).

[41] Article 7 is discussed above under domestic jurisdiction.

[42] But compare Article 1, paragraph 1.

ing, and the threat that continued strife and possible intervention could erupt into nuclear war gave rise to justifiable "international concern" on the part of the United Nations.

The claim that states are under a duty not to intervene in the internal arena or external relations of a state may be asserted by both the governmental and revolutionary elites in an internal war to immunize the internal from the external arena. Whether this proves successful depends in part on the action taken by the United Nations, in which case collective intervention may result to the disadvantage of one or the other of the warring elites.[43]

VI

There are several doctrines of international law that can be used by states and other actors in the external arena, particularly intergovernmental organizations, in attempts to exert influence over persons, groups, events, and relations in a state's internal arena. We noted above that certain insulating doctrines were no longer completely effective, especially as the competence exercised by international organizations reflects the present realities of interdependence. The doctrines considered here, however, are clearly intended to link the external and internal arenas rather than insulate one from the other. The doctrine of the continuity of the state tends to favor the established, governmental elite, while the doctrine of humanitarian intervention tends to favor the revolutionary elite. These will be treated as a separate group, for the remaining doctrines of according protection to governments in exile, of recognition, and of the minimization of violence may be used by both elites to support their respective claims.

The eruption of an internal war and the ultimate seizure of power by a revolutionary elite often raises great uncertainty on the part of other states, in particular about the willingness of the revolutionary regime to honor the state's previous international obligations. To lessen this uncertainty by nurturing expectations of order and stability on the part of concerned states, the doctrine of the *continuity of the*

---

[43] See the Declaration on the Inadmissibility of Intervention in the Domestic Affairs of States and the Protection of Their Independence and Sovereignty, adopted by the General Assembly on Dec. 21, 1965. United Nations, General Assembly, Twentieth session, *Official Records*, Supplement no. 14 (A/6014), p. 11.

state was formulated.⁴⁴ In its traditional formulation, the doctrine states that "[c]hanges in the government or the internal polity of a state do not as a rule affect its position in international law. . . . [For] though the government changes, the nation remains, with rights and obligations unimpaired."⁴⁵ The most authoritative statement, however, remains that made by Borchard and adopted in the *Tinoco Arbitration* (1923):

> A general government *de facto*, having completely taken the place of the regularly constituted authorities in the state, binds the nation. So far as its international obligations are concerned it represents the state. . . . An exception to these rules has occasionally been noted in the practice of some of the states of Latin-America, which declare null and void the acts of a usurping *de facto* intermediary government when the regular government it has displaced succeeds in restoring its control. Nonetheless, acts validly undertaken in the name of the state and having an international character cannot lightly be repudiated, and foreign governments generally insist on their binding force. The legality or constitutional legitimacy of a *de facto* government is without importance internationally so far as the matter of representing the state is concerned.⁴⁶

It would be inaccurate to contend that this sanctions any direct intervention into an internal war on the side of the existing government. Rather it reflects the concern of third parties over internal events and could inhibit efforts of the revolutionary elite to determine its own destiny and to undertake widespread reforms in vital areas, especially economic, of its internal system. This was certainly true of many states that recently attained independence.⁴⁷ Less recently, the Soviet government's repudiation in 1918 of the debts incurred by

---

⁴⁴ In this situation authoritative decision-makers have distinguished two kinds of factual situations, characterizing one as "succession of governments" and the other as "state succession" and attaching distinct legal consequences to each. The doctrine of the continuity of the state embraces both of these, but for this discussion only the doctrine of the succession of governments is relevant. The accuracy of this distinction, it should be noted, may be doubtful: the occurrence of substantial alterations in the structures and processes of governments poses the question of whether it is meaningful to speak of the same "state." See McDougal, "Law, Power and Policy," pp. 224–25.

⁴⁵ John B. Moore, *A Digest of International Law* (Washington, D.C.: Government Printing Office, 1906), 1:249.

⁴⁶ *AJIL*, 18 (1924): 147; see also The Sapphire, 11 Wall. 164 (U.S. Sup. Ct. 1871). For general discussion, see Herbert W. Briggs, ed., *The Law of Nations: Cases, Documents, and Notes*, 2d ed. (New York: Appleton-Century-Crofts, 1952), pp. 209–13.

⁴⁷ See J. J. G. Syatauw, *Some Newly Established Asian States and the Development of International Law* (The Hague: Martinus Nijhoff, 1961), *passim*.

the tsarist government was roundly condemned by other states as constituting a flagrant violation of international law. Nevertheless, the adherence to this doctrine may be growing less rigid, especially in those cases where the "social and political upheaval accompanying a revolutionary change of government is such as to render equitable and reasonable a modification of the obligations incurred by the former regime."[48]

The doctrine of nonintervention in the internal arena or external relations of a state is one of the most firmly established principles of international law. It is nonetheless subject to several exceptions, one of the most prominent being that of *humanitarian intervention.* Although it is generally agreed that a state may treat its nationals as it pleases, there exists a "substantial body of opinion and of practice" that would limit that discretion: "when a State renders itself guilty of cruelties against and persecution of its nationals in such a way as to deny their fundamental human rights and to shock the conscience of mankind, intervention in the interest of humanity is permissible."[49] This doctrine and practice, which emerged in the nineteenth and early twentieth centuries, rested upon the premise that international law required a state to guarantee certain minimum rights to the people within its territory and sphere of competence.[50] Instances of humanitarian intervention include those undertaken in Greece (1830), Syria (1860), Crete (1866), Bosnia, Herzegovina, and Bulgaria (1878), and Macedonia (1903). With the League of Nations and thereafter the necessity for humanitarian intervention was obviated to a great extent by multilateral treaties ensuring protection of religious and linguistic minorities[51] and by more universally adhered to conventions of a humanitarian character.

World War II and its aftermath seemed to make a mockery of the efforts to protect human rights. Its protection was indeed flimsy in moments of national and international crisis. The doctrine of humanitarian intervention itself has been dismissed as obsolete, ineffectual,

---

[48] Lauterpacht, *Oppenheim's International Law*, 1:154, n. 2.

[49] Ibid., p. 312. See also Stowell, *International Law*, p. 349, and *Intervention*, pp. 51–227, for complete treatment with examples.

[50] See in general Ved P. Nanda, "The United States' Action in the 1965 Dominican Crisis: Impact on World Order," *Denver Law Journal*, 43 (1966): 437–79, and 44 (1967):225–74.

[51] Lauterpacht, *Oppenheim's International Law*, 1:712–16, and Loewenstein, *Political Reconstruction*, pp. 52–67.

and nebulous at best. Moreover, other critics have pointed to the principles of nonintervention, domestic jurisdiction, sovereignty, and even the duty of states to refrain from the use of force in their international relations as obstacles to the implementation of this doctrine.

It is true that the effective protection of fundamental human rights in the world today is very feeble. But the obsolescence of humanitarian intervention is denied by its very use in the Congo (1964) and to a very qualified extent in the Dominican Republic (1965).[52] Moreover, the principles of sovereignty and domestic jurisdiction, as we noted earlier, have been steadily qualified by the concept of "international concern."[53] Furthermore, while states are prohibited from intervening in the internal affairs of another state and from using force or the threat of force in international relations, the United Nations may lawfully utilize forceful measures in a collective manner to remove a perceived threat to international peace and security. Finally, the doctrinal foundations for the protection of fundamental human rights do exist, and while grave difficulties continue to impede their implementation, unceasing efforts towards this end are still being made.[54]

The policies underlying humanitarian intervention provide part of the limits on a government's permissible action against its citizens. Humanitarian intervention—by one state or by several states, for example, under U.N. auspices—is merely a modality of enforcing those limits. The revolutionary elite may be able successfully to call for such intervention by another state or perhaps by the United Nations if the governmental elite resorts to particularly brutal measures of suppression. But since this entails physical intervention into a state, it is likely to be undertaken only after the greatest deliberation—including attention to the political realities of the situation—and most likely under collective auspices.

A state may exercise a measure of control over events in another state's internal arena by giving *refuge to a government in exile* of that state if it has been forced to flee temporarily from its territory. In

---

[52] See Nanda, "Dominican Crisis," and Richard B. Lillich, "Forcible Self-Help by States to Protect Human Rights," *Iowa Law Review*, 53 (1967): 325–51.

[53] In the case of Rhodesia, see Myres S. McDougal and W. Michael Reisman, "Rhodesia and the United Nations: The Lawfulness of International Concern," *AJIL*, 62 (1968):1–19.

[54] Schwelb, *Human Rights*.

past instances this has occurred in the context of an international war in which a state has been occupied by a belligerent power. During World War II, governments of Greece, Luxembourg, the Netherlands, Norway, Yugoslavia, Belgium, Poland, and Czechoslovakia—despite their having no claims to effective control over any part of their national territories—were established in London and were recognized as the *de jure* governments of these states. This recognition was based on the principle of international law that belligerent occupation does not extinguish the sovereignty of a state: "The occupying power is not successor to the lawful sovereign in the occupied territory but is a government based on force as a war measure."[55] Such belligerent occupation places actual ruling power in the hands of the occupant, but his rights are provisional only, being incidental to the war. The sovereignty of the state remains vested in the legal sovereign, even though it is in exile.

The claim to sovereignty of a government in exile will apparently be recognized only as long as this loss of effective control is considered temporary. This requires the government to make continuous efforts to regain its control by means of war waged by itself or in union with other states against the occupying state. If its efforts prove unavailing, then its claims to sovereignty become nugatory.[56]

If the governmental elite is forced by the revolutionary elite to flee from its territory, it may seek refuge in a friendly state and attempt to prosecute its struggle from there. The struggle at this juncture may very well warrant the recognition by other states of belligerency, thus imposing on them the duties of neutrality. Any aid subsequently given to the governmental elite would then violate these duties. Finally, the revolutionary elite would in all likelihood obtain *de facto*, if not *de jure*, recognition as the government of the state, placing even greater obstacles in the path of return of the government in exile, for any aid to the displaced elite would then constitute an unlawful intervention into the affairs of the state.

---

[55] F. E. Oppenheimer, "Governments and Authorities in Exile," *AJIL*, 36 (1942):568–95, esp. pp. 571–72. See also State of the Netherlands v. Federal Reserve Bank of New York, 201 F.2d 455, 461–462 (2d Cir. 1953), and article 43 of the Annexed Regulations to the Hague Convention 4 of 1907 on the Laws and Customs of War on Land.

[56] Hans Kelsen, *Principles of International Law*, 2d ed. rev. (New York: Holt, Rinehart & Winston, 1966), pp. 411–12; see also Philip M. Brown, "Sovereignty in Exile," *AJIL*, 35 (1941):666–68.

Certain so-called governments in exile have been formed abroad while a recognized government is functioning on the national territory. Examples of this category include the (Spanish) Giral Republican Government established in Mexico in 1945, the Algerian government established in Cairo prior to the granting of Algerian independence, and Holden Roberto's "Government of the Republic of Angola in Exile" in Kinshasa. These governments may be established after the end of a war or after a successful revolution. In neither case can they be considered any longer the government of the state. They may also be established by elements of a revolutionary movement, particularly one whose aim is to free a territory from colonial rule (for example, Holden Roberto's group) or from rule by a government with a different ideological base. States that accord recognition to such groups do so for political or other reasons, but such recognition cannot alter the fact that "such groups are merely hoping to form a legitimate government or state, at some time in the future."[57]

This kind of government in exile today would be established by the revolutionary movement and would assert claims of formal authority over the national territory. Such claims initially may have no basis in fact, but if the rebels prove successful in prosecuting the internal war then claims to effective control and at least partially recognized authority may become genuine. Legal rights and duties, however, have never attached to the revolutionary government in exile per se but rather to the status of the warring elites.

The doctrines of recognition in international law essentially constitute a ceremony by which states acknowledge the existence of a new body politic or a new government and thereafter admit it to the established world arenas. Part of these doctrines concern the *recognition of a state of belligerency* in an internal war.[58]

The point at which the rebels in an internal war are accorded belligerency status is of crucial import, since this brings the rules of war into full legal effect. To justify such recognition requires (1) the existence in a state of an armed conflict of general proportions; (2) the occupation and administration of a substantial portion of national

---

[57] Max Sørensen, ed., *Manual of Public International Law* (New York: St. Martin's, 1968), p. 290.

[58] A comprehensive treatment is Hersh Lauterpacht's *Recognition in International Law* (Cambridge: At the University Press, 1947), esp. pp. 175–268. Cf. McDougal, "Law, Power and Policy," pp. 196–98.

territory by the rebels; (3) the conduct of hostilities by the rebels in accordance with the rules of war and through organized armed forces acting under a responsible authority; and (4) the existence of circumstances affecting the interests of other states, or of the governmental elite, that necessitate this recognition.[59]

The legal status of the internal war before belligerent status is accorded to the rebels is that of insurgency. Technically—and tautologically—this denotes "the condition of political revolt in a country in which the rebellious party has not attained the character of a belligerent community."[60] While it is unclear whether recognition of a status of insurgency in a country has any legal consequences,[61] if the governmental elite has signed the four 1949 Geneva conventions for the protection of war victims then it is subject to their provisions concerning the regulation of "armed conflict not of an international character."[62] Thus even before the recognition of the insurgents as belligerents, the governmental elite does not necessarily enjoy freedom to prosecute the internal war as it pleases. Finally, during this stage of insurgency other states may legally help the governmental elite to suppress the revolt. At the same time international law forbids these states to give any assistance to the rebels.[63] Until it is conclusively supplanted, the governmental elite is presumed to represent the sovereignty of the state. This presumption, however, apparently does not extend beyond the duty not to grant the insurgents premature recognition as the government of the state and not to permit a foreign territory to become a base of operations against the governmental elite.[64]

Recognition of the rebels as belligerents imposes on them for the duration and for the purposes of the war the rights and obligations of an independent state, such as the rights of blockade, visitation, and search and seizure of war contraband on the high seas.[65] At the same

[59] Lauterpacht, *Recognition*, p. 176.

[60] Ti-Chiang Chen, *The International Law of Recognition, with Special Reference to Practice in Great Britain and the United States* (London: Stevens, 1951), p. 398.

[61] Ibid., pp. 400–7.

[62] Morris Greenspan, *The Modern Law of Land Warfare* (Berkeley: University of California Press, 1959), pp. 621–25.

[63] Briggs, *Law of Nations*, pp. 922, 999–1000; Lauterpacht, *Recognition*, pp. 230–33. See also the Pan American Convention on Duties and Rights of States in the Event of Civil Strife, Adopted at Havana on Feb. 20, 1928, *U.S. Treaty Series*, No. 814, esp. Article 1.

[64] Lauterpacht, *Recognition*, p. 233.

[65] The Three Friends, 166 U.S. 1 (Sup. Ct. 1896); Brierly, *Law of Nations*, p. 142.

time those states conferring such recognition assume the rights and duties of neutrals in the conflict. This entails a complete abstention from aiding either of the belligerents and an impartial and equal treatment of both belligerents.[66] Of course, instead of adopting a status of neutrality, the state could ally itself with one of the belligerents,[67] but this freedom may be quite restricted by the role that the United Nations may assume concerning the internal war.

The international law of recognition described above is weighted in favor of maintaining the governmental elite in power, thus ensuring a measure of stability in international relations, by denying the rebels the possibility of belligerency status until late in the development of the internal war. Moreover, the governmental elite may request and lawfully receive foreign assistance in its struggles and may expect other states to refrain from aiding the rebels. The discretion that the governmental elite enjoys in prosecuting the internal war is also much greater than it would be if it had to recognize certain rights of an equal belligerent.

But this same body of international law can be regarded as favoring the revolutionary elite by advocating the recognition of insurgent rights at an early stage of the conflict—for example, the Geneva conventions on war victims—and by making their opposition something less than completely illegal.[68] It also urges the recognition of belligerency once the strife becomes widespread, conferring upon the insurgents some of the rights of a sovereign state and allowing partial access to such forums as the United Nations. Other states' duties of neutrality notwithstanding, this access may provide valuable assistance to the revolutionary elite.[69]

The efforts of states to *minimize and prevent the spread of internal war* have become particularly prominent in the present era as the United Nations, like the League of Nations, seeks to determine whether a conflict might threaten international peace and security and to contain, if not resolve, the conflict. The Charter of the United Nations, in pursuit of its primary purpose of maintaining international

[66] Lothar Kotzsch, *The Concept of War in Contemporary History and International Law* (Geneva: Droz, 1956), p. 144.
[67] Titus Komarnicki, "The Place of Neutrality in the Modern System of International Law," *Recueil des Cours*, 80 (1952):395–509, 403.
[68] Hershey, *Essentials of Public Law*, and James W. Garner, "Questions of International Law in the Spanish Civil War," *AJIL*, 31 (1937):66–73.
[69] Padelford, "Spanish Civil War," pp. 226–43.

peace and security, obligates member states to "settle their international disputes by peaceful means in such a manner that international peace and security, and justice, are not endangered" and to "refrain in their international relations from the threat or use of force against the territorial integrity or political independence of any state or in any other manner inconsistent with the Purposes of the United Nations."[70] The "primary responsibility" for the maintenance of international peace rests on the Security Council,[71] although the General Assembly may consider a situation arising under Article 2, paragraph 4 if the Security Council is prevented from acting because of the veto.[72] The Council also possesses certain investigatory powers,[73] but its most critical function, which must be performed before it can decide whether to take any action under Articles 41 (enforcement measures not involving the use of armed force) and 42 (enforcement measures involving the use of armed force), is to determine whether there exists any threat to the peace, breach of the peace, or act of aggression.[74] This determination, upon which the Security Council may or may not be justified in assuming competence, is by no means a strictly legalistic one, and the terms themselves are not easy to define.[75] However, the Council has consistently assumed a liberal attitude toward the policies underlying these terms in Article 1, paragraph 1.[76] Hence, the Council—and in some cases the General Assembly—has assumed jurisdiction over internal wars in Greece (1946), Indonesia (1947), Palestine (1947), the Congo (1960 and later), and Cyprus (1960, 1964).

This U.N. machinery enables the international community to intervene in different modalities in any internal war that it finds, through the Security Council or, if necessary, the General Assembly, constitutes a threat to or breach of international peace and security. The Council has not hesitated to act in the past, even though it has been

[70] Article 2, paragraphs 3 and 4.
[71] Article 24.
[72] This procedure is authorized in the United Nations Uniting for Peace Resolution passed by the General Assembly on Nov. 3, 1950.
[73] Article 33, paragraph 1.
[74] Article 39; Leland M. Goodrich and Anne P. Simons, *The United Nations and the Maintenance of International Peace and Security* (Washington, D.C.: The Brookings Institution, 1955), pp. 360–61.
[75] Goodrich and Simons, *United Nations*, pp. 363, 354–60; Friedmann, *Changing Structure*, pp. 254–55.
[76] See Kahng, *Security Council*, pp. 25–110; McDougal and Reisman, "Rhodesia."

hamstrung by the veto. In fact, one observer even concluded that the very gravity of many situations in the internal arena of states resulted in the "more or less automatic assumption on the part of the Council that it had the competence to deal with them, irrespective of whether or not it had made a prior determination as to the existence of a threat to the peace, breach of the peace, or act of aggression."[77]

Whether the extension of influence over events in a state's internal arena will benefit the governmental elite or the revolutionary elite depends on the circumstances. The involvement of the United Nations in a number of internal wars, however, reveals a "constant practice" of the organization's "condemning, and when possible preventing, the rendering of support to rebel forces against an established government." Moreover, during the Congo operation another precedent was established that "assistance to the government itself should be provided only through United Nations channels."[78]

The revolutionary elite, however, might assert that it is acting against an oppressive regime that denies the people the fundamental human rights guaranteed by the Charter and set forth in numerous human rights conventions and covenants. Perhaps the United Nations could intervene politically, for there is no insuperable obstacle, in such an internal war on the basis of the revolutionary elite's demands. But in this conflict between the interest of the United Nations in the maintenance of international peace and the right of a people to the enjoyment of fundamental human rights, the overriding consideration at this juncture appears to be that "every civil war, if not ended quickly, is likely to become a threat to the peace."[79] This may mean that effective United Nations practice is today weighted against the revolutionary elite's position.

VII

The disarming clarity of the traditional formulations of the principles discussed above all but vanishes when states, acting individually or collectively, attempt to apply them to situations in the contemporary world. The traditional international law regulating internal war

[77] Kahng, *Security Council*, p. 95.
[78] Louis B. Sohn, "The Role of the United Nations in Civil Wars," *Proceedings* (1963), pp. 208–15, esp. pp. 212–13.
[79] Ibid., p. 215.

sought to contain the conflict, giving little consideration to the merits of the conflict. This is not surprising, for states have a paramount interest in a modicum of peace and stability in the international order, including the sense of security arising from a mutual tolerance of regimes espousing different ideologies. In fact, the doctrines of sovereignty, independence, equality, and nonintervention evinced the willingness of states to tolerate even radical social experiments within a state, provided that the state made no attempts to export its particular brand of social organization. In the contemporary era, however, the assumptions—and to a degree the policies—underlying these principles have been undermined by the modalities by which modern revolutions are conducted, by the reasons for which they are undertaken, and by the conditions in the international system under which they are being initiated.

Internal wars today are generally prolonged and bitter conflicts, varying in intensity, between the established governmental elite and the revolutionary elite, which is committed to seizing power in the state in order to implement its particular program of modernization. Such internal wars will continue to occur in the underdeveloped areas of the world, in part because of the absence of institutions capable of exerting effective, centralized controls over individuals within the society,[80] in part because they are the peripheral areas of the great powers' spheres of influence. The whole underdeveloped world is the arena of intense ideological assaults by certain communist and noncommunist states in the "battle for men's minds and loyalties," a battle that has recently been less blatantly pursued. Moreover, present restraints upon the use of force in interstate relations have tended to transfer the locus of interstate conflicts to the internal arena of underdeveloped states through wars by proxy, thus exacerbating the conflict and furthering the disintegration of that society.

Most of the prolonged internal wars of the contemporary era have been waged by revolutionary elites for a combination of reasons: to achieve national independence, to seize power and preclude participation by other antigovernment factions, and to implement a particular program of modernization. In the past, international law could ful-

---

[80] See Cyril E. Black, "The Anticipation of Communist Revolutions," in *Communism and Revolution: The Strategic Use of Political Violence*, ed. Black and Thomas P. Thornton (Princeton, N.J.: Princeton University Press, 1964), pp. 417–48.

fill its containing and stabilizing functions while remaining indifferent to the aims of the revolutionary elite except when they affected international peace and security. Since the promulgation of the Universal Declaration of Human Rights in 1948, however, numerous states and organizations have sought to define and devise a modicum of international protection for fundamental human rights.[81] For example, the principal salient in the successful assault upon colonialism was based on conceptions of human rights. The intense interest that the international community, organized in the United Nations and in various regional bodies, has expressed in the protection of human rights has resulted not only in condemnations of the internal policies of Rhodesia, South Africa, and Portugal, but also, in the case of the OAU, in support to revolutionary elites struggling against such racist governments. The motivations of individual states may be subject to question, but the unmistakable trend within the international community, expressed in the expansive "international concern" rationale, is that international law can no longer remain indifferent to domestic deprivations of human rights or to motives of various revolutionary elites.

In the context in which internal wars are now fought, not only have the traditional prescriptions regulating such conflicts proved inadequate, but entirely new structural and power dimensions have greatly undermined the assumptions underlying them. The international system has been enormously expanded in the past two decades by the emergence of new states, particularly from the former Western European colonial empires in Asia and Africa. These new states, nominally sovereign and independent, together with the older states of Latin America which largely share their outlook, once attempted to form a significant third force in international politics. But today their territories constitute the arena in which the policies and politics of the great powers often clash as well as the focus of attention for efforts of international economic and social welfare programs. This expansion of the international community has affected international law in two ways. First, traditional international law emerged within the context of Western European civilization and evolved to meet the demands of that society and state system. The addition of these new

---

[81] Schwelb, *Human Rights*. See also the most recently adopted Covenants on Economic, Social and Cultural Rights and on Civil and Political Rights, including the Optional Protocol to the latter.

states has consequently caused the "increasing dilution of values and standards" that underpinned traditional international law.[82] Second, the ruling elites in many of these new states espouse various ideologies that at least officially determine what public policies they will pursue in both internal and external arenas. When combined with the strategic perceptions of the great powers, this has resulted in the bitterly fought but relatively inconclusive "battle for men's minds." These developments have already caused some alterations in the content of international law and doubtless will cause more. But international society is now truly a global society, and the law that attempts to order its dynamics can only do so if it reflects these new realities.[83]

These new states have also shown themselves to be less reluctant than the states of Western Europe and North America to use forceful measures against certain regimes whose policies, in their view, transgress the human rights provisions of the United Nations Charter and related documents. This advocacy of the use of force, even when it might technically violate Article 2, paragraph 4, of the Charter, has occurred not only within the United Nations but also in regional organizations and in the actions of individual states. For example, in the now historic United Nations General Assembly's Declaration on the Granting of Independence to Colonial Countries and Peoples, adopted on December 14, 1960, the international community not only recognized but solemnly proclaimed "the *necessity* of bringing to a speedy and unconditional end colonialism in all its forms and manifestations" (italics added). Moreover, the Organization of African Unity has publicly advocated violent measures to topple the racist regimes of Rhodesia and South Africa. This militant language, however, sharply contrasts with the effective power of these states to realize their expressed desires. The support, especially among the African regimes, of such revolutionary movements has been only token, the result in

---

[83] For general discussions, see Richard A. Falk, "The New States and International Legal Order," *Recueil des Cours*, 118 (1966):7–103; B. V. A. Röling, *International Law in an Expanded World* (Amsterdam: Djambatan, 1960); Syatauw, *Asian States*; "Symposium on International Law Standards in an Era of Rapid Historical Change," *Howard Law Journal*, 8 (1962); and Oliver J. Lissitzyn, "International Law in a Divided World," *International Conciliation*, no. 542 (March 1963). An interesting discussion of traditional international law and the contributions that could be made by "non-Western" legal systems is found in Syatauw, *Asian States*. But compare Friedmann, *Changing Structure*, pp. 53 et seq.

[82] Friedmann, *Changing Structure*, p. 6.

part of internal economic and political exigencies and of power struggles among third world states themselves. It is also interesting to note that many of the states that strenuously demand the protection of fundamental human rights, including that of self-determination, in other states, are very reluctant to implement such rights in their own societies.

Finally, the emergence of the new states has brought into sharp focus a hitherto unappreciated dimension of international society. The starkly contrasting levels of economic, social, and political development of these states, especially in relation to the modern industrial states of the world, have become strikingly evident as the United Nations and its specialized organizations have turned to meet the needs of the underdeveloped countries. That international economic development is perhaps the predominant concern of international relations today emphasizes the glaring stratification that exists within the international system.[84] These structural changes have been accompanied by an acute awareness of structural inequalities, especially economic, among nations, and they have given rise to increasingly desperate pleas for major commitments on the part of the rich industrialized nations to redress the inequalities. These pleas range from the scholarly research of a Gunnar Myrdal to popular but powerful briefs by Barbara Ward to chilling calls for worldwide class revolution by Lin Piao. Whether these voices will be heard in time—and which ones will be heeded—are still very open questions.

The states of the underdeveloped world have not succeeded—outside of the U.N. General Assembly and various international conferences—in forming a powerful third force in international politics. But their nominally sovereign and independent territories lie at the peripheries of the great powers' spheres of influence, and internal wars occurring there are very susceptible to great power intervention, usually through wars by proxy. Most of the internal wars in these areas do not affect any vital interests as perceived by the great powers, and their fundamental interest is in preventing the uncontrolled spread of violence that could involve them and raise the risk of escalation to the thermonuclear level. Ironically, it is this characteristic that enables the United Nations to intervene somewhat effectively in these internal

[84] Friedmann, *Changing Structure*, pp. 8–18.

wars.[85] The dangers to world peace inherent in these wars must nonetheless not be underestimated. It may be somewhat unlikely that these wars will escalate into a nuclear war, but the low levels of political, social, and economic development in underdeveloped states make them especially vulnerable to disintegrative forces that could inflame an entire region should an internal war become intense. Further, the "demonstration effect" of a seemingly successful internal war should not be overlooked, especially when there are widespread deprivations of rights and freedoms.[86]

Finally, the instabilities in the international system caused by conditions in the states of the third world have not rendered any less dangerous the nuclear sword of Damocles that hangs precariously over all mankind. On the contrary, the tensions that have been unleashed and the ease with which smaller, partly industrialized countries could produce primitive but devastating nuclear devices can only increase the real possibility of a nuclear holocaust. One notes, however, that the "nuclear problem" has now become institutionalized in international politics and that international society, at least temporarily, "has learned to live with the bomb."[87]

Two other characteristics of the modern world must be noted. The first is the vast network of linkages that bind all societies of the world together. In the legal-political arena of the United Nations, this is reflected in the expanding concept of "international concern." The second is the extensive development of universal and regional organizations. The U.N., though useful if not indispensable on the level of functional international cooperation, still lacks authority and power to maintain peace and security in all parts of the globe in all situations. Its accomplishments should not be underrated, especially in preventing the spread of internal violence and in fashioning collective intervention in some situations that might have resulted in unilateral intervention by a state. But the organization remains ill equipped to perform its most important tasks.

[85] Richard A. Falk and Saul H. Mendlovitz, "Towards a Warless World: One Legal Formula to Achieve Transition," *Yale Law Journal*, 73 (1964): 399–424.

[86] For a general discussion, see Richard A. Falk, "World Revolution and International Order," in *NOMOS VIII*, ed. Friedrich, pp. 154–77.

[87] Given the power stratification that exists in the world and the existence of nuclear weaponry, those states with effective power will probably tend to adopt policies emphasizing order and stability rather than justice in the international community. See Sohn, "Civil Wars."

VIII

The application of the various doctrines and practices of international law described above has reflected three fundamental policies that states have regarded as of great importance. The first is the policy of minimizing to the greatest extent possible the threat or use of force by states in interstate relations. Not only does this tend to promote a stable international order, but it also performs an absolutely essential role in preventing any outbreak of violence that could trigger nuclear destruction of the planet. The second is the policy of encouraging stability, though discouraging rigidity, in both the external arena and the internal arena of states. Not only is a stable world order necessary for the participants in both arenas to function normally, but efforts to prevent destabilizing situations from arising inside states are also essential. There is, quite obviously, an intimate reciprocal connection between instability within a state and in the external arena. Third, the policy of extending the international protection of fundamental human rights has in the contemporary period received great emphasis, particularly through the United Nations. The relationship between deprivation of human rights by states and the resulting sense of grievance, and possible social disorders, is clearly recognized.[88] Permanent stability, obviating the necessity of recourse to force, is attainable only if the order serves the goals of justice. This must apply both within states and in the international community if world peace is to prevail.

These three policies have become paramount factors in the application of the doctrines of international law examined earlier. The steady erosion of the concepts of sovereignty, independence, and domestic jurisdiction reflect the infinite linkages that now bind all societies into one global society. The doctrine of nonintervention, though difficult to enforce in light of interventionary techniques more subtle than armed force, provides a salutary ordering rule that encourages stability in the international system. The interventions that now take place in widely varying forms are predominantly, though by no means exclusively, by intergovernmental organizations, especially the United Nations. Such interventions are collective and are undertaken only after the international community has made a specific determination that the purposes of the community will be served by this action.

[88] McDougal and Reisman, "Rhodesia."

The doctrines of international law that allocate decision-making competence and reflect the three policies outlined above are not rigid rules. Rather they are the authoritative statements of certain policies accepted as useful and desirable. In fact, the reality of any conception of international law as simply "a body of rules governing the relations between states"[89] is manifestly denied by the environment within which the international legal order functions. States, we noted earlier, are today by no means the sole participants in the external arena. This arena itself is an intensely dynamic system in which an immense number and variety of interactions between the various participants occur simultaneously on several different levels. Often the interactions shift from one level to another, as when a government negotiates a contract with a private international corporation of another state. Consequently, the conception of international law developed by Myres S. McDougal is a far more accurate and realistic description of the comprehensive processes through which states in particular, but not exclusively, interact. McDougal conceives of international law as a *process* of authoritative decision-making whose separately identifiable but intimately linked phases include the formulation, invocation, and application of community prescriptions concerning values that the various authoritative decision-makers seek to maximize. It is a dynamic process by which the peoples of the world "clarify and implement their common interests in the shaping and sharing of values."[90] Because there is no centralized legislative or decision-making body in the international system to which all states are subject, a variety of claims are put forward by authoritative decision-makers in states as well as in different intergovernmental organizations. The claims by the former, while not themselves international law, must be justified by a standard of reasonableness, and the claim itself is subject to claims by other states rejecting or accepting in varying degrees this initial claim. This process, together with treaties and the decisions of the International Court of Justice and various arbitral tribunals as well

---

[89] Green Hackworth, *Digest of International Law*, 1 (1940):1.

[90] McDougal, Lasswell, and Reisman, "The World Constitutive Process," p. 275. See also McDougal, "Law, Power and Policy," pp. 180–83; McDougal, Lasswell, and Vlasic, *Law in Space*, pp. 3–137; and McDougal, "Some Basic Theoretical Concepts about International Law: A Policy-Oriented Framework of Inquiry," *Journal of Conflict Resolution*, 4 (1960):337–54. A useful overview is found in McDougal and Lasswell, "The Identification and Appraisal of Diverse Systems of Public Order," in McDougal *et al.*, *Studies in World Public Order* (New Haven, Conn.: Yale University Press, 1960), pp. 3–41.

as a kind of international legislation emanating from the United Nations General Assembly, comprises international law. It should be noted that the process of decision as well as the other sources of international law are essentially claims embodying certain policies put forward by organizations possessing different degrees of formal authority and effective control.

What has become clear from the preceding discussion is that the traditional prescriptions that have heretofore protected the internal arena of the state no longer constitute an impermeable barrier to controls exerted from the external arena. In part this is not an unanticipated development. All societies eventually would have been forced to recognize the increasing network of interdependence that links them all. In part, however, this development is the product of a deliberate policy pursued by the organized international community to further its recognized common interests. The prevention of nuclear devastation and the universal and effective protection of human rights have been the principal goals underlying these efforts. As the relationship between the deprivation of human rights and the possibility of resulting internal violence that might spread becomes more readily the cause for collective intervention by the international community, the legal barriers that performed a vital ancillary function in the emergence of the state system will erode even further.

What do these complicated and dynamic trends in contemporary international society imply for the right of revolution? This right, it will be recalled, is part of a still vigorous philosophical tradition that regards the individual as possessing certain fundamental, inalienable natural rights. The state is a form of social organization that itself possesses no inherent validity but that is created by men to serve their needs. Only when the ruler or the state becomes oppressive, denying to the citizens what it was created to preserve, and when no means of peaceful redress or reform exist, may the society resort to its ultimate sanction, the right of revolution. Only in this manner can the society "set up a government more nearly in conformity with justice and humanity." Where the society exercises this right of revolution against an oppressive government, the doctrines of sovereignty, independence, domestic jurisdiction, and nonintervention would support its right to do so without external interference. Of course, the complementary interest of the international community in maintaining international peace may cause it to intervene. What is crucial, then, would be that the interest of the international community in fundamental human rights, which is also vital, results in an amelioration of the internal conditions that created the problem. If the universal and effective protection of fundamental rights is a paramount goal of the international community, then it must work out comprehensive strategies to attain this objective.

To the extent that permanent international institutions are created and can effect immediate and satisfactory redress for deprivations of human rights by a state (or by a group within a state that the government is unable to control), the right of revolution will become less necessary. This is clearly the object of the Universal Declaration of Human Rights, although its standards are far from being realized. It also seems quite certain that these standards will be implemented rather feebly in the near future. They will remain subordinate to other policies promoting order and stability in a violence-ridden and nuclear-equipped world. Yet international law can, while attempting to preserve order and the rule of law in the world, continue to articulate the policies underlying the whole area of human rights. For human rights are ultimately the *raison d'être* of the very conception of a legal system, be it national or international.

The creation of a universal and effective system for the international protection of human rights may render less necessary the recourse to the right of revolution. But this does not mean that it will no longer exist after a certain level of international protection has been attained. It is important to recall that this right is itself a modality, a means of protecting something even more fundamental. As long as men are conceived of as possessing fundamental, inalienable, natural rights, then this right of revolution, which is the ultimate protection for these rights in an organized society, will itself continue of necessity to exist, perhaps not in the positive prescriptions of international law but without question in its philosophical foundations.

BIBLIOGRAPHICAL NOTE

This essay has drawn upon materials dealing with the traditional international law of internal war, the fundamental alterations occurring within international society that affect both internal wars and the relevant international legal prescriptions, and the great emphasis now being given to the international protection of human rights.

Traditional International Law

The standard treatise is Hersh Lauterpacht, ed., *Oppenheim's International Law*, 2 vols., 7th ed. (1955). Excellent studies include J. L. Brierly's *The Law of Nations*, 6th ed. (1963), and Arthur Nussbaum's *A Concise History of the Law of Nations* (1947). The best treatments of the individual legal doctrines examined in the essay are listed in the accompanying footnotes.

Modern Developments

Excellent studies of contemporary challenges to international law include Philip Jessup's *A Modern Law of Nations* (1948), Wolfgang Friedmann's *The Changing Structure of International Law* (1964), and Richard A. Falk's "The New States and International Legal Order," *Recueil des Cours*, 118 (1966). Of the recent analytical works the studies by Myres S. McDougal *et al.* are of great significance and importance. These include his "International Law, Power and Policy: A Contemporary Conception," *Recueil des Cours*, 82 (1953); with associates, *Studies in World Public Order* (1960); and with H. D. Lasswell and I. A. Vlasic, *Law and Public Order in Space* (1963).

Of the recent works on modernization, the most comprehensive is Cyril E. Black's *The Dynamics of Modernization: A Study in Comparative History* (1966). Samuel P. Huntington's *Political Order in Changing Societies* (1968) is also useful. Recent studies of internal war include J. N. Rosenau's *International Aspects of Civil Strife* (1964) and H. Eckstein's *Internal War* (1964).

Human Rights

Important conceptual studies are Hersh Lauterpacht's *An International Bill of the Rights of Man* (1945) and *International Law and Human Rights* (1950), and Egon Schwelb's *Human Rights and the International Community* (1964).

Peace and War:
The History of the United States, 1939–1999
ARTHUR I. WASKOW

No CONFERENCE ON ANY ASPECT of American history that I can remember has ventured beyond "recent history"—the thirty years or so before the moment the conference opened. If we are setting a precedent in trying to look at history so new that it has not yet happened, it is not surprising that a meeting sponsored by the Conference on Peace Research in History should do so. For the Conference would not have gathered itself into being if its members had not cared about the future, as well as the past. We were concerned to study the makings of peace in human history partly in order to understand how peace might be created in the human future. Se we were less likely than most historians to assume that our territory stops at the knife edge of now.

On top of these predilections, there is our topic for this meeting. If the choice of subjection to law versus absolute sovereignty has posed a dilemma to Americans in the past, we are exploring the issue chiefly because we think that dilemma is at a crisis stage and will be resolved within the next generation. Perhaps through their whole history, the majority of Americans have dealt with that dilemma by seeing war as the successful instrument of an absolute sovereignty by which to impose their own forms of law and order on successively larger parts of the planet.

But there is recent evidence that the shadow of a great doubt has crept over that formulation. One index is the resistance to the American war in Vietnam. There have been peace movements before in American life, but they have collapsed during wars. There have also been antiwar (that is, anti–particular war) movements in American history, but they have held no brief against wars in general—only against particular errors of judgment like the War of 1812, or the Civil War, or World War I. What is new—certainly in extent, and perhaps in kind—is that since 1965 opposition to all war has, instead of collapsing when the government made war, fed into opposition to this one, and that the opposition to this war has nurtured opposition to all war. Whether this is a strange aberration or represents a major departure with a serious future is an important question for us to face.

But why not leave this peculiar field, the future, to those other professionals who make it their chief business—the technological forecasters, the social planners, the religious prophets, the utopians, the science fiction writers? I would argue that there are some important understandings that historians are much more likely than these others to bring to the study of the future. To begin with, the historian is trained to study social change: to understand the linkages among social movements, ideas, the state, economic processes, technology, and individual men as those linkages create change. It is, of course, precisely those connections, in all their subtlety, that go to make up the future; and no one is better equipped than the historian to remember, for example, that technology is not an entirely self-generating, independent factor in social change. (In the 1960s, many students of the future seemed to think it was.)

Second, most historians have learned from their painstaking scrutiny of the past that choice is real for mankind. They have lived with men who have faced into *their* futures and made choices, and so they are able to sense the open, branching pathways that lie before men now. At the same time, the historian is aware of how hard it is to make great changes happen swiftly, how even revolutions grow out of the past and preserve much of it. For these reasons the historian is perhaps the best equipped of all the students of society to write not flat predictions and not utopias, but what might be called "possidictions" —projections of change that are possible, depending on the social and political decisions that men make, rather than changes that are certain or changes that are merely infinitely desirable.

And third, I think the historian remains the scholar who most often sees his audience as the public, not a closed coterie of experts. In the study of the future, nothing could be more important. For at least in a democratic society, the future should be created by the citizenry generally, not by a group of professional planners and reformers. Indeed, the growth of such a group of elite futurists in the United States in recent years is one urgent reason for others, more oriented to the democratic public, to work out new ways of studying the future.

II

The analysis of the threads of change—the possible impacts of recent major trends on the future—is the first contribution the historian can make to the study of the future. Naturally, this analysis will not simply project recent trends in a straight line. For example, the American military budget has constantly increased over the last twenty years. We can possidict that the political strength of the military institutions may keep multiplying that increase over the next twenty years. But we might also possidict that people will decide to disarm precisely *because* the military machine has grown so large—a demonstration, I think, of what used to be called the dialectic. Of course, one has to have a serious analysis of how the military system would either create its own opposite, or continue in its own pattern, or create something quite different. In addition, one has to be able to take several factors of this kind and knit together the possible changes in each in order to see the way a whole society might develop. For example, one would have to knit together the direction in which the American military machine might go and the way the American underclass might develop in order to see how they might interact and what the results in American society might be.

But the problem would remain: this is speculation, not evidence. Is there any way to do research on the future?

I would argue that there is. If the work of projection is done with realism, models of alternative futures can be turned into research projects in the present. The sole condition is that the projectors and the public with whom they work be prepared to build, in the present, circumstances like those they have imagined for the future. The success or failure of these projects, the response of the society to these events, will be a test of the accuracy of the possidiction. In short, the methodology of the study of the future is inextricably bound up with action research and with the kind of participant observation that a good anthropologist might undertake as well as with the more traditional craft of the historian.

I will try to show how this process of action research on the future might be undertaken. But first I want to essay the function that is closer to the traditional work of the historian, by pointing out the threads of change in the recent past that I think may—I repeat *may*—be increasingly important in the future.

It seems to me that there are three major directions of development in the United States (and to some extent in the world at large) in the last twenty-five years that offer the possibility of change in new directions. Each of them has begun to form the bare seed of its own negation, in dialectical fashion. But if the negations flower *in all three,* the result would be not a societywide dialectic in the sense of the turning inside-out of American society as a whole, not a revolutionary negation of the society of the kind Marx would predict or Marcuse would possidict, but a very odd kind of reconstruction from within. In a sense, I am saying that the specific dialectical negations I project in each of three major social areas would themselves create a dialectical nonnegation of the society as a whole. The dialectic would have, in a very dialectical way, eaten itself up. If one or another of the negations failed while others succeeded, however, there would almost certainly be a bitter political struggle ending in repression, civil war, or revolution.

I suggest that the three major trend events of the last generation are these:

1. What Walter Millis has called the hypertrophy of war, or what might be called its elephantiasis: that is, the swelling up of war to such a size that, by its very swollenness, it becomes irrelevant to the purpose for which war was once carried on—the winning of political victories in foreign affairs. That development of the past thirty years affects chiefly those in every major power who "own" war: the "establishments." In the United States this process has coincided with the emergence of a large long-term standing military force for the first time in American history, and also with the emergence or at least the great strengthening of a relatively restricted group of men with major control over the foreign policy of the United States—men whom C. Wright Mills called "the power elite," John Kenneth Galbraith called "the New York foreign policy syndicate," and my colleague Richard Barnet more neutrally calls "the national security managers." For these reasons, I am suggesting that the first major trend-event of the last generation in America has been the emergence of what could almost be seen as a new segment of the establishment (or, if one prefers, the ruling class): a new segment defined more by its relationship to the means of total destruction than by a relation to the means of production.

2. The emergence in the past generation of another new grouping,

this one indeed named "the new class" by David Bazelon. Bazelon defines it as the class of the educated: those whose only property is what they carry around in their heads, but who *do* have the property they can carry around in their heads—as against the old working class, which owns no property, but also as against the old middle class, which owns a corporation, a farm, a shop, or something. Not that this "new class" is literally new in the sense of never having existed before, but it is new in the sense that it is, or is becoming, a *class*, an independent large group of people able to attach to each other, able to build a new kind of vision of the society.

3. The growth both in the United States and in the world at large of what Gunnar Myrdal has called "the under class": that is, those who are cut off from the majority of Americans and from about one-third of mankind generally, not in one fashion only, but simultaneously in wealth, status, and power. These—the terribly poor, the black or brown, the militarily negligible—are not only cut off for the present, but are or believe themselves to be increasingly cut off from the future, from the social mobility systems that used to exist, either in the world at large or in the United States.

III

Now to examine these trends. I suggested that each of them has shown the seeds of its own negation. First of all, among some—as yet a minority—of the owners of mass destruction there is growing a deep doubt about that aspect of their property. To some it begins to look like a wasting asset. Not that they are ready to abandon their control over foreign policy or their belief that a great power should have an active—even an imperial—foreign policy. But they have begun to wonder whether military means in fact can any longer achieve foreign policy ends. The hypertrophy of war is probably clearest in terms of nuclear war, and it became most apparent perhaps during the Cuban missile crisis, at the one moment of confrontation between the two great nuclear powers, when the rulers of the United States realized that a three-to-one superiority in the most powerful weapons known in human history was not enough to change the social system of a minor island ninety miles off their coast.

The lesson has not been so clearly learned in other kinds of warfare, but it seems to me that it is now being learned in Vietnam. I think that in the remarkable American opposition to the war, the moral objections are very closely connected with a sense of the impracticability of the war. In modern counterinsurgency warfare, just as with nuclear weapons, the major alternatives are to do practically nothing or to commit genocide—there is almost nothing in between. The whole nature of thermonuclear weapons and of counterinsurgency is to be unable to win victories in the normal sense. The reason this is true about counterinsurgency is that the insurgents force it to be true; where once, as in the Philippines in 1901, they would have given up, now they don't give up—even under far greater pressure. And I will come to why that is so when I take up below the negation of the under class. But from the standpoint of the great power, it seems to me the reality is that when confronted with a fully revolutionary struggle the traditional aims of the great power's foreign policy go to pieces. Those who owned the war machine in almost every great power did not normally expect to use it to commit genocide; they expected to use it to win military victories, and that becomes impossible. As a result, for example, in the greatest power on the planet, an attempt to suppress militarily a social revolution in a small, weak, agrarian nation puts enormous strain on the social system of the great empire —intensifying its internal problems until its cities burn, its monetary system trembles, its philosophers and the sons of its key managers seek imprisonment, and even its administration is toppled.

Confronted with these baffling results of the hypertrophy of war, in almost every great power a "right wing" assails what it thinks is a "no-win" foreign policy and demands more weapons. But in most of the powers there is also the emergence of a "left wing" of the establishment, which identifies the malady as having not too few weapons but too many. This dialectical response to the enormous growth of the war machine is so far only a seed; it is clearly not yet the dominant view of the American government, for example. We begin to see the invention of what might be called the strategy of disarmament—strategy because it is based not on a moral judgment but on the pragmatic analysis that the best way of disposing armed forces so as to advance the "national interest" is to dispose *of* the armed forces. And we see the invention of "unarmed forces"—Sputnik by the Russians, the Peace Corps by the Americans. But by itself this new turn within the foreign policy establishment would probably not be sufficient to reverse the traditional assumptions of the usefulness of the threat, if not the actuality, of war. For antiwar establishmentarians to rein in the military is one thing; for them to dismantle the war machine is quite another. It is the possibility of insurgencies in other arenas that offers the chance of there emerging enough power to make basic changes in the war system.

The second major trend has been the emergence over the last generation of the "new class" in America and increasingly in the other developed countries. It has a whole new kind of politics, which is the face of its classness. Its classness is based upon education, upon culture, upon a definition of conscience; and its politics is a defense for those things. It is a defense of education or a use of education, of its highly intellectualized vision of what the world should be like, therefore, of conscience and culture, rather than a defense of ownership or a demand for new ownership in the sense that labor politics was a joint demand of the working class for a change in economic distribution.

The new class is, of course, the bureaucratic class *par excellence*. It exists in the great government bureaucracies, the great business bureaucracies, and the universities—or rather the multiversities. I suggest that in the past decade we have begun to see the chance—only the bare chance—of the emergence of something like its own opposite from within the new class. The first signs of this negation were the Stevensonian reform democratic movements of the mid-fifties and then the nuclear peace movement of the late fifties. More recently, the negation has been growing in the student movement and in those who are even younger than college students: the communitarian "hippie" civilization, or what seems to be emerging in the high school generations. And that newest growth may be—it is too early to tell—not a cop-out from political rebellion, but a vigorous rejection of the old American politics.

So we have a new class, affluent, certain of its own security because its members do carry their property in their heads, and intimately knowledgeable of the sometimes subtle, sometimes brutal dehumanizations of bureaucracy. What I am suggesting is that out of this class comes for some of its members, and especially some of its children, both the demand for and the opportunity for a remarkable freedom. This opportunity has taken a number of political as well as cultural-civilizational directions. The major thrust of this movement has been against the very bureaucracy that nurtured and became the home of the new class.

So far as war and peace are concerned, there is another important facet of the new class: much more than any class in American history, at any rate, it is able to live transnationally, to live in other countries, or to live in other countries intellectually and emotionally when it doesn't live there literally. Out of this comes quite a new freedom from the assumptions of the national government—partly because of this transnationalism and partly because of freedom from the old economic system. So the new class has a fantastic new freedom to move around (socially, geographically, politically) in the society, and indeed in the world society. Its turned-on youth become the "activators"—the missionaries of participatory democracy to all those (in Africa or Mississippi, in Chicago or Ann Arbor) who have been excluded from a share in making the decisions that affect their lives. Their transnationalism is enormously strengthened by the discovery that in other parts of at least the developed world they have brothers and sisters. And they are kin without much regard to different official ideologies or national histories, for in Tokyo and Prague as well as in Paris and Berlin the youth of Berkeley and Morningside Heights find a transnational movement.

Whether this new freedom becomes the major thrust of the new class or remains a minor counterpoint to the bureaucracy and the multiversity is still open to question, just as it is still open to question whether the major thrust of the great power establishments becomes the strategy of disarmament or continues to be the hypertrophy of war.

Finally, there is the emergence both in the world at large and in the United States of what Gunnar Myrdal calls the "under class." That is, for the first time in the United States a clearly conscious group of people has discovered that it has been cut off from the mobility ladders—not only the individualist ladder but even the trade union kind of collective ladder. These people have been cut off in part because of the automation of certain kinds of old jobs and the proliferation of other, newer kinds of jobs. The only jobs available are those of the new class, and the kinds of mobility ladders that would have allowed the poor to move upward one step at a time are no longer available. They have also been cut off in part by the ingrained American racism, which has taken new and more subtle forms as the mammoth bureaucracies of the past generation, shaped in the white image, use formally color-blind standards and assumptions to exclude all but a few of the black and brown. And they have been cut off in part by the very breadth of affluence that has left the dispossessed a minority unable to mobilize by conventional means even that limited political power that the poor majority used to have. Thus one finds among the black poor in America a decline relative to the rest of the society over the last decade despite all the talk about the civil rights advances. So one finds the emergence of an often racially defined majority of the globe in desperate poverty, and *conscious* that it is in desperate poverty: that is, conscious that there are rich people in the world and that it is possible to *become* rich.

From this knowledge comes the possible negation of the cutting off of the under class—that is, the emergence through the new self-consciousness and through modern communications of the possibility of a shared technology of rebellion or revolution. Today we see not the mere sporadic guerrilla rebellion of the Maccabees, who rebelled successfully but did not get the word out to the rest of the Middle East, let alone the rest of the world, that it was possible to run a revolution. We see instead the modern situation in which a Gandhi, a Mao, a King, and a Nkrumah do get the word out to one another. So there begins to grow a shared social technology that is cumulative and that people can build on to create a revolution against their underclassness. Inside America this has taken the forms of the nonviolent Southern freedom movement; *la huelga* among Mexican-Americans; community-organizing projects in Black, Puerto Rican, and Appalachian-white ghettoes; and the Black rebellions of Detroit, Newark, and Washington.

Now it is not yet clear whether this negation, although it is the furthest along of the three, will be a successful one. We see the Chinese revolution—successful so far, but it has not yet demonstrated that it can power the take-off into industrialization. We see the failed Gandhian revolution, failed in the sense of not achieving major change in India. We see the failed and stagnated revolution of independence in Africa. And it must be asked whether in fact the under class of the world is going to be able to create an effective social technology of rebellion. The possibility exists; that *is* clear. Whether it will work, whether it will become real, is not clear.

IV

If one sees all three of those seeds of change growing and flowering, then one can see a very different America and a very different world by 1999. What we see is not an America that has undergone what the radical student movement calls "the revolution." Rather it is an America that has changed in a very peculiar reconstructive fashion, without overturning the main power structures but with considerable weakening (though not destruction) of the establishment. On this basis we could possidict a very different world—but not one in which the nation-state has dissolved, the poor are in power, or power is replaced by love.

What would it mean for antimilitarists from the establishment, "activators" from the new class, and effective rebels from the under class to emerge—all at about the same time? I think that we can identify some of the interconnections that might be made among the three forces of change.

For example, the very size and extensiveness of the American military system means that it is more vulnerable to analysis and criticism than when it was tiny and seemed truly "foreign" policy. For now that one-tenth of the gross national product has been spent on the armed forces for an entire generation—twenty-eight years—Americans have realized that the military is a domestic policy question. At the same time that the military-industrial complex becomes a powerful political force, its very power brings upon it the scrutiny of the people affected by it. Add to that the transnationalism of the new class, the bafflement of the part of the establishment that understands, or at least feels, the hypertrophy of war, and the anger of the rebellious part of the under class, and the military-industrial complex becomes vulnerable to attack from many fronts.

Or take another convergence of the three changes: the desire of the new class for jobs that use education and human relations and offer excitement and novelty; the desire of the detached establishment for a nonmilitary way of carrying on foreign policy; and the desire of the world under class for training in technical and political skills. Result: the Peace Corps, which tries to serve all three desires—more or less. Which it serves most depends on the strength of each of the three classes and especially their "negative" thrusts.

Or take the fact that the rise of consciousness of the new class and the under class coincide (for good economic and technological reasons), and that the two therefore meet each other in the early stages of formation. What impact do Blacks thus make on the new class, and the new class on Black America? The political alliance and personal contacts between the white and the black movements have already brought a cultural interchange. Rock music and perhaps the whole new "youth culture" may be one result, as the new affluence and the old, but in a working society repressed, sexuality explode together. Others may be the effort of Black poverty workers to bypass the dead end of manual labor and move straight toward the new-class jobs of human contact and, perhaps, their attempt to bypass the patriarchal family and move straight toward a more open, permissive, and democratic family life.

Such interconnections could be multiplied. But drawing simply on the ones I have suggested, it is possible to sketch a model of what 1999 might look like. I should like to do this first for the international scene, and then to look more closely at America.

V

Internationally, if all this worked by 1999, disarmament would have been achieved. There would be no world government, no world harmony, and no successful world revolution, but the continued intense conflict between the powers would be carried on by nonmilitary means. The third world would be developing by playing off the great powers against each other and would be building an effective social technology of change by using the many different pressures—carrots, sticks, and so on—provided by the great powers. In such a world there would be the growing edge, but by 1999 it seems to me only the growing edge, of a commitment to mankind growing out of the transnationalism of the new class.

It would be a world in which political change had become much more possible than it is today: a world not frozen by the fear of thermonuclear war, not frozen by the kind of absolute confrontations of social revolution and genocide that we see in Vietnam, but a world able to carry on political change because the means being brought to bear are those of politics and economics.

There would be three major new factors in the international life of that world. The first is that disarmament would be enforceable by an international institution, one not capable of acting like a world government except under very special conditions, but quite capable most of the time of checking, preventing, and deterring rearmament.

Second, in such a world the nation-states would continue to carry on their foreign policies, but this time using nonmilitary means, using what one might call the "unarmed forces" instead of the present armed forces as the major way of carrying on foreign policy. (We are assuming that the various national establishments have reformed themselves and still survive, still pursue "world power" but do so by more workable means. If they refused to reform and were broken by popular upheaval, the likelihood of a broader world community and perhaps world government might be greater.) In the world where nationalist great power establishments continue to exist, the Peace Corps and the space agency (or the space race, looking at it from both the Soviet and American sides) are the precursors of the unarmed forces. One would expect the proliferation of teacher corps, farmer corps, engineer corps, the use of revolutionary agents by revolutionary powers and of more establishment-oriented managers and manipulators of change by more established powers. Some of these unarmed forces would be small, as the Peace Corps is, and closely attached to a given constituency in the country as the Peace Corps is attached to the campus. And there might also be a redirection of the existing armed forces: the Strategic Air Command might be stripped of its bombs and turned into a strategic cargo-carrying command for the service of the underdeveloped countries; destroyers would make good hospital ships; perhaps the infantry would be turned into a world conservation corps, and so on.

So far as the unarmed forces of the great powers would be concerned, the great struggle would be over the underdeveloped world, the hungry world: in what direction and by what processes will the hungry develop, with what kind of politics, what kind of alliances, and the like? In that situation the hungry states themselves might well be able to define their futures more independently than in any other situation. They may not be able to define wholly how they develop; that is scarcely possible in a world where you don't have much power. But this may be the situation in which their power would be maximized. For they would be able to refuse a kind of aid they did not like and go elsewhere for one they did; they would be able to play off the great powers against each other; they would be able to draw on various competing ideologies, social patterns, and institutions to build what they liked. And the simple amount of capital available to them would be so large that they would not have to choose between stagnation and squeezing investment capital out of the peasant's work time, as they now must.

And third, there might well be in such a world a rather different kind of institution, one that would represent what might be called the "growing edge of mankind." These institutions would not have the sorts of power that national governments or governments joining the United Nations have available to them—that is, military or quasi-military power. But they would have available transnational kinds of commitments and the kinds of power that go with that. I mean the kinds of power that churches have had in the past and may gather again to use propaganda, boycotts, nonviolent interventions. Such institutions might conceivably be built through revitalization of the transnational religious and philosophical institutions of the world—Christian, Buddhist, Marxist—and also through such groups as a world student movement, a world association of scholars and scientists, or a transnational managerial association taking into its membership both the Soviet "socialist" managers and Western "capitalist" managers.

If we turn away from world affairs and look back again at the United States in 1999, it seems to me that one might possidict a considerable political change inside the United States.

First of all, by 1999 towns like Berkeley and Ann Arbor and Madison could be transformed by the fact of being university centers, if the new class moves in the direction I have suggested. Berkeley is obviously the key example; already what began around 1960 as a student movement on the campus has become a major political and cultural force in the city. So imagine a transformation of those places in the country where the new class is the strongest. Imagine the reconstruction of those places so that they are not hierarchical, so that the very best image of the university operates within them—full academic freedom and faculty self-government writ large for the whole community, institutions following the movement's lead into workers' control, people following the movement's lead into free-floating social mobility, a large proportion of the population acting as "activators" of the formerly disfranchised, poetry and politics the dominant jobs. And these places, remember, would be much larger in proportion to the general population by 1999 than they are today because these are the places of growth.

Second, a number of fairly large cities, from Newark up to Baltimore, that now have very large Black populations will almost certainly be mostly Negro much earlier than 1999. Some of them might well go the way of the Black movement, and instead of following the style of Adam Clayton Powell or Bill Dawson might be black in the styles of Carmichael, Seale, or King. There might very well develop two different ways of being Black in America, analogous to the twin phenomena in parts of Europe of an assimilated and an orthodox Jewry. That is, a set of "Black power" institutions and a separate Black culture or at least Black society might emerge, proud and independent; and alongside it, many Negroes might have joined the white society and found equal places within it. And from the children of the Black society some might push off into integrated America, while from the children of integration some might choose to become socially Black. It seems quite likely that if Black Americans have very considerably more power in the society than they do today, they will demand that American foreign policy be much more oriented toward the underdeveloped world and toward Africa specifically. The result might be a new version of the ethnic revolutionary politics of the Irish-Americans who in the nineteenth century were bitterly anti-British and wholeheartedly committed to the freeing of Ireland, or of the Zionist Americans who were committed to the achievement of a separate Jewish state and to its defense once it emerged.

And finally, to look at the national political picture, it seems to me conceivable that in one fashion or another there might emerge a loosely linked political alliance that would bring together the major elements of change that I have described, since on some issues they would have *some* interests in common. Such a party would probably often act, at least in part, like a movement as well as like a political party, not sealing off electoral politics but merging it into other kinds of politics. For example, parts of it might very well marry the neighborhood government of the schools in a city to the neighborhood political club and both to sit-ins against the hospital system. If such a party came to exist, its major opponent might well be not the right wing but the great American center—the part of the establishment that had opposed disarmament, the worn-out middle class of farmers and shopkeepers, the old craft unions and maybe even the diminished and defensive industrial unions. But the center might well be a normal majority, subject to national defeat only on special occasions, as were the Republicans from 1900 to 1932.

VI

How, then, can we go about doing research on the possidiction I have just laid out? There are many aspects to this conceivable future, many particular institutions within it, that could be constructed in the present to test the hypotheses involved.

One test of the concept of the movement-party that I have sketched would be an effort to marry local electoral political action to non-electoral projects that would bring together members of the new class and the under class. Such projects might include:

1. Group legal centers in which lawyers hire themselves, in effect, to a large group of people who pay small amounts of regular "insurance" (as happens now in group health centers in some places). The lawyers would serve their employers' needs in criminal and civil law and would teach them law. Such services would help the public to become less dependent on experts and would enable poor people, especially, to begin to find their way into politically potent professions.

2. Local consumers' unions that test the reliability and the prices of local businesses and picket or otherwise pressure high-interest auto loan companies, pollution-producing factories, etc.

3. Centers for the actual practice of "social psychiatry." Here liberal and radical psychiatrists, psychologists, and other specialists would practice individual or group therapy with the emotionally ill in a neighborhood. They could channel the energies of those who are thus recovering into various forms of self-fulfillment (art, poetry, politics), lead discussions or focus attention on those aspects of the community that are causing emotional illness and can be changed by political action, and encourage action that will make the change happen.

We might test these hypotheses concerning the new class by trying deliberately to train, support, and use "activators" whose vocation would be to spur change at home and offer a new way of carrying on foreign policy abroad. They would spend two years in Nigeria, two or three in Mississippi, a few with *la huelga* in Texas or Oregon, and several in the suburbs of Chicago. At every point they would learn how to turn people loose politically who had believed that there was no way for them to act politically to shape their lives.

Such a group of activators might well begin building some transnational organizations—perhaps a world student movement, perhaps a peacemakers' academy in which a new profession combining the roles of international peacekeeper, conciliator, and development energizer could be created and the seeds of a true transnational peacemaking force could be sown.

In each such development—and there are already many under way that are approximately relevant, though not perhaps carefully constructed out of someone's possidiction—the historian who has decided to loosen the boundaries of his own profession could be crucial. He should be present to assess such projects from a critical stance, to note where possidictions of the future are borne out and where they prove absurd, to apply his sensitivity to the particular event as an element in long-term change.

And finally, there are ways in which we—who are, after all, members of the new class—might create such projects of our own. A transnational commission of historians from nations whose governments are at war or at odds over war could investigate and write independent histories of such ongoing conflicts as that in Vietnam. What better way could we nurture that "growing edge of mankind" that would act as a check on national governments and make it more difficult for them to fight?

Or there might be a transnational association of scholars, historians included, whose deepest commitment would be to act against any perversion of scholars as secret researchers or secret agents of the military and paramilitary establishments of their various governments. What better way is there to make clear that our loyalty to open research and the increasing knowledge of mankind—*all* mankind—is stronger than our loyalty to the war machines of our different states? (And this suggestion is no idle notion. Surely we know of cases where historians who are American have done secret research for the military or have taught overseas and then filed reports with the Central Intelligence Agency.) If we both undertook such efforts and studied what we did, we would at once be fulfilling our profession as historians and advancing our historical knowledge.

And what is more, we would be undertaking to meet a responsibility that perhaps George Orwell laid before us most vividly. You remember his portrait of the antihistorian at the memory hole; you may remember too, that he warned: "Who controls the past controls the future; who controls the present controls the past." Our effort must be to show that *whoever frees the future frees the present*, and thus to make his warning come full circle in the service of liberty.

In this endeavor the historian as truth-teller, like other social scientists, is necessarily a radical. For by confronting the social myths propagated by those who rule our society—any society—he undermines the structure of power. Particularly by envisioning alternatives to the present order, he necessarily attacks that unconscious but pervasive ideology which holds that there *is* no alternative to the present order. Historians of the past have a special obligation to examine those defeated social alternatives that the victors of the present would far rather see buried than remembered; and it is in fulfillment and extension of this obligation that historians may have a special duty to examine those not-yet-defeated future alternatives that the victors of the present would far rather see buried than created—among them, peace.

PART IV

The Discussion Reviewed

The Historian and the Dilemma
BERENICE A. CARROLL

The idea of dilemma—of deep contradiction recognized and considered but not yet reconciled or resolved—recurs throughout this book. In the hands of the contributors various meanings of the idea appear, but concern with the war-or-peace issue as something primary is consistent from first to last. This mood is new among scholars, but already it is affecting the teaching and writing of history.

The Historian and the Dilemma
BERENICE A. CARROLL

AMONG THOSE WHO ATTENDED the Plattsburgh meeting there was no doubt at the end that the conference had posed many hard questions to which the answers remained unclear. But two central questions were little touched on, both of which deserve to be confronted more directly and, if possible, to be answered. We need to ask first, what is the nature of the dilemma itself, and second, what contribution can the historian in particular make toward its resolution?

In his opening essay, Charles Barker defines the American dilemma of power and law as a conflict between moral commitment and contradictory practice. None of the other authors addresses himself at length to the problem of definition, but each may be seen to fall into one of two groups—those who appear to accept Barker's definition and those who, while not explicitly rejecting it, appear to offer an alternative definition. In the first group we find Rosenberg, LaFeber, Neumann, and Nish. In the second group we find Chai, Sumida, and to a lesser extent Bruce; here the dilemma appears as a conflict between competing principles representing competing or conflicting interests.

Barker's essay describes two conflicting patterns in the American past. One is the moral commitment to peace and to the "multilateral recognition of the rights of all nations and persons and a systematic sharing of obligation and authority." This commitment Barker sees as rooted deeply in the traditions and beliefs of the American people: traditions and beliefs that helped to shape the Constitution, the early guidelines of U.S. foreign policy, the absorption of new states into the Union, the growth of the American peace movement, and the role of the United States in creating the League of Nations and the United Nations. The conflicting pattern is the practice of "unilateral violence against other peoples," the practice of Manifest Destiny and the Monroe Doctrine, Hiroshima and Vietnam.

Defined in these terms, the dilemma may also be seen as a conflict between the "ideal" and the "real," and so it appears in the papers of

Rosenberg, LaFeber, Neumann, and Nish. Nish even brings the point into his title, "Canada and the American Dilemma: Realism versus Idealism." A conflict between the real and the ideal is not the same as one between realism and idealism, but for the moment the main point is that all four authors conceive the dilemma primarily in terms of a disparity between what *is* and what *should be*.

Thus Charles Rosenberg refers repeatedly to examples in American history of a "tension between existing institutions and the demands of the ideal"; the "historical tension between the real and the ideal"; the "conflict between the is and the must be." In the papers of LaFeber and Neumann, emphasis falls heavily on the unilateralism of U.S. foreign policy as actually practiced, in contrast with the weakness or hypocrisy of American commitment to ideals of peace and multilateralism. Similarly Nish emphasizes the disparity between the "ideal of Canada as the keeper of peace" and the fact that Canada's economic commitment to armaments has been overwhelmingly greater than that to international cooperation.

The papers of Bruce, Sumida, and Chai also give some support to this position. Bruce points out that in matters of multilateral authority, nonintervention, and human rights, the United States often fails to match its actions to its words. Sumida notes that "many of the same states which strenuously demand the protection of fundamental human rights, including that of self-determination, in other states are very reluctant to implement such rights in their own societies." And Chai suggests that the ideals of international law and world order have been used to mask a harsher reality: the use of law as an instrument of subjugation and exploitation of colonial territories.

II

Defining the dilemma of power and law as a conflict between the real and the ideal may produce a highly pessimistic outlook, at least in those Americans who, true to their reputed pragmatism, tend to doubt the force of abstract ideals and idealism. But the dilemma may also be defined in another way, as a conflict between opposing principles arising out of conflicting interests. For ideals and idealism are not inherently in conflict with reality and with interests. Some ideals may be so removed from reality as to seem forever unrealizable, such as the ideal of a universal harmony expunged of all seeds of conflict.

Other ideals are so modest as to converge with commonplace reality: for example the ideal of individual service to the community. Peace, justice, liberty, and human rights are widely held ideals that are neither fantastic nor mundane. They are far from universally realized in practice, but they are not mere abstractions; they are reflections and extensions of witnessed and experienced realities. Moreover, they are rooted in the real interests of individuals and communities. Unfortunately, they may come in conflict not only with certain special interests of individuals or nations but also with each other.

This interpretation of the dilemma is suggested by the papers of Bruce, Chai, and Sumida. As noted above, these authors recognize disparities between ideal and reality in the international arena. But their conception of "the ideal" is tempered by their conceptions of the nature and functions of international law.

From the viewpoint of the first group of authors, international law and adherence to multilateral authority appear to lie in a realm of the ideal that stands opposed to interests. Emphasis is placed upon the need to sacrifice national interests to achieve the ideal. The problem then appears to center on our unwillingness, in practice, to make any such sacrifices. As Neumann puts it, we are unwilling even "to pay a small price for peace in the form of a sacrifice of some national interests." Similarly, it is viewed as an accusation to say that the United States is "using" the United Nations "as a means for achieving U.S. national interests."

Students of international law see the matter in a different light. They see international law and the exercise of multilateral authority not as abstract ideals but as a body of rules and procedures growing out of the actual practices, customs, and behavior of states in their relations with each other, and out of the relations between their nationals. And they see the broader principles of international law, such as the doctrines Sumida discusses, as arising out of conflicting interests and the need to control and resolve them within an orderly framework. Frequently, however, the conflict of interests between nations, or between ruling and revolutionary parties, leads to conflicts of principle that are inherently irreconcilable. Herein lies the true dilemma, the necessity of choosing between the sacrifice of one or another valid principle.

To develop these points a bit, we may note first that Bruce defines international law as "the legal system that has grown out of the continuous practice in the relations between sovereign, national states." He also cites the "functionalist" approach to international relations, a view which

> recognizes a direct correlation between the development of international law and the operations of organizations in various spheres of contemporary life. The functionalist view sees a progressively larger interrelation among international organizations—private, regional, international, and supranational—each pressing forward to provide order and stability in its own field of activity. These organizations are forced to recognize and promote a growing number of legal and institutional patterns in the international community—so the functionalist reasons—and by the ever greater variety of their structure and scope the world develops a new "common law" of international practice.

From this point of view, international law develops in response to the proliferation of transnational, international, and supranational organizations and their interactions; it reflects their individual, joint, or intersecting interests.

International law is also seen by some of its close observers as "processive," that is, not merely reflecting and responding to widespread behavior, but serving also to formulate new standards and shape behavior to meet them. This is the point Sumida raises in quoting McDougal's view that international law is "a *process* of authoritative decision-making whose . . . phases include the formulation, invocation, and application of community prescriptions. . . . It is a dynamic process by which the peoples of the world 'clarify and implement their common interests in the shaping and sharing of values.' "

This processive aspect is undoubtedly what those who see international law as an ideal have in mind: it includes the formulation of human rights conventions that are still widely disregarded in practice; declarations and resolutions of the U.N. General Assembly on international crises or on disarmament, which go ignored or unfulfilled; and so forth. But even this aspect of international law and multilateral authority is most properly seen as rooted in reality, itself a part of current reality, and helping to shape future reality. The ideals involved—peace, multilateralism, human rights, and the like—are not inventions out of thin air but, as noted above, are extensions of experienced or perceived realities. There are people who enjoy the human rights specified in the conventions; there are countries that live in peace and even disarmament (vis-à-vis each other) over long periods of time; there are states that comply with resolutions of the U.N. Security Council or General Assembly. The idea that such experiences can be extended to all peoples and to relations between all states remains an ideal, far removed from realization, but *not* far removed from reality, if we accept that what exists and has been experienced, if only in limited numbers, is real. Nor is it to be denied that the demand for extension of these experiences to all peoples and states is real and growing, forming an important element in contemporary international life.

Moreover, like all widely held ideals, those that pertain to international life reflect and serve real interests. The papers of Bruce, Sumida, and Chai refer to many interests served by international law and international organization. Among these, and others not touched on by them, are: the need for international stability, to secure safe conduct of persons, goods, and information in international travel, commerce, and communications; the settlement of private claims of individuals, corporations, and other groups against foreign governments or their nationals; the opportunity to advance national interests by methods less costly, risky, and injurious than war, and potentially more profitable; efficient and reliable channels for benefits in the forms of grants and loans to be extended from one country or region to another; benefits in health, welfare, education, and technology not only to poorer peoples but also, through international professional organizations, to those already possessing advanced technologies; opportunity to appeal intolerable abuses of human rights to international authority; and freedom to carry domestic conflict even to the point of revolution without external intervention.

Seen in this context, the complaint that the United States "uses" the United Nations to serve its national interests appears quite misdirected. The trouble is rather the opposite: the United States does not use the United Nations and other international structures nearly enough; it bypasses them and acts *alone* (not merely "unilaterally" in the sense of trying to shape the United Nations to its own will). After all, we do not object if India or Sweden "uses" the United Nations to further their national interests, as both certainly do, though in very different ways. Like domestic institutions of law and government, international institutions are made to serve interests, and the best test of their vitality is the extent to which they are used rather than disregarded and bypassed.

It may be argued that the interests legal systems, both domestic and international, are made to serve are "the general interest" of a community, a nation, or humanity. But this would be only a partial image of the truth. In practice both systems are used by individuals, groups, and nations to redress injuries, secure legitimate benefits, and establish rights—that is, to serve the interests of claimants—as much as (or perhaps even more than) they are used by society to deter crime or to constrain or punish delinquents.

This is not to deny that rich and powerful nations, by virtue of their wealth, prestige, or military power, may find themselves able to exercise so disproportionate an influence over international institutions that they may "use" them as instruments for exploitative or oppressive purposes. This is certainly what those who criticize the United States for "using" the United Nations have in mind, as becomes particularly clear in Neumann's remark that when Americans demand a "just peace" what they really want is "open frontiers for American investors and exporters," implying "the injustices of economic colonialism." It is the intent to exploit and its consequences that are the true objects of criticism in this process. Moreover, it should be noted that we are far less critical of small countries that use the U.N. even for exploitative purposes than of the great powers when they do the same. In fact, what we mean to condemn is really the abuse of power. But the abuse of power is a phenomenon common to domestic political, economic, and juridical systems as well as to international society. It poses its own dilemmas, of great severity, but it is not peculiar to the problem of achieving world order. Indeed, as suggested by Chai's paper, the abuse of power might be as severe (or more so) under a "world rule of law" as under the present relatively less ordered and lawful conditions.

When the abuse of power leads to the subjugation of the weak by the powerful, we have injustice, which is not in itself a dilemma. It becomes a dilemma when we seek means to deal with injustice and find that the means that serve the ideal of justice are, at least sometimes, in conflict with ideals of peace and order. This argument can be misused by those who expect to profit from war or from war preparation to cover their profiteering in an idealistic cloak. This is why Neumann treats with cynicism America's preference for values "higher" than peace, such as "freedom, . . . security, prosperity, honor, and inviolable commitments to allies"; too often, these values are called upon as cover for policies designed to perpetuate "the injustices of economic colonialism."

But it is not hard to conjure up examples from the past and anticipations of the future in which at least some of these values, especially that of freedom, and some others, such as the righting of injustice, do legitimately prevail over peace. Only the pure pacifist would argue otherwise, and since the leaders of governments and revolutionary movements are hardly that, we cannot very well accuse them of hypocrisy. That *some* wars are just, at least within the context of an armed and oppressive social and international order, nearly all of us would agree. Cameron Nish appears to grant that the American Revolution, if no U.S. war since, was a just war; Charles Barker notes that World War II "seemed then, as it still seems to all but a handful of deep dissenters, a war of self-defense and the guarding of essential ideals and loyalties"; those of us who have opposed U.S. intervention and pursuit of the war in Vietnam, though we may condemn atrocities on all sides, find it difficult to condemn the National Liberation Front and North Vietnam for pursuing the war itself.

We are therefore in danger of being accused of hypocrisy ourselves unless we recognize that the hypocrisy of which we accuse American and Canadian leaders is not that of pledging peace and making war, but that of pledging a just peace and just war while pursuing injustice both in peace and in war, or the hypocrisy of calling by the name of "defense" a military establishment that is not only the most bloated war machine in history but is also clearly used for aggressive purposes.

The conflict that arises between the ideal of order, on the one hand, and ideals of liberation on the other is well illustrated by Chai. He describes thus the dilemma faced by newly independent Asian nations:

They, more than anyone else, need a stable world order. They need it so that they can devote their attention to ordering their newly won statehood with the least bother from the big powers. But by the same token the last thing they will do is to accept the existing world order, for that would forever put them in an inferior bargaining position in the world political arena. They would remain bound by unequal treaties and unwanted legal shackles. They are also too eager to start a new national life with a clean slate to permit themselves to be hemmed in by old obligations.

Here the principle of world order is pitted against the principles of independence (desire to be rid of "unwanted legal shackles"), of equality (desire to be rid of "unequal treaties"), and of self-determination (desire to "start a new national life with a clean slate").

Sumida delineates the conflicts of principle in greater detail. He shows that the same principle (such as nonintervention) may be used by opposing sides against each other: both ruling and revolutionary elites may cry "intervention!" or "puppet!" to discredit the opponent. Different principles, equally valid, may also come into conflict with each other, as in the case of nonintervention versus human rights, or sovereignty versus self-determination.

"States have a paramount interest," writes Sumida, "in a modicum of peace and stability in the international order, including the sense of security arising from a mutual tolerance of regimes espousing different ideologies." The traditional doctrines of sovereignty, independence, equality of states, domestic jurisdiction, and nonintervention are designed to protect this interest in stability, security, and mutual tolerance. They serve, in Sumida's words, to "immunize the internal arena" from the influence or control of external parties; the intended effects are to limit and contain internal violence so as to cause the least possible disruption of international affairs, and to protect by international sanction each individual state from attack or interference in its domestic affairs. Thus the doctrine of national sovereignty, though often viewed as an obstacle to the achievement of multilateral world order, is itself intended to secure order and limit violence. So, too, is the doctrine of nonintervention, which multilateralists would generally expect a world judicial authority to uphold.

On the other hand, Sumida notes the growing concern for principles of human rights and self-determination. These principles sometimes come in sharp conflict with doctrines of nonintervention and sovereignty. At present, Sumida notes, the doctrines of sovereignty, independence, domestic jurisdiction, and nonintervention are most often used as obstacles to the achievement of human rights and self-determination. Oppressive regimes and colonial states use them to discourage intervention by other powers or by international authorities in behalf of oppressed individuals, groups, or peoples. It is by no means clear, however, that the solution would be to abandon these principles. For to do so would be dangerous to international order and would contradict one of the main immediate goals: self-determination. What is self-determination, after all, if not sovereignty, independence, equality, and freedom from external intervention? New nations, indeed, are more in need of the protection provided by such doctrines than any others.

It is true that this problem would disappear if humanity were to agree to abandon the nation-state entirely, to establish a true world government with a uniform system of law, and thereafter to treat all conflicts as "internal." There would be no sovereignty but that of humanity, expressed through its agreed organs of government and law. There might be rights of regional or local self-government, but certainly no independence. Different localities might have equal representation and be treated equally under the laws, but "equality of states" would disappear. There would no longer be "external actors," hence no such things as "intervention" or "aggression." There would very likely still be abuse of power, and it might be either more or less restrained than it is today, depending upon many unpredictable factors. World government would leave us with injustice and its attendant dilemmas, but it would certainly eliminate the dilemmas of seeking peace and multilateralism in a world of sovereign nations.

It must be observed, however, that not one of the authors has seen fit to argue directly for world government as a solution to the dilemma. This does not represent any oversight but rather reflects a lack of conviction—perhaps in the desirability of world government, certainly in its coming to pass in the near future. Thus Arthur Waskow explicitly refuses to "possidict" world government by the year 1999, though he sees disarmament as within the realm of possibility by that date. In fact it does appear that the nation-state will remain with us for some decades, whereas our own imperative national interests may persuade us sooner to abandon the war system, at least among the great powers and their willing or unwilling surrogates in the cold war. War itself seems likely to survive at least on a small scale between or within new nations and in continuing struggles for self-determination, just as violence survives on a limited scale within nearly all societies. Whether violence and war can ever be totally eradicated is not in question here; we can all agree it is not likely to be in the next thirty years. But if we fail to control the *levels* of violence and war in that time, we are unlikely to survive even that long.

The dilemma must therefore be faced, for the immediate present and the near future, within a context of nation-state sovereignty. This sovereignty need not be taken as absolute; indeed, as Sumida points out, it is not so either in the eyes of international law or in the practice of international relations. In the eyes of international law, and in day-to-day practice, the nation's sovereignty is already limited by the body of custom and accepted rules and treaties to which nations do normally adhere; and in special circumstances it is limited by certain doctrines such as "humanitarian intervention," protection of governments in exile, and recognition of belligerency under which nations or international bodies may violate or repudiate the sovereignty of other states with the sanction of international law.

In this context, the problem is how, given a mixed system of nation-states and supranational institutions, to maximize the existing elements of order and multilateralism, minimize resort to the destructive procedures of warfare, and yet provide effective channels of recourse against the abuse of power.

The first two of these three goals would be much more readily achieved, on the basis of the experiences and interests of the advanced industrial nations, if the third could be ignored. If we could disregard the Dominican Republic and Czechoslovakia, Biafra and South African *apartheid*, or the legitimate competing claims of peoples in the Middle East and in Vietnam, the great powers could very well (under the threat of nuclear disaster) arrange the world nicely to suit themselves, much as the great states of Europe used to do in the era before nationalism and anticolonialism took center stage. But fortunately or unfortunately, as the European experience clearly shows, such arrangements are inherently unstable; those uppity subject peoples keep stirring up trouble. Liberation and justice (ideals based on the interests of the oppressed) keep demanding satisfaction. If put down for a time, they come back later, with bombs instead of petitions in hand.

This is why Sumida calls for recognition of a right of revolution and for institutionalized channels of revolutionary change. This may or may not be realistic. It may be that liberation and order are ultimately always at odds and that true revolutionary change cannot be institutionalized. On the other hand, it is not clear that revolutionary disorder and disruption *require* physical violence and destruction of life, limb, and property. Without entering into discussion of the theory of nonviolence here, it may be observed that doctrines of nonviolence and tactics of nonviolent civil disobedience or disruption have spread markedly in recent decades. This is not to deny that, in face of retaliatory resort to violence on the part of the custodians of order, nonviolence today appears to be suffering a setback. On the other hand, it is clear that, to this extent, the control of violence *is* in the hands of the powerful, the "owners of war," as Waskow puts it, who at present have the strongest interest in the limitation of violence on the international level. If they withhold violence in response to nonviolent disruption, they risk a kind of defeat and losses (as in the case of Britain's withdrawal from India); but if they respond with violence, they still risk defeat with even greater losses (as in the case of France in Vietnam and Algeria and perhaps the United States today in Vietnam). They also risk disruption of the system of order (whether the fragile one of today or an improved one of the future) that protects them from nuclear annihilation.

In the end, the best hope—and the reason for hope—for achieving the goals delineated above is that they are in the rational self-interest not of some abstract entity called "humanity," but of the nations, groups, and individuals of which humanity is composed. The task before those of us who are already committed to these goals is to clarify and strengthen awareness of the interests served by peace, multilateralism, and international justice. Richard Falk and Saul Mendlovitz have written:

> the strengthening of international law depends upon the discovery by various groups of states that their interests are generally served by conforming to the legal expectations of the international community. . . . The major groups of states must perceive that their interests will be best served by working to solve the transition problem and by bringing a system of war prevention into being. Not all states have a comparable interest in the avoidance of a major war, and their acceptance of a new international system will undoubtedly depend upon its promise to realize their additional high priority interests.[1]

In the process of discovery and growing perception of such interests, historians have a major role to play.

III

Historians have been regrettably prone to neglect peace both as a subject and as a value premise in their professional work. The role of value premises in scholarship and social research is a large subject that cannot be elaborated here; it has been excellently treated by

---

[1] Richard A. Falk and Saul H. Mendlovitz, eds., *The Strategy of World Order*, vol. 2, *International Law* (New York: World Law Fund, 1966), p. 3.

Gunnar Myrdal in several works, most recently in *Objectivity in Social Research*.[2] Suffice it to say here that value premises are an essential element in scholarship and social science and that the scholar should strive not to eliminate them but to make them as explicit and as free of false assumptions as possible. It may happen that to make the value premises and assumptions explicit will suffice to have them rejected or altered; not infrequently we work from false assumptions that, once exposed to light, are readily discarded.[3]

Unstated value premises and unspoken, often untested assumptions have played a significant part in shaping the historian's treatment of war, peace, diplomacy, and related topics. To take peace as a value premise is to ask that prevailing value premises and assumptions be made explicit and to address questions to the past that have been largely ignored or neglected. A classic example of this process and how it contributes to the growth of historical knowledge is a type of historical study that has become well established only since World War I: investigation of the origins of wars. The initial value premise of such studies—white papers and blue papers on war guilt—was that blame for the sufferings of the war could or should be fixed on one belligerent. Subsequent scholarship, concerned rather with learning *how the peace had been lost*, exposed these earlier tracts to withering and definitive criticism, examined documents and events in exhaustive detail, and taught us a great deal about the complexities of historical processes.

Peace enters also as a value premise in stimulating other kinds of historical studies. The problem of how wars end, for example, seems to elicit serious study only in times of war when the demand or yearning for peace grows high: the first great study of the subject was Coleman Phillipson's *Termination of War and Treaties of Peace*,

---

[2] (New York: Pantheon, 1969). See also Myrdal's *Asian Drama: An Inquiry into the Poverty of Nations*, 3 vols. (New York: Twentieth Century Fund, 1968), 1: Prologue and chaps. 1–3, and 3:1536–38. A somewhat different critique of "value-neutrality" appears in Johan Galtung, *Theory and Methods of Social Research* (Oslo and London: Universitets-forlaget, 1967), pp. 484–90.

[3] A failure to make value premises and related assumptions explicit is partly responsible for the numerous histories of the United States that ignore Blacks except where they appear as an issue between whites. Had the premises been made explicit at the start (that only what whites do and think is important, or that Blacks haven't done, said or contributed much worth reporting, etc.) they might quickly have been rejected, making way much earlier for different value premises and a different perspective on American history.

which appeared in England in 1916; after a long hiatus, H. A. Calahan's *What Makes A War End?* appeared in the United States in 1944; the subject has been revived only in recent years by the war in Vietnam.[4] Similarly, concern for the prevention of war has led to recognition of the need to study "nonwars" of the past, or serious crises resolved without war. Concern for disarmament and arms control has led to studies of past experience with disarmament, less weighted with negative value premises than earlier studies. The search for peace today has also led to a rapid proliferation of studies in the history of pacifism and peace movements. All these types of studies need to be continued and expanded. But the history of war origins and war endings, of nonwars and disarmament, of pacifism and peace movements, is not the history of peace itself.

Peace is very rarely treated as a subject by historians.[5] Indeed, they hardly know how to conceive it as such, giving rise to the puzzled stare that greets the historian who declares his field to be "peace research." The difficulty is paradoxical, arising partly from the almost unrecognized fact that peace really is the condition of life for most of humanity, over most of the globe, most of the time. This is so because peace serves human interests, individual, group, or national, on the whole better than war. Evidently there are times when statesmen or revolutionary leaders conclude, rightly or wrongly, that war would serve certain overriding interests better than peace. But the survival and strength of the ideal of peace (which is not identical with pacifism) rests on this bond between the ideal and the interests it serves. It is for this reason that Charles Barker's treatment of the ideals of peace and multilateralism as deeply rooted traditions is closer to reality than a position which dismisses those ideals as hypocritical or weak, concentrating attention on the practices of violence and unilateralism.

---

[4] Coleman Phillipson, *Termination of War and Treaties of Peace* (London, 1916); H. A. Calahan, *What Makes a War End?* (New York: Vanguard, 1944). See also Berenice A. Carroll, "How Wars End: An Analysis of Some Current Hypotheses," *Journal of Peace Research,* 1969, no. 4, pp. 295–320, and other articles in the same issue dealing with war endings in selected wars from the fifth century B.C. to the present. Note also the November 1970 issue of *The Annals of the American Academy of Political and Social Science,* "How Wars End," ed. William T. Fox.

[5] A. C. F. Beales's seminal work, *The History of Peace,* is more accurately subtitled *A Short Account of the Organised Movements for International Peace* (London: Bell & Sons, 1931).

The statement that peace is the normal condition of human life is affirmed here as a conclusion of the author from her reading of history, from current research on wars since 1775, and from common sense observation of life. The affirmation is probably correct, as the reader may agree upon a few moments' reflection. But it does not appear that any historian has troubled to demonstrate it, nor even to proclaim it as a fact. In the face of widespread belief in the inherent warlikeness of man, however, it would seem to be an important point for historians to examine and verify.

The verification would not be a trivial task and would have to start by making explicit certain definitions and assumptions on which the assertion rests. It might be impossible to prove, for example, if one began by equating "war" with "conflict" or if one accepted Thomas Hobbes's view that "the nature of war, consisteth not in actual fighting; but in the known disposition thereto, during all the time there is no assurance to the contrary." Even with a much more limited definition of war, for example, restricting it to "organized armed combat," it would still be necessary to deal with the well-documented *frequency* of war. It is often pointed out that hardly a year can be found in the annals of history unmarked by at least one war somewhere on the face of the globe. And Quincy Wright offers an appalling estimate of the frequency of battles and skirmishes ("hostile encounters between public armed forces") on land and sea: "There have probably been over a quarter of a million such hostile encounters in the civilized world since 1500, an average of over 500 a year."[6] But though this in turn gives an average of more than one "hostile encounter" per day, it could almost certainly be shown that while the hostile armed forces have been so engaged, however large or small their number and however destructive their engagement, the majority of the human population has at the same time been engaged elsewhere in essentially peaceful (though not conflict-free) pursuits.

This does not in any way, of course, dispose of the war problem and the threat it now poses (given modern weapons of mass destruction) to all humanity. Nor does it deny or explain the fact that governments often devote more of their resources to war or war preparation than to peaceful concerns, nor the fact that minorities directly engaged in combat sometimes have the psychological and economic

[6] *A Study of War*, 2d ed. unabridged (Chicago: The University of Chicago Press, 1965), p. 687.

backing of majorities in the belligerent populations. Nevertheless the point is worth establishing in itself, in view of the fact, noted most recently by Franz Schurmann, that "today many Americans betray a view of the world in which war, not peace, is the norm."[7]

Demonstrating the contrary, that peace has been the normal condition of human life, is one way in which peace itself can be considered as a subject by historians. But where can they go from there? Peace is often defined as the absence of war. War can be defined by certain characteristics that recur, not perhaps in every case, but often enough to make the phenomenon recognizable and subject to study by historians. But how can historians study an *absence*? Alternatively, peace could be defined as everything people do that is not war. But how does one study "everything"? One way is to chop it up, as historians do, into national histories, regional history, economic history, intellectual history, and so on. But there one seems almost to come full circle, for war surely plays a part in all these.

Nevertheless, peace emerges here again as a subject. For the question arises, what part is played by peace, as compared with war, in the national, economic, intellectual, and social history of mankind? Sociologists write of the social functions of conflict and war; we are sadly lacking in works by scholars of any discipline on the social functions of peace. Like the normality of peace, its positive social functions are ignored. Though it may seem that this is because they are self-evident, there is a serious and increasingly influential school of thought which contends that war makes more fundamental contributions to human progress than peace and that violence is an indispensably creative force in social evolution.[8] For those who see as

---

[7] Franz Schurmann, "On Revolutionary Conflict," *Journal of International Affairs*, 23, no. 1 (1969):37.

[8] See Hannah Arendt, "Reflections on Violence," *Journal of International Affairs*, 23, no. 1 (1969): 1–35, and works cited therein. Also Lewis Coser, *The Functions of Social Conflict* (Glencoe, Ill.: Free Press, 1956) and later works. The list of authors cataloging or extolling the positive uses of violence and war is too long to enumerate here, but one may note that it extends in muted forms into and throughout the universe of historical writings. As a single example, one might mention the impressive work of William H. McNeill, *The Rise of the West: A History of the Human Community*, which, perhaps unintentionally, conveys the impression that war and conquest have been the primary means of diffusion of culture and the rise and fall of social systems throughout the history of civilization. No objection is intended here to the examination of whether war serves positive functions; the objection is to the failure to examine the same question about peace in an equally serious way.

urgent the need for transition to an international system capable of preventing World War III, the record of rapid social change in the past seems discouragingly tied to great outbursts of violence: revolutions, civil wars, wars of national or imperial conquest and consolidation.

A rare historical study (perhaps even unique) that seeks to respond to this position is John U. Nef's *War and Human Progress*.[9] Ironically, the book was taken by some for a tract extolling the contributions of war. In fact it was more nearly the opposite, and it fulfilled its aims impressively (at least for those who read the book rather than the title). But surely historians as a profession have more to contribute to this debate than a single volume, under whatever title. Arthur Waskow writes that "the historian is trained to study social change: to understand the linkages among social movements, ideas, the state, economic processes, technology, and individual men as those linkages create change." War is not even mentioned here as a source of social change. Perhaps this goes too far in the other direction, but historians would do well to seek a more balanced understanding of the role of peace and war in changing social, political, and international systems.

Historians might also take a cue from the students of international law, who tell us that "to a very large degree states do observe most of the principles of international law and fulfill most of their international obligations" (Sumida). Though this is undoubtedly true, one suspects it comes as news to most historians, who are inclined to see the history of international relations primarily as a dismal record of treaties broken and obligations evaded. If it is true, where are the historical works that show it—to the public, to teachers of history, to students, to the makers of foreign policy? Or for that matter, where is the critical analysis of this admittedly gross observation?

Historians seem to be guided in this area by the premise that those international agreements and regulations that are widely observed are unimportant, whereas those that are broken are important and worthy of the historian's attention. The point is made explicitly by W. K. Hancock, who remarks that states feel little obligation to international law when their "vital interests" are threatened: in international law "efficacy reaches its maximum in the zone of minor interests and falls to

[9] (New York: W. W. Norton, 1968); originally published by Harvard University Press, 1950.

its minimum in the zone of major interests."[10] But is this premise valid? How are "vital interests," "minor interests," and "major interests" defined? Who so defines them?[11] We have noted above that the interests for which states and revolutionary groups go to war evidently override, in the perceptions of those who decide for war, the interests served by peace. But need the historian accept and perpetuate this evaluation in every case? *Were* the interests for which the United States went to war against Mexico in 1848, against Spain in 1898, and against the Viet Cong in 1964 "vital"? To whom? Is every act of war or of international lawlessness deserving of the justification that it served the "vital interests" of the violator?

One might also ask, how far do states ordinarily go in breaking or evading international regulations? It may be that even while engaging in serious violations of international obligations, as in the case of illegal rearmament in Germany in the 1920s, states do nevertheless observe certain limits that keep their behavior, ordinarily, within the general intent of the international standards.[12] It may even be argued that Germany was able to repudiate openly her obligations under the Treaty of Versailles in March 1935 only because her rearmament did at that time conform to the military standards of the day—a fact witnessed in June of that year by the signing of the British-German naval pact. On the other hand the behavior of Germany from at least 1938 on, with her rearmament well advanced, gives the classic proof of the ability of nations under a system of sovereignty and war to defy all international standards when the will and the power are both available. The problem of achieving international order is that of controlling or preventing such instances of total defiance. It does not help in that endeavor, however, to make it appear that disregard and defiance of international agreements and standards on this level are the rule rather the the exception. Like peace itself, compliance with international law is the *normal* condition of international behavior. This again is affirmed here in the absence of adequate historical study of the subject.

[10] W. K. Hancock, "*Civitas Maxima*," in his *Four Studies of War and Peace in This Century* (Cambridge: At the University Press, 1961), p. 99.

[11] See in this connection Kenneth Boulding's review of six textbooks on international relations, *Journal of Conflict Resolution*, 8, no. 1 (March 1964): 65–71, in which he questions current conceptions of "national interest."

[12] See Berenice A. Carroll, "Germany Disarmed and Rearming, 1925–1935," *Journal of Peace Research*, 1966, no. 2, pp. 114–24.

More generally, it may be suggested that historians need to give more attention to the development of international law and the history of international and transnational institutions, associations, and exchanges. Is it true, as Bruce suggests, that these are rapidly developing and proliferating phenomena? Gunnar Myrdal seems to suggest otherwise; in *Beyond the Welfare State* he argues that since World War II we have been in a period of international *dis*integration, at least in economic relations.[13] Myrdal is highly critical of the accomplishments—or rather lack of accomplishments—of many pretentious international institutions. On the other hand, he places some hope in the sheer survival of intergovernmental organizations, both for the experience they provide in practical cooperation, even on a very limited scale, and for the vested interest in internationalism they create. The "secretarial drive for the self-preservation of the organization" would not alone suffice, he notes, but around every international organization "there are a great number of persons everywhere, often hundreds or even thousands, to whom the organization represents a means of serving an internationalist ideal."

In this connection, it may be noted that the Union of International Associations reports that there were more than 2,200 international organizations in 1968, and that more than 3,000 international congresses are held annually involving more than 2 million people. Contemplating these facts, the historian is led to wonder: where is the history of these associations? Who or what are all these organizations? What do they do? Who do they reach? What is their impact? How do their numbers and activities compare with those of international associations in the period between the two world wars, or even earlier? If it is true that we are witnessing international economic disintegration, in the sense of rising tariff boundaries, more inflexible currencies, and similar trends, is it nonetheless possible that we are also witnessing a highly significant rise in transnational exchange and cooperation, below the governmental level, which historians should be recording?[14]

[13] (New Haven, Conn.: Yale University Press, 1960).
[14] If historians have been giving any attention to international associations, their history, and their implications, the fact is so little known to other historians that it has entirely escaped the indexers of the *American Historical Review* in recent years. There are no index heads for international associations or international organizations, and under international relations, at most a few works dealing with the United Nations, the OAS, the OAU, or NATO

Historians do a great deal to shape, as well as to reflect, the self-image of nations and groups and their perceptions of the social universe they inhabit. As Arthur Waskow writes, "the historian remains the scholar who most often sees his audience as the public, not a closed coterie of experts." Waskow's recommendation is that the historian should turn his attention to the future: using his understanding of the past to "possidict" the future, he should engage himself in action research projects directed toward realization of his "possidictions."

But it may be that the historian can make as necessary a contribution within the framework of his own trade by a shift in value premises and subject matter. The new directions, both as value premise and subject, are peace, internationalism, and transnational and international institutions. The lesson of making such a shift has already been well learned in the racial dilemma: black consciousness demands black history. Peace, international integration, and transnational orientation also need a history. They have a history. The historians have yet to write it.

—nothing at all on "lesser" intergovernmental and nongovernmental associations (except those of historians themselves). Several of the questions raised here will be dealt with from the viewpoint of the social scientist in a forthcoming thesis by Kjell Skjelsbaek, International Peace Research Institute, Oslo. He reports that of the 200 intergovernmental organizations existing in 1966, 76 percent were founded since World War II. Of international nongovernmental organizations, 50 percent were not more than sixteen years old and 25 percent were less than seven years old. The organizations are increasing not only in number but also in inclusiveness of membership and level of activity.